Y0-CCO-666

The Beatles: Untold Tales

The Beatles: Untold Tales

by
Howard A. DeWitt

Copyright © 1985 by Howard A. DeWitt

All rights reserved. No part of this work, including text, photographs, etc. may be reproduced or transmitted in any form or by any means, electronic or mechanical, including photocopying and recording, or by an information storage or retrieval system, without permission in writing from the publisher or in the case of the photographs, permission from the legal owners.

Published by: Horizon Books
P.O. Box 3083
Fremont, California 94539

ISBN: 0-938840-03-7

1st Printing, January, 1985
2nd Printing, October, 1991

Library of Congress Catalog Card Number: 84-82314

Consulting Editor: Dennis Roby
Cover Design: Dennis Loren
Original Drawing: Beth Hughes

Table of Contents

Acknowledgments

This book owes a great deal to the people close to the Beatles during the early 1960s. Joe Flannery, Clive Epstein, Tony Sheridan, Horst Fascher and Bob Wooler gave freely of their time. They also provided a great deal of new information about the Beatles. In Hamburg Tom Shaka and Christian Kluver were helpful, and Liz and Jim Hughes of the Cavern Mecca Museum were important in tracing early Beatles activity. At the Cavern Mecca Eddie Porter, Connie O'Dell and Steve Phillips were cooperative. Charlie Lennon spent an inordinate amount of time answering questions, and Bob Wooler and Joe Flannery went beyond the call of duty. The Aachen Hotel in Liverpool provided food, lodging and pleasant conversation. In addition, the patrons of Ye Crack and the Grapes recalled their days with the Beatles and bought a poor American scholar a number of beers.

Much of the material for this book was the product of a visit with Morten Reff and Anita Hansen in Drobak, Norway. They provided shelter and leads about European rock music. In Antwerp, Belgium Willy and Lutgarde Pauwels were helpful in this research, and Jacky Huys, Belgium's premier rock critic, shared his knowledge of American music. Dave Caryl, a record dealer in Liverpool, was able to provide many leads, and he secured much of the recorded material used in this study.

In California Eric "Dr. Rock" Isralow, columnist for the San Francisco Examiner, criticized the manuscript as did Dennis Roby, Shelia Krishnaswany, Carolyn DeWitt, Dennis DeWitt and Steve Marinucci. Tom Schultheiss of Pierian Press provided a number of leads as did Barry Miles of Omnibus Press. Dennis Loren of RPM suggested many of the individuals and ideas which grace the following pages.

Although not directly involved in the writing process a number of people endured late night phone calls and were sympathetic to the project. Among these were Fred Worth, Ron Kovic, Lee Cotten, Jim McCue, Ed Diaz, Grant Morlock, and Guitar Mac. Veteran rock and blues performers Bo Diddley, Mark Naftalin, Tommy Roe, Donnie Brooks, Memphis Slim, Mary Wells and Little Willie Littlefield aided in the research.

My wife Carolyn and our two children, Melanie and Darin Dion were very sympathetic to the project. Ohlone College granted a sabbatical leave for the research. My parents Anthony A. and Howardine DeWitt were encouraging. The final responsibility for the manuscript, however, resides with the author. Enjoy the book. It is the product of five years' work and over fifty in-depth personal interviews. Two more volumes will follow. Anyone with suggestions for material in these books please write to PO Box 3083, Fremont, CA 94539.

Howard A. DeWitt

Introduction: The Untold Tales

The myths and realities of the rock and roll entertainment business are difficult to separate, because of the widespread differences in viewing the impact of rock music upon American and British culture. This book will not end the tendency to mix fact with fiction in rock journalism. However, the following essays will present an in-depth analysis of people close to the Beatles during their formative years.

In this period, the feeling of raw energy and exaltation that rock and roll music provided for the Beatles helped to shape their musical direction. Since 1963 the Beatles have been one of the most written about groups in the rock music industry. Yet many of the books on the Liverpool four fail to examine the individuals and influences that shaped the Beatles' early years. *The Beatles: Untold Tales* is an attempt to remedy this problem by analyzing the rise of the Beatles in the early 1960s.

By concentrating upon Liverpool people like Bob Wooler, Joe Flannery and Clive Epstein, it is possible to see how they shaped Brian Epstein's business attitudes as well as the Beatles' musical development. In addition, the influence of two Hamburg, Germany residents, Tony Sheridan and Horst Fascher is important in the early evolution of the Beatles' sound. The first section of the book appropriately entitled: "The Hamburg-Liverpool Influences," examines these five individuals, and the manner in which they helped the new music to evolve.

The second section of *The Beatles: Untold Tales* is an analysis of John Lennon's creative process. By focusing upon three pubs which John frequented, it is possible to examine his intellectual growth. In these pubs, John combined rock music and literature to channel his rebellion against Liverpool's stark socio-economic background. In 1956 when sixteen year old John Lennon heard Elvis Presley's "Heartbreak Hotel," he knew that rock and roll music was his future. "My whole life changed," John remarked. "I was completely shaken by it." Like many young people, Lennon's intellectual growth was influenced by Presley's rebellious, non-conformist image. In John's small, spiral notebooks he jotted down his personal thoughts, and these ideas were translated later into rock music songs. The combination of rock music and serious literature allowed Lennon to mature into one of the most creative artists of the 1960s.

Tony Sheridan, a Hamburg musician, and John's uncle, Charlie Lennon, were very close personal friends to Lennon in the 1950s and early 1960s. An essay entitled: "Remembering John: Tony Sheridan and Charlie Lennon" suggests that much of John's character was formed by his family background and rock music. These two influences tend to surface again and again in Lennon's background. The working-class Liverpool environment which shaped John's literary talent is combined with the personal tragedies in Lennon's life to produce a portrait of a tortured artist.

The final segment of *The Beatles: Untold Tales* examines the reaction of the media to the new music. The sensationalist-minded English press initially attacked the Beatles. An important English newspaper that ridiculed the Beatles' music was *Melody Maker*. As England's most prestigious rock publication, *MM* was in a position to make or break most acts. In the Beatles case, the snide comments and juvenile coverage only increased their popularity. In an essay entitled: "Will The Beatles Please Go Away? *Melody Maker* Reacts To the New Music," it is clearly demonstrated that *Melody Maker* did not understand the new music. The book concludes with an article on the *New Musical Express* and the Beatles. The close relationship which the *NME* established with the Beatles resulted in some of the finest reporting on the English rock music scene in the 1960s. Not only were John Lennon and Paul McCartney inordinately candid with *NME* reporters, but they also provided many of their personal thoughts on the English rock and roll revolution. Unlike its competitor, *NME* was a far-sighted and progressive voice in rock journalism.

The material in this book is the product of more than 200 hours of interviews with more than fifty people close to the Beatles in the late 1950s and early 1960s. In addition, every major English rock newspaper and many of the minor newspapers were combed for caveats of Beatle knowledge. What is obvious from this collection of essays is that there is still a great deal to discover about the Beatles.

PART I

THE HAMBURG—
LIVERPOOL
INFLUENCES

The Hamburg-Liverpool Influences

As the Beatles' music evolved in the early 1960s, there were a number of influential people who helped to popularize and refine their sound. The whirlwind success of the Liverpool beat resulted in many of the Beatles' early supporters slipping into the background. Soon they were simply brief footnotes in the history of rock and roll music. This section of *The Beatles: Untold Tales* will examine the role and influence of five important individuals in the Beatles' formative years.

Tony Sheridan was the first person to record with the Beatles at a makeshift Polydor Record studio in Hamburg, Germany in 1961. Sheridan's record, "My Bonnie," was the catalyst to Brian Epstein listening to the Beatles and signing them to a management contract. The rest was history as the Beatles became musical superstars. Yet without Sheridan's musical tutoring the Beatles would not have been nearly as successful. An essay entitled: "Tony Sheridan: The First Beatle" clearly points out the enormous debt that the Liverpool group owes to this obscure Irish rock singer. Not only did Sheridan teach George Harrison most of his important guitar licks, but he coached John Lennon and Paul McCartney on stage presence. In a lengthy interview with Sheridan, he details his contribution to the Beatles music.

Horst Fascher is an elusive figure in the Beatles' story. He was a well-known German boxer who acted as the Beatles bodyguard. His advice, knowledge of obscure rock records, and ability to understand what moved a crowd was very important to the Beatles. Few people realize how significant Fascher was in the development of the Beatles music. In an essay entitled: "Horst Fascher: Hamburg Boxer as Teacher," the subtle influence of this German personality is examined.

When the Beatles began playing at the Cavern Club on Mathews Street in Liverpool in 1961, it became the vehicle to their subsequent stardom. The disc jockey/compere at the Cavern, Bob Wooler, was one of the best known figures in local Liverpool entertainment circles. In addition to promoting the Beatles' music and introducing them at the Cavern with a special flair, Wooler was also a shrewd judge of musical material, stage mannerisms and original rock songs. In Liverpool, Wooler is still referred to as "The Fifth Beatle," and he is credited with helping to educate Brian Epstein as well as the Beatles concerning the direction of British rock and roll music. An essay, "Bob Wooler: The Fifth Beatle" suggests that Wooler's musical advice began the Beatles on the road to stardom.

Clive Epstein was another relatively obscure but important individual who helped the Beatles climb to fame and fortune. Although Brian Epstein's younger brother, Clive was virtually ignored by the show business moguls, he was a significant force in shaping the Beatles career. Brian Epstein depended upon his brother for advice about the business end of the music industry. Consequently, Clive became a major influence upon the Beatles' career. "Clive and Brian Epstein: The Beatles' Legacy" is an essay which develops the close family relationship among the Epstein's.

The last essay examines the career of Joe Flannery, a local Liverpool promoter who masterminded his brother, Lee Curtis, to a position of prominence in the Merseyside music scene in the 1960s. Flannery is often referred to as "The Invisible Beatle," because he was involved in shaping the careers of John Lennon, Brian Epstein and the Beatles in 1961 and 1962. As the only Liverpool businessman with entertainment business experience, Flannery was an indispensible adviser to the Beatles. "Joe Flannery: The Invisible Beatle" pays a long overdue tribute to one of the giants of Liverpool rock music.

There is no doubt that without Tony Sheridan, Horst Fascher, Bob Wooler, Clive Epstein and Joe Flannery, the Beatles' music would not have had such a revolutionary impact upon the history of American popular culture.

The Hamburg Beatles, 1960

Bo Diddley: A Beatle Influence

TONY SHERIDAN

Tony Sheridan: The First Beatle

Tony Sheridan is a well-known figure from the Beatles' Hamburg days. He was the first person to record with the Beatles, and Sheridan's song "My Bonnie" reportedly has sold more than a million copies. When it was revealed that Sheridan's backup group, the Beat Brothers, were in reality the Beatles, there was a great deal of public attention focused upon Sheridan. Unfortunately, an in-depth analysis of his importance to the Beatles' music is ignored in most books. Peter Brown's *The Love You Make: An Insider's Story of the Beatles* includes two brief references to Sheridan, and Brown dismisses his impact upon the Beatles' music. Philip Norman's well-researched *Shout: The Beatles In Their Generation* concludes that Sheridan was "too blithely erratic to suit the rock and roll starmakers." While these descriptions of Sheridan's personality are not necessarily inaccurate, they do ignore his influence upon British rock music in general and also his impact upon the Beatles' songwriting. This essay will examine the influence of Tony Sheridan upon the Beatles' music.

Tony Sheridan was born Anthony Esmond Sheridan McGinnity in Ireland in May, 1940. After a calm and undistinguished childhood, Tony attended Worwich Art College in 1956, and practiced his rock guitar in nearby pubs. That same year he also formed his first band, the Saints. The group played the skiffle music which had become so popular in the United Kingdom due largely to Lonnie Donegan. In 1956 Donegan had six tunes on the British charts including "Rock Island Line." Donegan's songs were folk and skiffle tunes, and he inspired thousands of young English musicians to form skiffle bands.

Soon rock and blues also became a part of the musical landscape with the emergence of Tommy Steele, whose two big 1956 hits were "Rock With The Cavemen" and "Singing the Blues." Steele's career as a rock singer began almost by accident. After sailing to New York on a cruise ship and performing as "Chick Hicks," Steele returned to London with a suitcase full of records by Elvis Presley, Bill Haley, Guy Mitchell and Chuck Berry. By imitating their styles, Steele quickly became England's first teenage idol. Both Donegan and Steele were strong influences upon Tony Sheridan, but he did not want to model his career after either artist. Consequently, Sheridan developed his music slowly over a four-year period. From 1956 to 1960, he shied away from recording offers and often performed material which was different from that which was currently popular. Very early in his performing career, while still relatively unknown, Tony acquired a reputation as an independent artist. This was due to his view that selling out for hit-records would kill his rock-and-roll talent. As Sheridan expanded his repertoire by incorporating the music of Ray Charles, Fats Domino, Gene Vincent, Conway Twitty and Chuck Berry into his act, he developed a strong cult following. His early fame was the result of a reputation for fine performances and genuine rock and roll guitar work.

In 1958 when Sheridan left Ireland to play his brand of rock and roll in London, the state of English music was dismal. Cliff Richard and Tommy Steele were the only superstar English teen idols. In 1958 Richard's two chart records "Move It" and "High Class Baby" brought an entertainer of tremendous talent and staying power into the British music scene. But neither Richard nor Steele were raw, energetic rock and roll talents. While the Fleet Street newspapers and the music magazines might have compared these singers to Elvis Presley, the British audiences yearned for a more substantial form of rock music. In small clubs and little art college tea rooms, Tony Sheridan provided a blues and rock electric guitar which earned him the name: "The Teacher." He was a breath of fresh talent at a time when British rock singers were imitating Elvis.

There were a number of other singers who also aspired to be teen rock-and-roll idols. Such singers as Terry Dene, Marty Wilde,

Tony Sheridan, Early 1960s (far right)

Dicky Pride, Duffy Power, Billy Fury, Johnny Gentle, Vince Eager and Vince Taylor attempted to copy the sultry style of Elvis Presley, the boyish vulnerability of Buddy Holly, and the raw energy of Gene Vincent. Generally, these British rock and rollers were as talented as many of their American counterparts, but the demand for the real thing, American music, made it impossible to develop large numbers of British rock acts. A British promoter, Larry Parnes was responsible for most of the minor league teen idols. He had launched Tommy Steele's career, but he was unable to duplicate the feat. For years, Parnes traveled throughout England looking for new rock and roll talent, and he passed the Beatles up a number of times. This was because there was more to creating a rock marketplace than Parnes and most of the other early British promoters realized. The rock revolution was building slowly in small clubs, art colleges, and local town halls. These venues were neither appealing nor profitable to promoters like Larry Parnes, and the musicians who played them were overlooked.

In a club known as the 2-Is in London's Soho district, some of the new and undiscovered British acts toiled for a few dollars a night. In 1959-1960, Gene Vincent and Eddie Cochran toured

England, and their influence gave birth to a new brand of English rock. In December, 1959, the *New Musical Express* heralded Vincent's arrival by pointing out that his English fans gathered at Heathrow airport despite the fact that Gene's plane arrived at 6 a.m. Although he had not placed a song on the English charts for three years, Vincent was still a strong concert draw, and his influence helped to set the stage for the emergence of Tony Sheridan's brand of British rock and roll.

When Sheridan went on tour with Gene Vincent and Eddie Cochran he was already a budding rock and roll star. Sheridan's training with English musicians was excellent, and his most valuable experience was as a member of the Playboys, Vince Taylor's backup band. "The tours with Taylor helped me to understand the rock music business," Sheridan stated, "it was a time in which my music matured."

Sheridan also had fond memories of playing at the Liverpool Stadium in 1960 with Rory Storm and the Hurricanes and he heard about the Beatles at this concert from the Hurricanes drummer Ringo Starr. Sheridan had no way of knowing that John Lennon and Stu Sutcliffe were in the audience, and that in a few short months they would be playing together at Bruno Koschmider's Kaiserkeller Club in Hamburg, Germany. It was during this concert with Gene Vincent in early 1960 that Sheridan became a star in his own right. He was the only English act called back time after time for an encore.

Although he played in Hamburg in 1960, Tony Sheridan was also a popular performer in England. His popularity was demonstrated in January, 1961, when promoter Larry Parnes booked a tour he billed as "A Fast Moving Anglo-American Beat Show." Every night in movie theaters throughout England a 6:15 and 8:30 p.m. performance featured Gene Vincent, Eddie Cochran, Georgie Fame, Billy Fury, the Tony Sheridan Trio and others in concert. Sheridan learned a great deal from his exposure to Vincent and Cochran's music, and he also watched these two master entertainers control the crowds. In Glasgow, Scotland, the tour package stopped to play the raucous Empire Theater. Billy Fury had been attacked on stage in Glasgow, thus confirming its dangerous reputation. Vincent and Cochran mesmerized the audience with their strong rock art, and Tony Sheridan was the only English musician brought back for an encore.

By 1960 British audiences recognized Sheridan as an English performer whose style was similar to American rock and roll. Yet jazz and skiffle groups continued to dominate the small London clubs, and there was little chance for rock musicians to obtain decent bookings. The burst of energy in small clubs (which a decade later brought such pub rockers as Nick Lowe, Dave Edmunds, Graham Parker, Joe Jackson, Elvis Costello and Brinsley Schwartz into the mainstream of British rock) was missing in the late 1950s and early 1960s. A musical revolution was building slowly as the British evolved their own distinct brand of rock music, but from 1958 to 1960 the British club scene was sterile, and most rock acts simply covered American songs. It was probably the worst possible time for a talented, blues-oriented, rock guitarist like Tony Sheridan to break into the business.

In time, Sheridan discovered the 2-Is club in Soho. This small coffee bar served only soft drinks and accommodated no more than 40 people. Soho had a Damon Runyan atmosphere akin to "Guys and Dolls," with British hipsters dressed as American gangsters mingling with young ladies whose fashions resembled Marilyn Monroe's. English wrestler Paul Lincoln was in charge of the 2-Is, and he introduced Harry Webb and the Drifters as one of the earliest acts. They soon changed their name to Cliff Richard and the Shadows and became international rock music superstars. Lincoln, who wrestled with a mask under the name Dr. Death, was an unusually generous person who booked most of the early English rock acts.

In addition to rock music, the 2-Is encouraged such blues musicians as Peter Green, Eric Clapton, John Mayall and Alexis Korner. These young artists often wandered into the basement club to play with the house band. Tony Sheridan became resident guitarist at the 2-Is, and his band included future Shadow musicians Brian Bennett and Brian Locking. One night, Jack Good wandered into the 2-Is club intent upon hiring Tony Sheridan as a TV backup guitarist. The presence of this well-known English television producer was an indication that rock music was quickly becoming a strong commercial phenomena in England.

Jack Good, a young man in his mid-20s who had recently graduated in philosophy and English from Oxford University, was almost single-handedly responsible for English rock music appearing on national television. In February, 1957, Good helped to launch the BBC-TV program "6.5 Special." This was a magazine-type show appealing to young adults. Part of "6.5 Special" programming was to present new, undiscovered rock music acts as well as to showcase current teen music favorites. The program was

George Harrison, John Lennon and Tony Sheridan, 1961

an immediate success, but Good soon left BBC to work for England's Independent network ATV. Good was placed in charge of "Oh Boy," a critically acclaimed rock music show. What made Jack Good unique was that he was able to select talent which did not mimic American acts. Adam Faith and P.J. Proby were two good examples of Good's astute judgment. As a result of "Oh Boy," a group of English rock stars emerged. Good championed Cliff Richard's first hit, "Move It," believing that the song was the first British hit with an authentic rock sound. He also made a strong pitch for developing England's own rock talent. This helped to create a number of minor British rock stars who paved the way for the Beatles' popularity.

The late 1950s were an exciting period in Sheridan's life as fellow musicians turned out to jam with him nightly on the 2-Is stage. Each evening at 7 p.m., a guard at the 2-Is upstairs door collected 2 shillings from 30 to 40 people who wandered down into the dark cellar to listen to what London's "hip set" considered real rock music. Tony also spent a great deal of time on Oxford Street each day searching out the latest American records and magazines to strengthen his musical knowledge. By 1959, the 2-Is was a legendary entertainment spot. Sheridan's music increasingly reflected a rockabilly sound as Buddy Holly, Warren Smith, Gene Vincent, Eddie Cochran and Jerry Lee Lewis became the chief inspirations for Sheridan's sound. As the 2-Is' popularity grew, record and television executives curiously wandered into the basement coffee bar. Most of the talent scouts in the British entertainment industry left the 2-Is convinced that rock and roll music was a temporary phenomena. They did not believe that rock records had mainstream commercial possibilities in the English economy.

But Jack Good recognized Sheridan's enormous talent, and he was able to showcase Tony on the "Oh Boy" TV show. As a result of this television exposure, Sheridan became a minor league British music star. There were, however, few other outlets for Sheridan's talents. No major English record label offered him a contract, and he found it difficult to secure bookings. Another problem as far as Sheridan's commercial appeal was concerned was his insistence upon performing his own intimate and highly autobiographical songs. "I write my songs the way I feel them," Sheridan once remarked.

It was to be some time before the singer-songwriter syndrome became an important part of the music industry; Sheridan was simply a decade ahead of his time. Furthermore, from the music promoter's viewpoint, Sheridan's music was too broadly based in blues, rhythm and blues and 1950s style American rock and roll. In other words, Sheridan's range was too broad for the limited English audience. This aspect of his performance, combined with his autobiographical material, prompted many promoters to label Tony an erratic act.

Recently, as Tony Sheridan reflected upon English rock music in 1958-1959, he suggested that the strict morality and stuffy conventional attitudes prevented an English brand of rock music from emerging. "A good example of England's conventional morality," Sheridan remarked, "can be seen in the Terry Dene case." Dene, a young singer who grew up in London's Elephant and Castle district, worked days packing records in HMV's Oxford Street store, but he harbored dreams of becoming a rock star. One night, Dene jumped on the 2-Is stage with his guitar while Sheridan's band was taking a break. With his good looks and sensual sound, Dene was an immediate hit. Shortly after his 2-Is debut, Decca Records signed him and he released a string of minor hits. Soon Dene was a rising young rock singer in Elvis Presley's mold. However, he suffered a nervous breakdown and was black listed after he was found allegedly wandering down Oxford Street in his underwear. Sheridan believes that the pressures of the rock music business, combined with the threat of military conscription, caused Dene to suffer a nervous breakdown. He was never able to perform again with any degree of consistency, and the English record companies were no longer interested in his talent.

Since Tony had witnessed Terry Dene's tragedy, he was determined not to fall into the same mold. Sheridan's act was one of England's popular shows as he successfully fused the stage gyrations of Elvis with the sullen personality of James Dean. This was a perfect combination for English audiences, and Sheridan soon developed a rabid cult following. But the manner in which Dene fell from public favor frightened Sheridan and he was determined to control his own career. It was this fierce personal independence which most music promoters and record executives found exasperating. In addition the English rock music scene was still in an infant stage.

The crowds at the 2-Is coffee bar were of a bohemian-beatnik variety, and they were often too cosmopolitan for earthy rock songs. The poetry of Allen Ginsberg and Lawrence Ferlinghetti and the books of Jack Kerouac reflected the mentality of the 2-Is audience. They loved Sheridan's music, but these audiences were not as responsive to experimental rock songs as Sheridan desired. Like his audiences, Tony Sheridan was a voracious reader, and he, by reading a wide variety of books, was able to write many original songs. Yet record company executives did not ask Sheridan for his material. This is one of the tragedies of the London years because Tony was a creative songwriter who had few outlets. "I am not your typical rock and roll singer," Tony quipped. "I don't write songs to just produce hit records or fill albums." This highly independent attitude did little to endear Sheridan to promoters and record company executives.

It was only natural, therefore, for Tony Sheridan to accept a new opportunity in the summer of 1960. Tony had been approached one night at the 2-Is by Horst Fascher, a bouncer at Bruno Koschmider's Kaiserkeller Club in Hamburg's notorious Reeperbahn section. Fascher was visiting London, and he liked Sheridan's show. He suggested that Tony come to work in Hamburg. Sheridan agreed on the spot, and as soon as Fascher returned to Hamburg, Koschmider sent Tony money for the trip. Koschmider was a shrewd businessman, and he knew that the free

John Lennon

spending audiences at his club enjoyed rock and roll music. A talented performer like Sheridan would be a big hit. As for Tony himself, he was ready for a change. "I couldn't wait to see Hamburg," Tony remarked, "and show the Germans real rock and roll music."

When he arrived in Hamburg, Tony Sheridan was mesmerized by the energetic and open German civilization. He found the Reeperbahn populated by Indonesian bands with an Elvis Presley type sound. They mouthed the words to American rock hits without understanding the subtle nuances of rock and roll music. After a two-year apprentice period in London, Sheridan was ready to inaugurate Europe's rock revolution. "The Germans were unaware of Ray Charles, Little Richard and Chuck Berry," Tony remarked, "and I was ready to educate the locals." However, Tony was in for a big surprise. The Kaiserkeller Club was not the rock and roll paradise that Fascher had described in his visit to London.

When Sheridan walked into Bruno Koschmider's Kaiserkeller Club, he was horrified by its appearance. The club had no sound system, the stage was a makeshift affair, and there was no dressing room. Immediately, Tony felt deceived because he was told that the

Kaiserkeller was a major night club with modern facilities. "The Kaiserkeller was the pits," Sheridan remarked, "orange boxes and one amplifier was all that the musicians had to work with." This made it difficult to achieve a good sound level. "We used the amp for the guitar and bass," Sheridan remarked.

After the first night, Sheridan admitted that he was depressed and considered the move to Hamburg a mistake. But on the second night as the Kaiserkeller was packed with 800 people, Sheridan was elated by his music's acceptance. A week later there were lines down the Grosse Freiheit and Tony Sheridan was a star. The schedule at the Kaiserkeller, however, was a gruelling one. Sheridan and his three-piece band, the Jets, played from 6 p.m. until 6 a.m. on Friday and Saturday and from 7 p.m. to 3 a.m. from Sunday through Thursday. The use of Preludin pills, commonly known as "prellies," was necessary to stay awake. In fact, the publicity surrounding Preludin tablets was so vast that the German government forced the manufacturers to change the pills to make them less attractive. "Only the Germans would add a laxative to the prellies," Sheridan chuckled.

As Tony looked back upon his early years in Hamburg he smiled as he recalled the Kaiserkeller's nightly fights. "One night, Bruno Koschmider was kicking a ruffian with his tin leg, the leg fell off, Koschmider picked it up and resumed beating the patron," Tony remarked. There was a decided underworld atmosphere in Hamburg in 1960. In scenes reminiscent of the movie "The Godfather" local gangster types reserved tables as their henchmen stood around looking menacing. The Germans responded warmly to Sheridan's music, and soon he was a favorite.

Shortly after Sheridan arrived in Hamburg, Bruno Koschmider brought in Rory Storm and the Hurricanes from Liverpool to play in a converted movie theater, the Indra. This was Koschmider's smallest and least attractive club, but it was an excellent venue for a young, untried group. Rory Storm was an immediate hit and quickly graduated to playing with Sheridan in the Kaiserkeller.

When Rory Storm and the Hurricanes moved to the Kaiserkeller, Tony Sheridan offered to help them restructure their act. It was largely due to Tony's suggestions that Rory Storm became a more effective singer on stage and the Hurricanes an asset as a backup band. Storm was afflicted with a stuttering problem which vanished the moment he went on stage. As a result of Tony's suggestions, Rory Storm and the Hurricanes were one of Hamburg's most polished stage acts.

In the process, Sheridan became very friendly with the drummer, Ringo Starr. Ringo was impressed with Sheridan's virtually encyclopedic knowledge of rock music, and they spent hours together talking about the influence of blues sounds and American rock and roll music upon local bands. In many respects, Tony Sheridan was Ringo's tutor in the tough world of Hamburg's Reeperbahn district.

After a particularly hard night at the Kaiserkeller, Tony would wander down the street to meet Ringo at Harold's, a small cafe that stayed open all night. Sitting in the soft morning shadows eating Kellogg's corn flakes and sausages, Tony and Ringo spent an inordinate amount of time dissecting the music of Ray Charles, Chuck Berry, Johnny Burnette and Little Richard. Often Horst Fascher, the bouncer at the Kaiserkeller, and by now one of Tony's close friends, joined them for breakfast. Everyone in Hamburg respected Fascher's boxing feats, and he was also known as an astute judge of musical talent. As the three young men sat in this obscure Reeperbahn cafe, they were convinced that a new age of rock music was dawning. "We could play as long as we liked; there was plenty of booze and women ... when you're twenty it's great," Sheridan reflected.

During his first engagement in Hamburg Tony brought along two accomplished English musicians, Ian Hanes and Colin Milander. But unlike Sheridan these musicians had trouble adjusting to Hamburg's life style and they returned to England. This placed Sheridan in a difficult position because he no longer had a back up band. When the Beatles arrived in Hamburg a few months later, Sheridan believed that the young Liverpool group was the perfect backing band. An immediate rapport developed between Tony and the Beatles. Although Sheridan had kind words for the Jets, many Hamburg residents recalled that Tony sounded much better with the Beatles. The Jets had a soft pop musical sound and found it difficult to play the biting brand of rock and roll which Sheridan favored. The Beatles were perfectly suited to play this type of music, and soon they were backing Sheridan or playing with him at the Kaiserkeller. When the Jets returned to England with Sheridan, they rechristened themselves the Echoes and toured with minor league British pop idols Vince Eager, Ricky Valence and Dicky Pride. The Jets were simply musically too shallow to fit into the Hamburg rock scene.

When the Beatles arrived in Hamburg in August, 1960, to play at Koschmider's Indra Club, Sheridan was immediately struck by their strange clothing. Not only did the Beatles wear cowboy boots, leather jackets and Elvis type hairdoes, but they played rock music. John Lennon's callous attitude was one of Sheridan's earliest impressions of the Beatles. Reflecting on his first meeting with the Liverpool band, Tony also remembered how impressed he was with the notebook of 100 plus songs that John Lennon carried around. These songs, Tony reflected, were raw, energetic rock tunes. After the Beatles began their string of hits in 1963, Tony wondered why John Lennon and Paul McCartney had rewritten so many of these songs. Tony believed that the Beatles had softened their music for commercial reasons. "I could never redo my songs for a wider market," Tony remarked. "Rock music is a type of poetry and to change its meter and rhythm is to destroy it." In Hamburg the Beatles's original songs were not tunes like "Love Me Do" or "Please Please Me." Brian Epstein convinced the Beatles to sell out," Sheridan concluded.

George Harrison's excellent guitar playing was the result of careful tutoring by Tony Sheridan. When the Beatles played in Hamburg, Sheridan spent hours teaching George various styles. Although he had played guitar for a number of years, Harrison found it difficult to play blues and rhythm and blues songs effectively. Tony used his Chess Record collection featuring Bo Diddley, Chuck Berry, Muddy Waters, Howlin' Wolf and Little Walter to teach Harrison the subtle nuances of rock guitar playing. Since he was only 17 years old, Harrison was not always included in the hell raising. As a result, George had an inordinate amount of free time, and he practiced his guitar at least two hours a day. By the time he left Hamburg, George had developed extraordinary guitar skills. He also learned a great deal about stage presence and playing to an aggressive audience from Sheridan.

When the Beatles arrived in Hamburg on August 17, 1960, they were under contract to Bruno Koschmider until December 18. They began their Hamburg engagement at the small Indra Club but soon were promoted to the Kaiserkeller. The crowds at the Kaiserkeller quickly became capacity ones due to the strength of the Tony Sheridan-Beatles bill. After four months playing from ten to twelve hours nightly, the Beatles were skilled live performers. As American singer Tommy Roe observed: "The Beatles sounded better in person than on records. The Hamburg training made them Europe's tightest rock band in the early 1960s." Just before John Lennon returned to Liverpool in December, 1960, he went with Tony Sheridan at the Gretel and Alfons bar to reminisce about the Beatles four months on the Reeperbahn. Tony Sheridan confided to

Tommy Roe and Tony Sheridan

John that the Beatles were a unique act. "I told John it was the visual impact of the group which appealed to the German intellectual crowd, but it was the raw, pulsating energy of the music which moved the sailors, workers, local gangsters and college students."

After John left Hamburg in December, 1960, Tony believes that he was unprepared for the Beatles' future successes. "He was a very confused mixed-up person," Tony reflected. "He didn't accept his success; he didn't allow himself to accept it." In 1963 when the Beatles returned from their last appearance on the Reeperbahn, Tony remembered that John Lennon swallowed almost a bottle of pills to stay awake for two nights. "He was aggressive and poured a large glass of beer over Brian Epstein's head.... It was an attack upon Epstein's softness." Tony felt John strongly resented Brian Epstein's solid upper-class family background and envied the stability and sense of purpose which Brian demonstrated in his day-to-day life.

Although Tony Sheridan was very close to John, he found it difficult to establish a close friendship with Paul McCartney. "Paul is a genius," Tony stated. "They tend to be cold, intellectual and

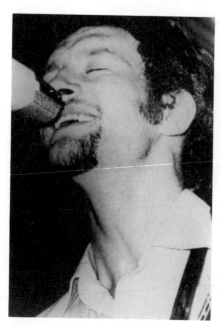

Tony Sheridan

selfish." During the early years in Hamburg, Sheridan found McCartney was very arrogant. "McCartney's arrogance was an aloofness, he didn't have much warmth, and he looked after his own interests." As McCartney honed his musical talents in Hamburg, he was an enigmatic figure. Paul would spend solitary hours listening to a Little Richard record and then follow it with songs by Bing Crosby or Frank Sinatra. At first Tony thought that this was strange, but he realized that this was the key to McCartney's genius. The combination of early rock music with the deft stylings of pop crooners developed McCartney's extraordinary songwriting skills. For months McCartney arranged, rearranged and tinkered with the song "Till There Was You," and his careful attention to style, detail and presentation is a good example of why the Beatles were so successful. "Paul McCartney, musically speaking," Tony remarked, "was the most sophisticated Beatle."

The influence of bass-player Stu Sutcliffe's German fiance Astrid Kirchherr is well-known. A beautiful twenty-two year old art student with long blond hair and a penchant for stark black clothing, Kirchherr is credited with revolutionizing the Beatles' hair style and clothing. What is frequently ignored, however, is

The Hamburg Beatles

Astrid's intellectual influence. She introduced the Beatles to German art, literature, and music. She also impressed upon John Lennon and Paul McCartney the importance of mood, design and theatrics in music.

As Tony Sheridan remarked: "We all wanted to impress Astrid; she was the most beautiful and intelligent woman in Hamburg." She was also something of a den mother to the Beatles. Despite her love for Stu, Astrid was close to all the band.

There were also light moments with Astrid, and as the Beatles rode the train home from her parents suburban Altona home they had fond memories of the sumptuous dinners and lengthy conversations. Soon the Beatles were undergoing a subtle metamorphosis. As Astrid Kirchherr and her friend Klaus Voorman became friendly with the Beatles, they educated the group about art, and soon the Beatles were intrigued by the German art school— the Meister Schule—once the Beatles became aware of design, color, lighting and artistic subtlety, they were able to develop an artistic approach toward rock music.

Astrid's influence was so strong that the Beatles often fought publicly on stage for her attention. As she drove her small sports car to the Grosse Freiheit, Astrid was a picture of elegance with her stylish clothing, expensive camera equipment, and sophisticated artistic attitudes.

"She influenced everybody," Tony Sheridan remarked. "I remember a fight between Stu and Paul over Astrid on stage at the Top Ten Club...She was the girl everyone wanted to impress." The Beatles were pleased that Astrid spent a good deal of time photographing them. With the exception of Pete Best, the Beatles loved Astrid Kirchherr. She was an important friend, and Astrid's parents had a genuine personal concern for the Beatles.

Since John, Paul and George had such strong feelings for Astrid, they did not object when Stu Sutcliffe left the group to study art with Astrid in Hamburg. Before Astrid began living with Stu, she designed and tailored a black leather suit with skin-tight pants for him. Soon the other Beatles adopted this mode of dress, and the Hamburg crowds applauded the new outfits. Few people realized how profound Astrid's influence was upon the development of the Beatles' style. As Tony Sheridan pointed out she was a beautiful, classy woman with an aggressive, intellectual nature; Astrid Kirchherr continues to haunt serious writers. It is often alleged that she lives on the fringes of the Reeperbahn. Still another story suggests that she continues to mourn Stu Sutcliffe's death. Neither story is close to the truth. The adjustments Astrid made after Stu's death were difficult ones, but she was a strong person and survived the trauma.

Astrid is presently married to a Hamburg businessman and she helps operate the Klimperkiste Club at Esplande 18 in Hamburg. The Klimperkiste is described by locals as a jazz bar catering to the whims of Hamburg's "noveaux riche." Walking into the Klimperkiste one frequently sees an attractive woman in her 40s directing the help. Astrid remains, in the 1980s, a beautiful woman who has made a nice life for herself. The club has a touch of class typified by a sumptuous champagne brunch served on Sundays. The Klimperkiste also features the best in traditional New Orleans style jazz. The crowd is young in their 20s, and the presence of art students is a notable feature of the Klimperkiste's atmosphere. When the Magnolia Jazz Band begins playing, the music ranges from a Louis Armstrong inspired version of "Mame" to Major Lance's "The Monkey Time." Astrid remains a trend setter, but equally significant, she is an intelligent business woman.

Another source of controversy that Tony Sheridan witnessed during the early years of the Beatles' career was the firing of Pete Best and the signing of Ringo Starr as the Beatles' drummer. Although he possessed smokey good looks and a James Dean manner, Pete was not an accomplished drummer. His replacement was already something of a legend in local music circles. Ringo Starr was Merseyside's most experienced drummer when he joined the Beatles. Although he was a shy, almost introverted, young man, his entire personality changed once he appeared on stage. After playing with Rory Storm and the Hurricanes, Ringo was spotted by John Lennon and Paul McCartney in the clubs in Hamburg and Liverpool. They liked Ringo's unorthodox drumming style and

Tony Sheridan, Polydor Recording Artist, 1963

recognized a strong country-western singing voice. Before he signed with the Beatles in August, 1962 Ringo was persuaded by Peter Eckhorn to join Tony Sheridan's band at the Top Ten Club. At a salary of $75 a week, Ringo was making a livable wage, and he was also acquiring valuable musical experience. Had Ringo not tired of the Hamburg grind, he might not have been the Beatles' replacement drummer. In June, 1962, however, Ringo was homesick and he left for Liverpool. A few days later, he went to the Cavern Club to hear the Beatles, and talked with John Lennon for hours about the good times in Hamburg. On August 16, 1962, Pete Best was called into Brian Epstein's office and informed he was no longer a Beatle. At the time, Ringo was on a brief tour with Rory Storm and the Hurricanes, and when the Beatles appeared at the Riverpark Ballroom in Chester, Pete refused to play one last night. Consequently, Johnny "Hutch" Hutchinson of the Big Three filled in on the drums. One of the main reasons that Ringo quickly accepted the Beatles offer was Tony Sheridan's prediction that the Liverpool group would soon be superstars.

For a brief period of time, Tony and Ringo lived in a small room above the Top Ten Club. "He was a nice guy," Sheridan remarked.

Tony also believed that Ringo was the most accomplished and consistent drummer in Hamburg or Liverpool. Perhaps the most important quality in Ringo's music, Sheridan stressed, was the enthusiasm he projected on stage and his crowd-pleasing antics. "There was a quiet charisma to Ringo," Tony stated. When Peter Eckhorn and Tony Sheridan persuaded Ringo to spend four months playing in Sheridan's band, they helped to develop one of the foremost drummers in modern rock music.

Despite his influence upon the Beatles, Tony is remembered as the singer the Beatles backed on the Polydor Record song, "My Bonnie." Sheridan's energetic lead vocals, combined with the Beatles rave-up background, propelled "My Bonnie" into the German charts. Although Sheridan's record sold in excess of 50,000 the first year, he was unhappy. "I wondered why it had to be this record. It was not one of my best efforts," Tony reflected. He had a number of acetates which had a sound similar to that of Elvis Presley or the Everly Brothers. However, Polydor Records was not interested in Sheridan's original songs because they hoped to capitalize on the beat-group popularity sweeping Germany. While recording "My Bonnie," Tony played guitar riffs similar to those employed by Scotty Moore and Buddy Holly. Sheridan spent a great deal of time listening to Elvis Presley's Sun Records. As a result, he was a master of Moore's rockabilly guitar style. But Tony was such an accomplished guitarist that he was able to perform someone else's material in his own unique manner.

From 1963 to 1968, Sheridan recorded a series of songs which were included on a Polydor album issued in Germany. The LP, entitled: "What'd I Say" and advertised as 'Tony Sheridan with the Beat Brothers' has sold more than a million copies in the last decade. The songs on this LP include "Sweet Georgia Brown" and "Why" with the Beatles listed as the supporting musicians. The remaining tunes are advertised as Tony Sheridan and the Beat Brothers and include "Ruby Baby," "Let's Dance," "Unchained Melody," "You Better Move On," "Jambalaya," "What'd I Say," "Save the Last Dance For Me," "Just a Little Bit," "Ya Ya" and "Let's Slop." The LP is a strange mixture of songs recorded from 1963 to 1968, and although it is well done, the tunes are not Sheridan's best ones. To this day, Tony is known primarily as the man who recorded "My Bonnie." Although it has not been a strong chart song "My Bonnie" was No. 48 on England's *Billboard* Top 50 listing for the week of July 6, 1963. In February, 1964, the single was reissued and sold well in both the British and American

Tony Sheridan, Late 1970s

marketplace. Sheridan's "My Bonnie" was modeled after Ray Charles' version released on August 6, 1958 by Atlantic Records. In fact, when the Beatles and Tony Sheridan practiced "My Bonnie" Sheridan jokingly referred to John Lennon and Paul McCartney's vocals as a budget version of Charles' backup group the Raelets. But Charles was not the only American musical pioneer to influence the Beatles first recordings. Bill Haley and the Comet's version of "When the Saints Go Marching In" was the model for the Beatles and Tony Sheridan's recording of this song. During the next few years, however, the atmosphere slowly changed in Hamburg.

By the mid-1960s, the rock music scene on the Reeperbahn was beginning to fall apart. American rock acts like Johnny and the Hurricanes no longer excited German audiences. But some of America's best rock acts, notably Fats Domino, Gene Vincent, Tommy Roe and Chuck Berry continued to perform in various Hamburg clubs. Tony Sheridan remained the most popular rock musician in Hamburg. However, many people believed that he was wasting his talents in venues like the Top Ten and the Star-Club. The Beatles and later the Searchers attempted to pull Tony out of his comfortable Hamburg setting. Always a maverick, Sheridan would not leave Germany, and he toured only with the artists who represented his own musical direction. As a result, Tony traveled to Israel with Gene Vincent, did two European tours with Conway Twitty, and a short series of dates with Jerry Lee Lewis.

During the late 1960s Tony continued to perform in Germany. "If you are a historical figure, you can always fall back upon it," Sheridan reflected. Tony also toured Vietnam with Horst Fascher acting as his manager and booking agent. They were very popular with the American soldiers and Sheridan's hits, "My Bonnie" and "Skinnie Minnie" were requested again and again by rock enthusiasts in Vietnam. After two marriages and a rollercoaster career in the music business, Tony concentrated upon his songwriting and engaged in marathon reading sessions in the 1970s. Always an intelligent, reflective individual, Tony studied religion, philosophy and Irish literature. "The Celtic things afflicts all of the Irish," Sheridan remarked.

As he reflects on life, Tony has a personality very similar to Van Morrison. They are both interested in religion, the problems of personal relationships and they have an existential view of life in their songs. Tom Shaka, an American singer who performed in Hamburg, remembers that Tony knew as much about the blues as any musician he had ever met. "Tony Sheridan is a genuine musical talent," Shaka remarked, "and he was as helpful to me in the 1970s as he was to the Beatles in the 1960s."

From 1972 to 1974, Sheridan achieved a new type of fame in Germany with a revolutionary radio blues show. After 15 years as a professional musician, Sheridan mesmerized the blues hungry German audiences with live guitar solos, in-person blues songs, and some of the finest blues records heard in Europe. Sheridan's show broadcast over NDRZ in West Germany brought renewed touring opportunities for such American bluesmen as Little Willie Littlefield, Memphis Slim and Billy Boy Arnold. These previously unrecognized American bluesmen found German audiences receptive to their music as a result of Sheridan's radio show. Memphis Slim was already living in Paris and operating two night clubs when his records began to sell in Germany. Little Willie Littlefield, who sold Jerry Leiber and Mike Stoller the hit song "Kansas City," for $100, was playing in Angelo's Cocktail Lounge in San Jose, California, when he went to Germany to play a series of twenty concert dates. Eventually, Little Willie Littlefield moved to West Germany. "The audiences love me and I am in Germany to stay," Littlefield says.

Tom Shaka: American Bluesman in Hamburg

By the late 1970s, Sheridan was a follower of Bhagwan Three Rajneesh. This religious movement, originated in India and now based in central Oregon, U.S.A., has more than 2,000 followers in Hamburg. Dressed in red, the clothing of Bhagwan's followers, Tony Sheridan now is an articulate, slightly grey, middle-aged man who remains an impressive physical and mental figure. He credits his intellectual growth to Bhagwan, but at home he has a large library on varied subjects. He continues to read, write and think intensely about life. His songs are excellent, and a portfolio of thirty to forty tunes awaits a major record company. Sheridan continues to perform throughout West Germany, and he is one of the strongest acts to appear in local clubs.

Tony Sheridan was in many respects the first Beatle. He wrote and performed original material. Sheridan experimented with art and changes in musical structure, and he was one of the first English musicians to master blues guitar riffs. He went beyond the stereotypical teen idol of the early 1960s with his music. Unfortunately, Sheridan was lost in the shuffle of the recording industry. Much like Van Morrison, he is a song-poet who is still capable of inspiring audiences. It is not too late for Tony Sheridan; he may one day achieve the elusive stardom that the Beatles experienced in the 1960s.

Tom Shaka and Tony Sheridan, 1983

HORST FASCHER

Horst Fascher: Hamburg Boxer as Teacher

In the early 1960s, as the Beatles were fine-tuning their music in Hamburg's notorious Reeperbahn district, they became friendly with a young German boxer, Horst Fascher. Most of the serious books on the Beatles portray Fascher as either a minor figure or a "gangster type" who hung around the fringes. Neither description is accurate because Fascher was a significant influence in the development of the Beatles' music.

As a knowledgable German with a strong interest in music, Horst was important in advising the band on its live performance style and selection of songs. He was an excellent barometer of local opinion. For a time Fascher was a bouncer at Bruno Koschmider's Kaiserkeller Club. Horst recruited a number of his friends from the Hamburg Boxing Academy, to maintain order in the club. Local Germans nicknamed Fascher's bouncers "Hoddell's Gang," and the gang often protected the musicians from irate drunks. There was also a very human side to Fascher's personality. Often Horst took the foreign musicians to his mother's home for sausage and soup. He was particularly attracted to these English musicians, because he was able to practice his English and sing a song or two late at night.

When the Beatles first appeared in Hamburg in late 1960, Horst Fascher was a well-known German featherweight boxer. He had been on the Hamburg and West German national boxing teams, and he had distinguished himself in a well-publicized series of London-Hamburg boxing matches. Unfortunately, during the mid-1960s, Fascher was jailed for accidentally killing a sailor in a street fight. This effectively ended his boxing career and also had a dramatic impact upon his life.

Sitting in Horst's sunny, tastefully furnished Hamburg apartment recently, we talked for hours about Hamburg and the Beatles in the early 1960s. "I have not given a lengthy interview in twenty years," Fascher remarked, "and no one has come around to ask me about my days with the Beatles."

Fascher began by dwelling on some of the myths surrounding his days with the Beatles. "I was never Bruno Koschmider's right-hand man," Fascher remarked. Horst went on to explain that many books suggest that he was Koschmider's assistant at the Kaiserkeller. The reality is that Horst was very close to the bands and able to help them find better performing venues while he acted as a bouncer. Eventually, Horst was fired for protecting the musicians' interests. Koschmider's clubs paid low wages, had poor working conditions and required long hours on stage. As a result, Fascher advised skilled bands like the Beatles to find better bookings. Soon clubs like the Top Ten and the Star Club offered improved working conditions. The main reasons for Fascher's benevolent attitude were that he loved rock and roll music and that he hoped to enter the business side of the music industry. Horst emphasized that he was an independent agent who booked acts for the Top Ten and Star-Club, and never more than an employee at the Kaiserkeller.

In May, 1983, as the interview took place, Paul McCartney continued to maintain a close personal friendship with Fascher. As I sat on the living room couch in Horst's apartment, a large picture of McCartney dominated the room. It was obvious that Paul continued to occupy a special place in Fascher's life. Just two years earlier they had gotten together for a brief reunion, and it was obvious that Fascher's relationship with McCartney was one built upon years of mutual trust and friendship. As Fascher talked, he unravelled some of the hidden mysteries of the Beatles early years. Fascher's experiences represent important reflections upon the rise of rock and roll music in England and Germany.

In 1959, Fascher's first contact with English rock and roll music developed as he traveled to London as a boxer to participate in the Hamburg-London city boxing matches. After his featherweight

Tommy Roe and Horst Fascher

bout, Horst went to London's Soho district to hear some music. There was a subtle revolution taking place as a new and distinct form of English rock and roll music was emerging in clubs like the 2-Is. This small venue was the one which essentially gave birth to English rock music by allowing skiffle, blues, and rock performers to sing for audiences of 30 to 40 people. Since there were very few rock music clubs in London, the 2-Is was unique because it attracted talent like Tony Sheridan, Cliff Richard and the Shadows, and Terry Dene among others.

Tom Underwood, the manager of the 2-Is, was introduced to Horst, and they talked for hours about the possibility of bringing English rock acts to Hamburg's famed Reeperbahn night club section. That night Horst heard Tony Sheridan, a veteran of England's television show, "Oh Boy," perform Elvis Presley-type rock and roll, some blues tunes, and a number of original songs. It was a heady moment and Horst was smitten by Sheridan's unique talent. He also listened to Vince Taylor and met future Shadow member Bruce Welch. During the middle of Taylor's set, even English rock star Cliff Richard walked into the small club. It was an exciting experience for Fascher, and he decided to bring a number of these talented performers to Hamburg. The small stage and the limited seating capacity at the 2-Is signalled to Fascher that the English rock revolution was still in its infancy. Fascher knew that German audiences loved rock music and therefore would cheer the 2-Is acts. His interest in importing British performers was to help shape a strong musical connection between Hamburg and both London and Liverpool. The first British musicians were to come from London. Once that available talent was used up, Liverpool would become the second city to supply Hamburg clubs with rock music groups.

Once Horst Fascher had returned to Hamburg, he began to tell his friends about the energetic, but unappreciated, brand of English rock music at the 2-Is coffee bar. His descriptions of the London music scene attracted the attention of the owner, Bruno Koschmider at the Kaiserkeller, where Horst worked as a bouncer. As a result of Horst's imaginative re-creation of the British music scene, Koschmider arranged for Tony Sheridan to appear at the Kaiserkeller Club. This garish club, located on a small street in the Reeperbahn section, resembled a posh house of prostitution. The wild colors and art deco appearance made the Kaiserkeller attractive to rock music aficionados. The entire street was lined with electric signs, and barkers at various establishments attempted to entice patrons in to see the mysteries of nude dancers, female mud wrestlers and beautiful transvestites. Indonesian bands blurted out cover records of Elvis Presley's music, and there were a number of little sidewalk cafes selling sausages and chips. The Roxy Club featured transvestites, the Indra juke box music, and the Kaiserkeller rock and roll. There was something for everyone in Hamburg's Reeperbahn section. Although it was a bizarre, often comical, area of Hamburg, there was a strong demand there for good rock music. In May, 1960 when Tony Sheridan arrived in Hamburg, he was a well-known two-year veteran of English rock music circles with appearances on the popular television show "Oh Boy" and a strong cult following in and around London. In addition, Sheridan had gained an enviable reputation as an accomplished blues guitarist.

As a result of Tony Sheridan's knowledge of the English rock scene and Horst Fascher's ability to translate Tony's thoughts into action, Rory Storm and the Hurricanes were hired to perform with Tony Sheridan. (Sheridan had brought his own band, the Jets, but they proved to be unsatisfactory.) Larry Parnes, a London booking agent, was also instrumental in convincing Koschmider to hire English bands. In fact, Parnes was so well known for discovering

English teen idol Tommy Steele, that Koschmider actually paid Parnes more than he had to for booking Rory Storm's band. When Tony Sheridan and other acts went to Germany, it was the beginning of the English invasion of Hamburg and the creation of a musical sound destined to change the course of rock and roll musical history.

Once Rory Storm and the Hurricanes came to Hamburg, Horst Fascher became very friendly with Rory Storm and the Hurricanes's drummer, Ringo Starr. Eventually Ringo was persuaded by Horst to leave Storm's group and join Tony Sheridan's band. It was while serving this brief apprenticeship with Sheridan that Ringo learned to play American style rock-and-roll music. Sheridan's band thrived on the music of Chuck Berry, Jerry Lee Lewis, Ray Charles, Eddie Cochran, Little Richard, Elvis Presley, Conway Twitty and Gene Vincent. In fact, Vincent once remarked that Sheridan's band was the best rock group he had heard outside of the United States. The result of this exposure helped Ringo to become one of England's best rock drummers as well as providing him with an encyclopedic knowledge of rock music.

Unlike the other English and Irish musicians who migrated from town to town or country to country, Tony Sheridan remained in Hamburg. He married a local girl, Rosie, and he became the father of a young son. Much of Tony's time in the early 1960s was spent with his good friend Horst Fascher. In fact, Fascher eventually became Sheridan's manager in the late 1960s. But in the summer of 1960, neither Fascher nor Sheridan were yet main figures in the burgeoning rock revolution. From the very beginning, Fascher, however, was convinced that Sheridan was talented enough to secure a record deal. After just a few months on the Reeperbahn, Fascher was publicizing Sheridan's solid rock and roll performances. Soon major music figures in West Germany were coming to the Kaiserkeller to hear the new "beat groups."

Bert Kaempfert, a well-known musician and Polydor Records A and R man, eventually heard Sheridan and the Beatles due to Horst's urging. Not only did Fascher help to promote the influx of new English musical talent, but he also complained bitterly to Koschmider about the squalid living conditions and poor pay the English bands received. Koschmider responded by firing Fascher and instructing the Kaiserkeller's manager, Willy Limpinser, to keep Horst out of the club. "I found Tony Sheridan was living in a room with no windows, little to eat, and not much money," Horst

Hamburg's Reeperbahn, 1983

remarked. So he often took Sheridan to Harold's, a small sausage shop, for a late night dinner of pommes frites, chicken and sausage. The tall articulate Irishman and the short, muscular German talked late into the night about rock music, the changing cultural milieu of Germany and the rise of the new English bands. Both Fascher and Sheridan read voluminously, if not secretly, and they recognized that a cultural revolution was in the making. They had the same ideas about music, discussed the business side of the industry, and vented their general anger over the paucity of money and the lack of popular recognition for rock music; Sheridan and Fascher continued to feel lost in the bowels of German culture.

Contrary to popular myth, Fascher was neither the "tiny, swaggering bully," described by Philip Norman in *Shout: The Beatles in Their Generation* nor the small time promoter pictured in Peter Brown's *The Love You Make: An Insider's Story of the Beatles.* A good example of Fascher's alleged small promoter mentality is indicated by a story in Brown's book. In this tale, Brown charges that Fascher was forced to bribe groups to play in Hamburg's Top Ten or Star Club, but these stories do not square with the facts. According to Peter Brown, Horst Fascher gave Brian Epstein a brown paper bag which contained one thousand pounds so that the Beatles would play in the Star-Club. The rumor was that Epstein had priced the Beatles out of the Hamburg market, because their records were selling well in England and bookings in the U.K. were lucrative ones. This was a story that was foisted upon an unsuspecting public to draw even more fans into the Hamburg clubs to see the Beatles. Since this $2,500 bribe would have made it virtually impossible for the club to have turned a profit; the story does not appear to be accurate. Fascher was a shrewd businessman and did not need to resort to bribes in order to attract the best musical talent. This tale is simply another example of the types of myths and legends which surrounded the Beatles early career.

Contrary to the legend, Fascher was not only an excellent entrepreneur, but also an astute judge of musical talent. Many of the rock groups in Hamburg depended upon Fascher for an honest critique of their music and stage performance. As Fascher's reputation grew, a young German seamen, Peter Eckhorn, approached him about running a new night club. Eckhorn's father owned a former Reeperbahn club named the Hippodrome. Like many German night clubs of the 1950's, the Hippodrome featured in-door horse racing and mud-wrestling ladies. When it closed in 1959, the featured acts were Indonesian rock groups singing Elvis Presley songs. Like his father, Peter Eckhorn was consumed by show business magic, and he believed that the growing interest in rock music would create a new demand for rock-oriented night clubs. As a result, Eckhorn reopened his father's former Hippodrome Club in November, 1960, and renamed it the Top Ten Club. Eckhorn realized that Fascher could provide the right type of music for his new club. By the spring of 1961, the Top Ten Club had become one of the more popular spots on the Reeperbahn and ended Bruno Koschmider's control of the Reeperbahn's music business. Tony Sheridan and his group, the Jets, opened the Top Ten Club, and there were already plans to bring in the Beatles and other Liverpool groups. Fascher had convinced Eckhorn that the German intellectuals, the rowdy sailors, and the music purists were all equally infatuated by the Liverpool sound.

The rise of Peter Eckhorn in the German entertainment business is an important reflection of how profitable rock music was in Hamburg's Reeperbahn. While Horst Fascher was still employed at the Kaiserkeller, Eckhorn persuaded Fascher to begin working on the Hippodrome Club. This was a shrewd move, because Fascher convinced Tony Sheridan and the Jets as well as the Beatles to consider performing in the new Top Ten Club. The Beatles had a contract with Koschmider which forbade them from performing in the vicinity of the Kaiserkeller, and this seemed to guarantee that they would not perform for another club in the Reeperbahn. Nevertheless, Horst urged John Lennon to talk with Peter Eckhorn about a possible engagement at the Top Ten Club.

In early December, 1960, just a few days before the Beatles completed their four month engagement at the Indra and Kaiserkeller, Eckhorn took Lennon out for dinner. Lennon informed Eckhorn that the Beatles would honor their contract with Koschmider. John was concerned over Koschmider's threats, and he also felt that honoring the contract would make the Beatles more attractive to other club owners. Although he was relatively new in the rock business, Lennon believed that the Beatles must develop some business skills. Eckhorn argued that Lennon was hurting the Beatles' career by staying with Koschmider. The Top Ten Club not only offered better living, working, and creative conditions, but Eckhorn also offered ten marks per man more a night. After a lengthy tirade against Koschmider, Eckhorn persuaded Lennon to sign a contract for a two-week engagement at the Top Ten Club in December, 1960.

On December 18, 1960, the Beatles played their last engagement at the Kaiserkeller Club. They returned to the Bambi Kino, the small movie theater where they slept, to quietly move out their clothes and begin their two-week engagement at the Top Ten Club. John Lennon wrote his uncle Charlie that he would not be home until January 3, 1961. However, as the Beatles prepared to move to another club, someone working for Bruno Koschmider informed the Hamburg police that George Harrison was only seventeen years old. That morning, Harrison was abruptly sent home to Liverpool.

As the police hustled Harrison out of town, Paul McCartney and Pete Best attempted to move their belongings from the small room behind the Bambi Kino. A fire broke out and the police arrived. The two young musicians were temporarily detained. The result was that Pete Best wanted desperately to go home, Paul McCartney was shaken by the police interrogation, and John Lennon was furious that the Beatles were not able to play in the Top Ten Club.

On December 19, 1960, the Beatles played for one night at Eckhorn's club. It was a disspirited performance since the Beatles could not cover George Harrison's absence. Despite some excellent piano work by Paul McCartney and John Lennon's attempts to play

George Harrison

lead guitar, the performance was not topnotch. John informed Eckhorn that the Beatles had received a telegram from Allan Williams telling them that they were scheduled to perform at Grosvenor's Ballroom in Wallasay on December 24 and at Liverpool's Litherland Hall three nights later. But John promised that the Beatles would return to the Top Ten Club.

When John Lennon returned to Liverpool, he was not as disspirited as many studies suggest because he knew that the Beatles would return shortly to Hamburg. Just prior to leaving Hamburg, John and Horst Fascher had had a long discussion. Horst urged Lennon to work on the Beatles' stage presentation. It was already excellent, but the act needed still more discipline. Fascher was also concerned with the Beatles' safety and he urged John Lennon to ignore the pimps, prostitutes, drug dealers and generally sleazy characters who hung out on the Reeperbahn when they returned.

During the Beatles' subsequent visits to Hamburg, Fascher was an important source of advice and encouragement to the Liverpool lads. "I was a big name—I protected the musicians," Fascher reflected. In his attempt to educate the Beatles to the ways of the Reeperbahn, Horst took John Lennon to the Sascha Beer Club. This small beer bar was a hangout for pimps, prostitutes and a wide variety of low lifes who hung around Hamburg's fringes. As Horst Fascher watched in awe, John Lennon was paid by a local prostitute to spend the night in her apartment. Horst was afraid the girl's pimp would come looking for John to beat him up, so Horst put out the word that he would protect Lennon from any assaults. He gave John a small button to wear, and this symbol indicated that Fascher would beat to a pulp anyone who bothered Lennon. Had it not been for Fascher's protection, John might not have escaped from Hamburg's Reeperbahn section.

As Horst's interest in rock music intensified, he inquired about booking American name rock acts in Hamburg. Soon he was in touch with English and American promoters, and he helped to bring such well-known rock stars as Gene Vincent, Carl Perkins, Fats Domino, Little Richard, Tommy Roe, Jerry Lee Lewis, Chuck Berry and Gene Pitney to the Reeperbahn. There were many other minor league rock acts such as Johnny and the Hurricanes and B. Bumble and the Stingers who also appeared in Hamburg due to Fascher's booking connections. As a result of the heightened interest in English and American rock music groups, a number of new clubs such as the Star Club and small beer bars like the Fleurs Schanke employed musical groups. There was not only an influx of musicians, but the crowds were large, boisterous, and prone to spending lots of money on beer, whiskey, and pills. In Hamburg in the early 1960s, there was an incredible gathering of musical talent provided by many of the best-known rock groups and individual singers of the decade. Hamburg was becoming a training ground for musical and financial success.

When the Hamburg returned to the Top Ten Club in April, 1961, there was an exciting musical atmosphere. Allan Williams was able to secure valid work permits and Peter Eckhorn wired train fare for the group. The Beatles alternated music sets with Tony Sheridan's band, beginning at seven p.m. and ending at three a.m. With Tony Sheridan and his reformed band, the Jets, living above the Top Ten Club in comfortable rooms with the Beatles, there was a non-stop party atmosphere. At these parties a number of new musical influences were opened to the Beatles. Perhaps the most significant new musical direction was country-western music. Rikky Richards, an obscure British country-western singer, passed through the Top Ten Club one night on his way to entertain American troops in Frankfurt. During a late night party, Richards

The Top Ten Club

introduced the Beatles to a number of new rockabilly songs. Richards, a Carl Perkins aficionado, sang songs like "Matchbox" and "Everybody's Trying to Be My Baby."

It was during the Beatles' Top Ten engagement in April and May 1961 that their musical act became the strongest one on Hamburg's Reeperbahn. Much of the Beatles success resulted from the support given to the Liverpool Four by local existential intellectuals from the nearby University and Art Colleges, but Horst Fascher was also an important force as he cajoled, coaxed, and publicized the Beatles musical skills. He continually buoyed the Beatles' confidence while critically commenting on their musical directions. Fascher was a friend who perceived that John Lennon and Paul McCartney possessed unusual songwriting skills, and he continually exorted the Lennon-McCartney duo to turn out new songs.

It was partially as a result of Horst Fascher's urging that Bert Kaempfert signed the Beatles to a contract with Polydor records as back-up musicians. Their first recording was made in Hamburg in May, 1961, backing up Tony Sheridan. They received 65 dollars for the session. Interestingly enough, Fascher kept urging Kaempfert to let the Beatles record their own music, but Kaempfert refused, and after a year and a half Polydor simply voided their contract.

One of the main reasons Fascher believed that the Beatles were so talented was that he compared them to the American rock-and-roll singer Gene Vincent. To revive his sagging career, Vincent toured throughout England and eventually Germany in the early 1960s. In 1961 the Beatles backed Vincent at the Cavern Club in Liverpool, and the first issue of *Mersey Beat* featured a front-page picture of Gene Vincent, as well as a story on the Beatles. The comparison between the legendary Vincent, whose "Be Bop a Lula" delighted European audiences, and the Beatles was important. As Fascher noted, both were great acts, but the Beatles were better songwriters and appealed to the young girls. Fascher realized that Vincent's slick, almost greasy, rock look was on its way out, and he urged the Beatles to become more conscious of fashion.

When Gene Vincent played in Hamburg's Star-Club, he became very friendly with Horst and his brother, Freddy Fascher. They talked a great deal about the changing direction of rock music and Vincent lamented the decline of straight-ahead rock-and roll music. Horst found Vincent to be an intriguing fellow, but he felt that the American's volatile temper and sporadic concert problems were killing his career.

In contrast to Vincent's decline, the Beatles talent continued to develop at the Cavern Club in Liverpool and clubs like the Top Ten around Hamburg. The growth of the Beatles' music was demonstrated during their April 13, to June 6, 1962 appearance at Manfred Weissleder's Star-Club. It was during this trip that the Beatles talked seriously about recording hit records. Not only was the group's confidence greater, but they were buoyed by the enthusiastic response of audiences in the clubs and theaters in which they performed. By 1962, the Merseyside sound was fast becoming the main type of rock music in England and Germany. As the Beatles and other bands emerged, the old American rockers like Gene Vincent faded as top musical acts. There was such a strong demand for new British rock groups that even Vincent's band, the Sounds Incorporated, were signed by Columbia Records. Sounds Incorporated immediately turned out a string of minor hit records, thereby giving credence to the growing belief that any English group could hit the charts. Although Sounds Incorporated were an excellent group, nonetheless, they were helped by the mania for English music.

Paul McCartney

In many respects Tony Sheridan failed to become a popular recording artist, because he refused to return to England or identify with English music. Fascher counseled Tony to consider marketing his music in the same manner as the English singers. One of the strange twists in Tony's career was that he was influenced by the Beatles. Initially, Sheridan was the Beatles' teacher, but they soon surpassed his influence.

In 1962, Tony Sheridan was the source of the Beatles's new musical skill. As the Beatles backed the Irish-born singer, they received a musical education which eventually made them superstars. It was Horst Fascher who helped steer the Beatles in Sheridan's direction. Horst pointed out Tony's virtuoso guitar skills, and he also suggested that the Beatles could learn a great deal about recent rock music, since Sheridan had toured with American singers Gene Vincent and Conway Twitty and had a good grasp of early American rock and roll.

One of the more interesting aspects of Tony Sheridan and the Beatles' career witnessed by Horst Fascher was the recording of the John Lennon-George Harrison composition "Cry For a Shadow" as well as John Lennon's vocal lead on "Ain't She Sweet." "Cry For a

Shadow," was a takeoff on Cliff Richard's group, The Shadows. John Lennon's vocal on "Ain't She Sweet" was his first professional recording, but Fascher could not convince Polydor Record executives to take the Beatles seriously.

When the Beatles backed Tony Sheridan on "My Bonnie" and "When the Saints Go Marching In" they were listed as the Beat Brothers. In Hamburg, everyone knew that it was the Beatles on Sheridan's record. And once "My Bonnie" began selling in England, it was known largely by word of mouth. As a result when Raymond Jones walked into NEMS on October 28, 1961 and asked Brian Epstein for "My Bonnie," Jones was typical of many young people who liked the record but found it difficult to purchase in record stores. Since it was Horst Fascher who helped the Beatles to secure a recording contract with Polydor Records, he was partially responsible for the beginning of their career. Before John Lennon signed his contract with Brian Epstein, he recalled that Horst Fascher gave him some sound advice. "Show business is two words—show and business," Fascher lectured. He made it very clear to John that if the Beatles were to become successful they needed sound business management. This advice convinced John to sign a contract with Brian Epstein. When John Lennon sat in Brian Epstein's office a year and a half later with the other Beatles and Bob Wooler, he remembered Fascher's words and asked Brian a number of pointed questions about how he was going to publicize the Beatles' music. John was satisfied with the answers, and in December, 1961, Lennon scribbled a brief note to Horst thanking him for his advice.

A year after signing with Brian Epstein, the Beatles left for their last engagement in Hamburg, and they eagerly anticipated some parties with their friend, Horst Fascher. "Love Me Do" was already in the British Top Twenty, and the Beatles were the hottest rock group in the UK. Yet, in their last Hamburg appearance, the Beatles were not the headliner act at the Star-Club. An American rock group, Johnny and the Hurricanes, had top billing. The oversight did not bother the Beatles, and they simply gave as energetic a show as possible to point out that they were now top recording stars. No one realized that this would be the Beatles' final appearance in Hamburg, and they were simply happy to be playing for old friends.

After their first night at the Star Club the Beatles returned to the Pacific Hotel to party with old friends like Ted "Kingsize" Taylor. As Horst Fascher sat with the Beatles, he realized that their

Hamburg's Star Club

careers were heading in a very successful direction. The rise of
"Love Me Do" on the English charts and the demand for the record
in Germany convinced Fascher that big things were ahead for the
Beatles. Fascher smiled as he recalled the naive, inexperienced
young men who had arrived in Hamburg in August, 1960. As a
result of his belief in the Beatles' talent, Fascher later flew to New
York to book some new rock acts for the Star Club and to see if he
could help his old friends, the Beatles.

During this 1962 trip to New York, Fascher met with the
manager of the Peppermint Lounge. The twist craze had taken over
America, and Joey Dee and the Starlighters were the Peppermint
Lounge's main attraction. Fascher hoped to bring Joey Dee to
Hamburg, and he offered the manager of the Peppermint Lounge,
Mr. Kay, to bring the Beatles to New York in return for Dee's
services. After Kay heard the Beatles' tapes, he turned the group
down because English musicians were not a draw in America.
Fascher attempted to convince the Peppermint Lounge to book the
Beatles, and he spent two days extolling their musical virtues. "The
Beatles have a wealth of original material," Fascher informed Kay,
"and they have filled clubs in Hamburg and Liverpool nightly." But

there was no precedent for bringing English musicians to America and the attempts to break Cliff Richard in the American market had not been successful ones. Fascher flew back to Hamburg undeterred by the rejection.

In order to build his career as a concert promoter, Fascher worked very hard from 1962 to 1965 to bring in name rock acts. Eventually, Fascher was responsible for some of the best rock groups appearing in the Reeperbahn. As he became a well-known concert promoter Horst found the pressures increasing, and one night in a street fight he accidentally killed a sailor. After a brief trial, Fascher was sentenced to two years in prison. "I was put in jail," Fascher stated, "and there was no more work at St. Pauli or in the Clubs."

When he was released from prison in the late 1960s, there were dramatic changes in the Hamburg music scene. No longer was it possible to make a decent living promoting music in Hamburg's Reeperbahn section. Since 1963, Horst had worked with Don Arden, an English booking agent. In 1969 Arden began looking for a rock group to manage and the following year Roy Wood's group Move was renamed The Electric Light Orchestra. The commercial success was strong enough to allow Arden to found Jet Records. Since Arden was no longer able to provide acts, Horst Fascher was forced to look for new business directions.

As a result of declining musical opportunities in Hamburg, Horst persuaded Tony Sheridan to embark upon a tour of American military bases in Vietnam. After negotiating a contract with the American USO, Fascher presented war-weary American GIs excellent rock and roll shows as well as Las-Vegas-type lounge acts. In Vietnam Horst met a beautiful young Filipino entertainer and married her. A son followed shortly and the Faschers returned to Hamburg. By the early 1970s, Fascher was a local businessman.

During the 1970s, Fascher's life veered away from the rock-and-roll world. He continued to engage in various business pursuits, and in the late 1970s Horst opened a new edition of the Star-Club. The new Star-Club featured Tony Sheridan, as well as other Hamburg talent from the 1960s. Ringo Starr was in the audience on opening night. However, the music scene had changed dramatically and Fascher failed to draw sufficient crowds to maintain the new Star-Club.

In the early 1980s, Horst's wife was hit by a runaway automobile, and she needed around-the-clock nursing care. Horst provided the best medical care for his wife, and he is now one of

Hamburg's most successful sport shoe businessmen. Still very friendly with many top level musicians, Fascher continues to maintain a historical interest in rock music. His days with the Beatles remain a pleasant, if somewhat distant, memory.

Sitting in his apartment in May, 1983, Fascher's eyes lit up when he talked about the old days on the Reeperbahn. The Top Ten and Star-Club experiences were among his favorites, and he is convinced that the Beatles and the Hamburg Clubs helped to usher in a whole new generation of rock-and-roll music. "In the old days it was common for 20,000 people to dance in a club during a 12 hour period," Fascher remarked. A few years ago Paul McCartney and Horst got together to swap old stories about the glories of the Top Ten days. Horst Fascher's life was changed by his brief friendship with the Beatles, and his memories and experiences remain fond ones.

The Who, It Would Have Been Impossible Without The Beatles

BOB WOOLER

Bob Wooler: The Fifth Beatle

During the early 1960s the Beatles' music made them an important, yet unrecognized, rock group at the Cavern Club on Mathews Street in Liverpool. It was while refining their act in this dark cellar that a disc jockey, Bob Wooler, helped the Beatles to perfect their music. A short, dapper, extremely articulate young man, Wooler was an integral part of the Liverpool and Merseyside music scene in the 1950s and 1960s. In addition to acting as a master of ceremonies at local dances, Wooler also spent an inordinate amount of time collecting American rock, blues, and rhythm and blues records. Since he possessed a virtually encyclopedic knowledge of rock music, Wooler was sought out by rock, jazz and skiffle groups for advice on songs which could be added to their concert repertoires. He was considered so knowledgeable in music matters that local promoters like Brian Kelley and Allan Williams used Wooler as a sounding board for their concert promotion ideas. Brian Kelley often hired Wooler to work on advance promotion for his dances at the Litherland Town Hall and the Aintree Institute. Wooler, also an independent entrepreneur, helped to promote historically important concerts like Little Richard's October 12, 1962, show in the Brighton Ballroom. The Little Richard show featured the Beatles and ten other well-known Merseyside groups. As a result of his concert promotions, his knowledge of records, and his ability to bring live audiences to their feet as a disc jockey, Wooler played a significant part in the Beatles rise to fame and fortune.

Before he became known as the "Fifth Beatle" among Liverpool music fans, Wooler was an unlikely rock music aficionado. He was a sauve, urbane man with a delicate sense of humor. Almost every Liverpool musician asked to comment on Bob Wooler remarked that he was a friendly, open man who would go to great lengths to help anyone in the music business. In the 1960s Wooler was instrumental in bringing London talent scouts and recording executives to the Cavern to hear local talent. Before he became a promoter and disc jockey/compere, Wooler worked for the British railroad as a shipping clerk. He gave up this line of work in 1960 to devote himself to journalism and the entertainment industry. A quiet, almost studious man, Wooler refused to move to London in the 1960s and this relegated him to a relatively insignificant role in the history of British rock music. Yet, in retrospect, it is obvious that Wooler was one of the most unique figures in the rock music field. It was Bob Wooler, for example, who took records by obscure American singers like Arthur Alexander to the Beatles, and once they heard Alexander's version of "Anna," it became a staple in the Beatles's early songbook. Selection of material is an important part of success in the rock music business, and Wooler had an uncanny knack for advising groups to do a certain song. When the Searchers "Needles and Pins" was recorded, it was due to advice from Wooler.

Another important aspect of Wooler's career is that he managed a number of local Liverpool bands. As the skiffle craze reached its high point of popularity in the late 1950s, Wooler booked and managed the Kingstrums. It was during this period in 1958-1959 that Wooler often saw the Beatles perform in local halls. Although he paid little attention to their performances, he simply remembered them as another suburban band. "I never noticed the Beatles," Wooler remarked, but he did evaluate a number of other local bands.

The most impressive early Liverpool rock band was the Bluegenes. They began playing in local clubs in 1959, and the following year they were one of the main attractions in the Hamburg Clubs on the famous Reeperbahn. Eventually they changed their name to the Swinging Blue Genes, and in the summer of 1963 their recording of "It's Too Late Now" reached the U.K. Top 30. Wooler remarked to a *Liverpool Echo* reporter that no local band could match the Bluegenes because they were the first Merseyside

Derry Willkie

band to popularize an American rock sound. Later their cover version of Chan Romero's "Hippy Hippy Shake" became an American top ten hit record. Although the Bluegenes recommended that the Cavern Club hire the Beatles, it was Bob Wooler who persuaded the Cavern to book them regularly.

As the Liverpool music scene underwent a transition from a skiffle-jazz sound to rock music, Wooler was busy promoting the new rock sound. By 1960 he hosted a twice-weekly dance show at Litherland Town Hall, and he wrote articles on the burgeoning rock music industry. In addition Wooler spent a great deal of time at Allan Williams' Jacaranda Club in Liverpool. He began to associate with newly emerging rock bands like Kingsize Taylor and the Dominoes, Faron and the Flamingos, Derry and the Seniors, and Rory Storm and the Hurricanes. Derry Willkie was one of the first musicians to mesmerize local Liverpoolians with tales of Hamburg's musical attractions. Each night in the local clubs, Willkie told stories of the appreciative German audiences, and he threw in examples of the exotic sexual freedoms that awaited local bands. Allan Williams was often a more attentive listener than the musicians, and he was eager to take a band to Hamburg. In fact, one night Williams stood on a table in the Jacaranda and toasted the coming British invasion. The customers looked around wild-eyed and had no idea that Williams was announcing his intentions of booking local acts in Hamburg.

As a group of drunken bystanders listened, Bob Wooler recognized that the popularity of Liverpool bands in Hamburg was an indication of a rich commercial music sound. Wooler also realized that skiffle and jazz music were on the decline, and he zealously encouraged every rock band in Liverpool to refine its act. When the Beatles returned from their brief stint in Hamburg's Indra and Kaiserkeller Clubs in December, 1960, they spun stories of Bruno Koschmeider's marvelous musical clubs. While the pay was low, the living conditions abysmal, and the crowds rowdy—the Beatles nonetheless recognized that for the first time they could play their music in a creative manner which allowed room for experimentation before a live audience. After talking with the Beatles and watching them practice, Wooler was amazed at the transformation in their talent.

Shortly after having dinner with the Beatles and talking with John Lennon at length, Bob Wooler sought out Allan Williams. In a lengthy conversation Wooler pointed out that the Beatles were a completely new musical act. The long sets at the Kaiserkeller in Hamburg had created a polished and sophisticated rock sound. Even though the Beatles had become professional and possessed a charismatic musical magic, Allan Williams was not convinced. Therefore he reiterated his desire not to have anything to do with the Beatles, because he felt they were simply too troublesome and too difficult to control while on stage. Refusing to give up, Wooler continued to push the Beatles' act and finally, on Christmas Eve, 1960, Williams relented and booked the Beatles into the Grosvenor Ballroom. He still failed to realize, however, that the Beatles would strike a commercially responsive chord with local Liverpool audiences.

The first example of the new Beatles occurred on December 27, 1960, when they played at the Litherland Town Hall. After being rebuffed by Williams, Bob Wooler had turned his attention to promoter Brian Kelley, and they spent long hours discussing the Beatles. Reluctantly Kelley agreed to use the Beatles at Litherland, and they received 6 pounds (or about $3.75) each for the engagement. After playing 4½ hours earlier that night in Liverpool, the Beatles came on stage for the Boxing Day show at the Litherland Town Hall and reeled off an hour of solid American music. Local audiences could not believe how exciting the Beatles' versions of Gene Vincent's, "Be Bop A Lula," Barrett Strong's "Money," and the Isley Brother's "Twist and Shout" were. Brian Kelley, a large, well-dressed man with strong business instincts, recognized the Beatles' unique talent and began to use them in local concerts. Another promoter, Sam Leach, also hired the Beatles to play his dances, but he promoted so many concerts that he didn't pause to notice the Beatles' enormous talent.

As a result of the important changes taking place in the Liverpool music scene, Rory Storm and the Hurricanes inaugurated rock music concerts at the Cavern Club on Mathews Street in Liverpool on May 25, 1960. This began the transformation of the Cavern and other clubs from jazz, skiffle venues to rock or beat music clubs. Soon Liverpool groups like Gerry and the Pacemakers, the Big 3, the Searchers, and the Beatles were playing nightly at the Cavern. Although rock music groups had performed before the May 25, 1960 date, there was suddenly a change in local Liverpool clubs as rock groups now dominated the club scene. In addition to the Beatles, Lee Curtis and the All Stars sparked a particularly enthusiastic response among the young girls. By June, 1961, the Liverpool sound was thriving.

The creation of the Liverpool sound had actually begun one year earlier in June, 1959, when the Silver Beatles (as they were temporarily known) and Gerry and the Pacemakers performed at local dance halls. Most of the Liverpool musicians had a pragmatic attitude toward a musical career. "In Liverpool there are only two things to do, play soccer or form a band," John Lennon remarked. So in the summer of 1960 Lennon attempted to finalize the band that he had kept together for almost three years. When Pete Best finally joined the Beatles on drums in August, 1960, he solidified the act. Yet there were few bookings and little interest in the group. As Philip Norman's book, *Shout: The Beatles in Their Generation,* has documented, the Silver Beatles hit their lowest point during the summer of 1960. At one time John Lennon lamented that Aunt Mimi was complaining about the three abandoned drum sets in her house. The final insult occurred when they were hired to back a stripper in one of Allan Williams' clubs on Upper Parliament Street.

Although no one wanted to hire the Beatles, there were some valuable lessons learned from these lean days. In addition to experiencing problems with local club owners like Allan Williams, the Beatles also found out that club and concert appearances were necessary to perfect their sound. They were determined to find some well-known singer to back on a tour. After watching American rock singers come through Liverpool, the Beatles were certain that all they needed was practice before live audiences to improve their sound.

The chance to tour with a well-known singer arrived almost by accident. As a result of the rock music explosion in Liverpool, Allan Williams began to operate a booking agency. Not only was Williams' Jacaranda Club the most popular in Liverpool, but he was also well known among London promoters. When Larry Parnes, a music empressario who had discovered Tommy Steele, traveled to Liverpool to audition a back-up band for singer Billy Fury, everyone in Liverpool was excited. On May 5, 1960, at the Wyvern Social Club on Seel Street, the audition took place with Johnny "Hutch" Hutchinson, from Cass and the Casanovas, on drums for the Beatles. Although Larry Parnes rejected the Beatles, Bob Wooler persisted and eventually changed Parnes' mind after a few drinks and a lengthy discussion. As a result the Beatles were signed to back another Parnes' singer, Johnny Gentle, on a brief tour of Scotland. When Parnes asked John Lennon for the group's name, he replied: "the Silver Beatles." For a time the group was also known as Johnny and the Moondogs, but the music of Buddy Holly and the Crickets soon prompted another name change. The insect selected by John Lennon was a beetle, but in typical Lewis Carroll fashion he altered the spelling to "Beatles."

It was difficult for the Beatles to accept Parnes' offer to tour with Johnny Gentle because they lacked a permanent drummer. There were few local drummers who would tour for the $43.20 a week plus expenses that Parnes offered, but John Lennon was intent upon backing Johnny Gentle. As a result he asked Bob Wooler for his help. After analyzing the situation Wooler suggested that the Beatles hire Tommy Moore, a 24-year-old forklift driver at the Garston Bottle Works. Moore's only previous experience was as a big band drummer, and he had little knowledge of rock music. After the first concert, John Lennon walked past Moore and hollered: "You bloody awful bastard." Moore threw his drum sticks at Lennon and finished the second set with one drum stick. The other one splintered to pieces. This incident set the tone for the remainder of the tour. After Moore was hit on the head by a suitcase falling from the rack on the tour bus, he told the Beatles that he would no longer play with them. Like Allan Williams, Moore returned to Liverpool with wild stories of the Beatles' personal excesses, and he vowed never to have anything to do with them.

John Lennon Practicing

In 1961 a number of Liverpool clubowners were influenced by Williams' and Moore's assessment that the Beatles were wild animals who could not be controlled. It was peculiar that Williams had such an impact upon the Liverpool music scene, but in 1961 he was the acknowledged kingpin of local rock music promoters. In spite of his negative view of their behavior, Williams realized that something about the Beatles' music was appealing to Liverpool crowds. A two year love-hate relationship between Williams and the Beatles followed. During the Beatles' later years of success in the 1960s and the solo careers which followed into the 1970s, they seldom mentioned Williams name. He was personally so repugnant to John Lennon that many years later Lennon broke a television set while listening to a review of Williams' book, *The Man Who Gave the Beatles Away,* on Los Angeles television. Lennon allegedly commented that Williams "was feasting off his past association with the Beatles." In a fit of rage one night in Los Angeles' Troubadour Club, John told Keith Moon that Williams "was the man who never knew the Beatles." Lennon laughingly recalled when Williams showed up in Los Angeles in 1973 looking for John. After speaking at a Beatle fan fest Williams was robbed as he walked back to his hotel. John laughed heartily at the thought of his former Liverpool employer walking Los Angeles' mean streets without money. An equally bizarre incident occurred on June 10, 1976 when Williams showed up at the backstage door of the Seattle Kingdome with an IOU for 16 pounds signed by Paul McCartney. The startled stage manager told Williams to wait, and McCartney sent a message which instructed Williams to mail the bill to his accountant for payment. The IOU was from August, 1960, when McCartney had borrowed the money to purchase some new clothes. Beatle collectors would have paid large sums for this piece of memorbilia, but Allan Williams mentality was not that of a skilled businessman. The incredulous McCartney could not believe the nerve of Allan Williams, and the incident brought back bittersweet memories of the old Liverpool days. To McCartney it seemed only yesterday that the Beatles were getting ready to begin their first Hamburg trip.

Before they left for their first appearances in Hamburg in August, 1960, the Beatles spent the early part of the summer hanging around Williams' Jacaranda Club. They would drink coffee and eat toasted bread with jam and listen to Williams brag about his influence in the music business. In addition, while they diligently practiced every afternoon at the Jacaranda, Bob Wooler frequently dropped in to listen to their music.

The Beatles often went to the Garston Baths, a rough area of Liverpool, to listen to the local bands. Since Garston was the area of Liverpool where Bob Wooler was born, he was able to provide the Beatles with quick access to local clubs. It was in the Garston Baths that the Beatles heard a group known as the Mars Bars. After their set John Lennon went up and introduced himself to the lead singer. His name was Gerry Marsden, and he soon fronted the Merseyside group Gerry and the Pacemakers. The Beatles were not only receiving a musical education, but also observing how other Merseyside groups crafted their music. But the Beatles found it difficult to persuade the best known local promoter, Allan Williams, to take them seriously, and he constantly belittled the Beatles' music.

The worst indignity that Allan Williams foisted upon the Beatles in the summer of 1960 was to convince them to play his New Cabaret Artists Club. This was a new venture for Williams, and it was modeled after the strip clubs in London and Manchester. In order to set up the club Williams convinced his West Indian friend, Willie Woodbine, to invest in the New Cabaret Artists Club. It was

George Harrison at the Cavern

typical of Williams' ventures, a sleazy, undercapitalized club with no class and little talent. Rather than bringing in professional strippers, Williams looked to local girls. He located the club in a section of Liverpool which was filled with houses of prostitution, and he attempted to appeal to Jamacians, Indians, and other immigrants who were unfamiliar with the more mainstream part of Liverpool's music scene. The New Cabaret Artists Club was a hit because of the novelty of the strip acts. No one in Liverpool had seen this type of entertainment and soon middle-aged businessmen, young boys and shy family men wandered into Williams' club. The Beatles were hired to provide background music for the strippers, but they were less than enthusiastic about working for Allan Williams. He agitated the Beatles continuously and used every conceivable means to criticize their music.

Allan Williams' book, *The Man who Gave The Beatles Away,* describes how a stripper named Shirley plied her trade as Paul McCartney played the drums and George Harrison and John Lennon furtively played their guitars behind her. What Williams' book fails to note, or perhaps even recognize, is that the audiences at the New Cabaret Artists Club in reality were booing the stripper while applauding the band. Even when Paul McCartney jokingly played a solo version of "Begin the Beguine," the patrons clapped continuously and stomped for the Beatles while hissing the stripper. Lord Woodbine furiously ran around the club threatening the patrons. Allan Williams, never one to confront trouble, vanished as the audience became uncontrollable. The Beatles revelled in the fact that the patrons preferred them to Shirley, and they chided Allan Williams for his lack of class and his humorless reaction to the crowds' catcalls.

One night after backing Shirley, John Lennon stood in front of the New Cabaret Artists Club and screamed "Allan Williams is a wretched bore." Startled observers had no idea what was going on, but the incident reflects the tensions the Beatles endured during their short stay at the New Cabaret Artists Club. Williams temporarily stifled their style by discouraging their rock music, which was reflected by the interjection of such songs as "Besame Mucho." Yet, during the days and nights they played at the New Cabaret Artists Club, Lennon and McCartney experienced some inspiration for mainstream pop songs. In later years Paul McCartney often spoke of the incident with Shirley, but he was too shy to point out that the audiences and the atmosphere led to the creation of songs like "P.S. I Love You," "Girl," and "This Boy."

As the Beatles perfected their music in 1960, Bob Wooler's career took a number of important turns. He was working as a railway clerk at Garston Docks and in November, 1960, quit his job to work for Allan Williams. After visiting Hamburg, Williams set up a Top Ten Club modeled after the German nightspot, but in typical Allan Williams fashion, it was undercapitalized and looked like a Salvation Army dining hall. As Williams sat in local Liverpool pubs bragging about his future profits, someone allegedly torched the building and the Top Ten Club quickly faded into oblivion. At this point Wooler expanded his disc jockey activities to support himself. In 1959, Bob had been the dj at Holyoake Hall near Penny Lane and worked for the promoter named Wally Hill. These dances at the Holyoake Hall had increased Wooler's popularity, and in a few months he had an extensive teenage audience following him to other halls. On Thursday evenings Wooler was the dj/compere at the Wavertree Town Hall. This was located in the neighborhood that George Harrison grew up in during World War II. Soon almost every young person in Liverpool was a fan of Bob Wooler. This would prove to be important for the Beatles' future success, because his support for their music was shared by his many fans.

Liverpool's Cavern Club

It was during 1961 that Bob Wooler was totally converted to the Beatles' music. On January 25, 1961, the Beatles performed at Hambleton Hall in Huyton and Wooler was impressed with their original versions of Little Richard's "Good Golly Miss Molly," and Gene Vincent's "Be Bop A Lula." Not only did the Beatles excite the crowd, but they also presented an emotionally draining stage show that produced howls from the audience. Wooler was initially surprised at the boisterous reaction to the Beatles, but he recognized that their music elicited a new response in local Liverpool audiences.

Another change in the Beatles' approach to rock music was their commitment to continual practice sessions. Unlike the Silver Beatles of 1960, the new Beatles in 1961 attempted to practice three to four hours, six days a week. In fact, much of Allan Williams' difficulty with the Beatles resulted from their continual demands to use his clubs as a practice hall. In a fit of rage one day Williams ran into the club holding a large pipe wrench and chased the Beatles into the street. He could not understand why they had to practice so intently. Yet, Williams was a shrewd promoter, and he continued to book the Beatles into local concert calendars. The rise of the Beatles led to a change in Liverpool's musical clubs. Soon lunchtime concerts were given, as well as evening performances, and the Merseyside sound rang out everywhere in 1961.

On February 24, 1961, when Allan Williams presented a show at the Grosvenor Ballroom, in Wallasey the crowd was unusually excited about the Beatles' music. Pat Chambers, a young girl who was following the Beatles from one concert to another, noticed a new seriousness in their stage presence. Their music appeared to be much tighter. This was partially due to Bob Wooler's continual lectures about the professional aspects of the music business. Also, the Beatles were preparing to return to the Reeperbahn section of Hamburg to play in the local clubs, and they were eagerly anticipating the type of night club work which had made them a professional act. After some serious discussions, the Beatles informed Allan Williams that he could book their return engagement. It was almost by default that the Beatles selected Williams, because they believed that he could obtain a quick visa from the German consulate in Liverpool.

On March 1, 1961, Allan Williams addressed a crude letter to the German consulate in Liverpool requesting permission to bring the Beatles into Hamburg's Top Ten Club. Since Williams was a high school drop-out, the letter was amusing to the Germans who announced that they could do a much better job, but they still granted the visa to the Beatles. In April, 1961 the Beatles returned to Hamburg for a three-month stint in the Top Ten Club. It was during this trip that Tony Sheridan persuaded the Beatles to back him in a series of recording sessions for Polydor Records in Hamburg. These sessions produced some of the most interesting stories about the Beatles' musical skills.

It was while they prepared to record that Sheridan began teaching George Harrison guitar riffs. Sheridan, like Eric Clapton and Peter Green, was able to influence a generation of guitar players, and he spent hours with Harrison in a dingy loft practicing blues guitar riffs. Sheridan was heavily influenced by Elvis Presley, and he taught the Beatles how to interpret traditional American blues and rock songs in their own unique manner. Every time he could find a record player, Sheridan played the English Elvis Presley LP's entitled *Rock and Roll, Volumes I and II*. These albums contained the best of Presley's music. Sheridan also urged the Beatles to add their own unique touches to other American music. Soon the Beatles were playing Chuck Berry's "Johnny B. Goode," "Rock and Roll Music," and "Memphis, Tennessee" with a frenetic

The Beatles at the Cavern

drive which made Berry's versions seem almost tame. Harrison later remarked to Wooler: "Tony Sheridan gave me a musical education when we recorded "Cry For a Shadow."

During the Polydor recording session, John Lennon sang the lead vocal on "Ain't She Sweet." Bert Kaempfert, the Artist and Repertoire man for Polydor, realized that Lennon and the Beatles had a highly commercial sound. As a result Kaempfert signed the Beatles to a three-year recording contract. But executives at Polydor believed that Tony Sheridan's music was all that was necessary to dominate the European rock market. Since Polydor failed to exercise their option to record the Beatles they were released from their contract when Brian Epstein subsequently informed Kaempfert that he wished to sign the Beatles to a management contract. It is Bert Kaempfert, the German musician and producer, who truly "gave the Beatles away." In fact, as Allan Williams watched this scenario, he picked up the phrase from a German who labelled Kaempfert as the man who had failed to realize the Beatles's enormous potential.

The Beatles returned to Liverpool in June, 1961. The third Hamburg trip had resulted in some significant changes in the

Star Club Ad, 1962

group. Stu Sutcliffe, the bass player, remained in Hamburg to study art and be with his girl friend Astrid Kirchherr. Although Sutcliffe was in ill health, he enrolled at the Hamburg Academy of Art where he showed great promise as an art student. This was a significant change because Paul McCartney shifted to the bass and George Harrison's lead guitar began to dominate the Beatles' music.

Just before the Beatles left for Hamburg, a young accounting student from the Liverpool Institute showed up to watch the Beatles. Neil Aspinall had rented a room in Mona Best's house, and he had talked extensively with Pete Best about the Beatles' music. After he went to one of their dances in early 1961, Aspinall was immediately smitten by the Beatles' talent. Soon he became their road manager and remained an integral part of the Beatles' organization through the 1960s.

The Beatles' tremendous appeal to local fans was demonstrated on August 31, 1961, when Bernard Boyle, Jennifer Dawes, and Maureen O'Shea, founded a Beatle fan club. After listening to the Beatles and reading Bill Harry's *Mersey Beat,* they decided to put out a mimeographed sheet detailing the Beatles' activities and future performances. A few weeks later Irish-born Liverpool-bred

Freda Kelly and Bobbie Brown founded a club which evolved into the official Beatle fan club. By 1963 Freda Kelly took over the club from her friend Bobbie Brown, and she spent numerous hours of her own time informing fans of important activities. Frequently Freda contacted Bob Wooler for advice on how to phrase a particular item about the Beatles, and Bob graciously offered excellent advice to the fledgling fan club.

An important catalyst to the Beatles' success was Bill Harry's rock newspaper, *Mersey Beat*. The first issue appeared on July 6, 1961, and it included an article by John Lennon on the history of the Beatles as well as a regular column by Wooler. *Mersey Beat* was a magazine far ahead of its time. It presented an in-depth look at the Liverpool music scene and provided a convenient guide to where local bands were playing. The most interesting aspect of *Mersey Beat's* first issue was the satirical brilliance of John Lennon's prose.

The Beatles' musical education was also expanding beyond the bounds of Liverpool. Throughout 1961 Bob Wooler supplied the Beatles with records by Little Richard, the Coasters, Eddie Cochran and Arthur Alexander. The Beatles also discovered a new American record label, Motown. This began a synthesis of crossover black soul music with traditional American rock and roll, and the result was the Beatles' own unique sound. In addition to providing the Beatles with an inexhaustible supply of records, Wooler also wrote a popular music column for the *Liverpool Echo* and contributed to Bill Harry's *Mersey Beat*. When Mary Wells toured Europe with a Motown revue in 1963 she commented that the Beatles were more aware of the Detroit sound than most Americans. During this tour the Motown revue had a night off in Liverpool, and it was a sight to see Marvin Gaye and Mary Wells dancing in the Cavern. The Beatles, dressed in casual clothing, watched in awe as the talented, well dressed Motown revue offered a lesson in showmanship on the dance floor. Bob Wooler jokingly told the Beatles to study the fashion conscious dress of Marvin Gaye.

Long before Brian Epstein met the Beatles, Wooler suggested many times that the group change their stage appearance by making improvements in their personal grooming. Another Liverpool musical personality, Joe Flannery, also gave John Lennon the same advice. Flannery held up a picture of his mother to demonstrate how the Frenchmen were styling their hair. In October, 1961, John traveled to Paris with Paul McCartney and Jurgen Vollmer for a brief vacation. John and Paul met Jurgen in Hamburg where he was a student at the art college. Along with

The Beatles: Ready for Stardom

Klaus Voorman and Astrid Kirchherr, Vollmer became one of the Beatles' closest friends. German intellectuals, known as exis' (existentialists) were attracted to the Beatles, and Vollmer was one of the conduits to this crowd. Vollmer was a brilliant photographer, and he took many pictures of the Beatles. In 1981 a book of Vollmer's photographs appeared under the title *Rock N Roll Times*. The book contained many intriguing photos of young John Lennon hanging out in Paris. It was while they were in Paris that John and Paul cut their hair like Jurgen Vollmer, and the Beatle haircut was born. After several glasses of wine one night near the Sorbonne, John Lennon raised his wine glass in a salute to his new haircut. Everyone laughed, but few people realized how significant this hairstyle would be for the Beatles' career.

    The Beatles did not know that the record they had recorded with Tony Sheridan was receiving airplay throughout Europe and that there was apparent interest in "My Bonnie" in England. In fact, only a few weeks after the Beatle haircut in Paris, Raymond Jones, a young music fan, walked into NEMS Department Store in Liverpool and asked the record department manager Brian Epstein for the Beatles' record, "My Bonnie." As a result of this record request Brian Epstein went to the Cavern on November 9, 1961 to see the Beatles. Since Brian had called ahead to reserve a table, Bob Wooler wisely used this advance notice to announce to the crowd that the Beatles music appealed to everyone. After watching the Beatles, Brian went out to a pub and talked with Wooler, and the result was that Brian went out the next night to hear the Beatles perform in a different setting.

On November 10, 1961, a concert known as Operation Big Beat took place at the Tower Ballroom in Brighton. The Beatles, Gerry and the Pacemakers, Rory Storm and the Hurricanes, the Remo 4, and Kingsize Taylor and the Dominoes did two shows. The first show at 6:30 resulted in an encore for the Beatles, but they did not reappear on the stage after peforming four numbers because they were also performing at 8:30 at the Village Hall in Knotty Ash. In spite of the lack of an encore, the Operation Big Beat concert established the Beatles as the most popular Merseyside rock group. As a result of this concert, they were deluged with offers to perform in the Liverpool area.

This increased concert activity led Neil Aspinall to purchase a van for 40 pounds in order to deliver Beatles' musical equipment to concert sites. Since he only was paid 1 pound each night, Aspinall continued to work as an accountant during the day. There were also more signs of an increased reaction to the Beatles' music. A good example of the Beatles' drawing power occurred on December 8, 1961, when they performed with a black soul singer, Davy Jones, at the Tower Ballroom, New Brighton. As the crowd rushed the stage, afterward Brian Epstein realized that the Beatles were now a valuable commercial property.

As a result of this performance, the Beatles signed a management contract with Brian Epstein on December 13, 1961 in Mona Best's Casbah Club. Rex Makin and Alistair Taylor witnessed the document, but Brian failed to sign it. Two nights later the Beatles performed at the Tower Ballroom, New Brighton, with Brian Epstein hovering conspicuously near the Beatles. Brian had many ideas about changing the Beatles' music, but their popularity prompted Bob Wooler to comment that it would not be long before they signed a recording contract.

On December 23, 1961 Mike Smith of Decca Records listened to the Beatles perform at the Cavern. Smith was an assistant A and R man at Decca, and he was aware of the Beatles' musical prowess. Before the Beatles set began, Bob Wooler casually dropped by Smith's table and explained how advanced the Beatles' music was

Bob Wooler: Live at the Cavern

compared to British superstars like Cliff Richard and the Shadows. Wooler suggested that a U.K. rock revolution was in the making and that the Beatles were simply the first sign of the commercial popularity of the Liverpool sound. The Beatles' music impressed Smith, and he also agreed with Wooler's arguments. As a result Smith convinced Decca to audition the Beatles. Although the Decca audition was not successful, nonetheless, Brian Epstein and Bob Wooler were still able to use this audition to publicize the Beatles.

From January until September 1962, Bob Wooler continued to praise the Beatles' music and champion their cause with the general public. Liverpool fans often jokingly referred to Wooler as the "Fifth Beatle." On January 4, 1962, when *Mersey Beat* reported that the Beatles were voted Liverpool's favorite musical group, Wooler read the article over the public address system at the Cavern Club. Yet the Beatles still found it virtually impossible to break into the record business. In March, 1962, they were shocked when Decca informed Brian Epstein that they would not sign the Beatles, because they lacked commercial appeal. Brian Epstein could not believe Decca's decision and he became more determined then ever to make the Beatles successful. In long discussions with Bob

Wooler, Brian vented his anger and frustration, but publicly he seemed unruffled by the rejections from every major British recording company.

After consulting with Bob Wooler, Brian decided a radical change of image was necessary for the Beatles, and he had them fitted at Burton's Multiple Tailors for suits with stylish velvet lapels. It was Wooler's idea to make the Beatles visually more appealing with the custom suits, handmade Spanish pointed-toe boots, and a shorter, more manageable hairdo. It was not difficult to convince Brian Epstein that the Beatles needed a new image, and as they flew to Hamburg, Germany for their fourth appearance on the Reeperbahn, the Beatles were dressed more like mods than rockers.

On April 5, 1962, just five days before they were to fly to Hamburg, the Beatles were honored by their fan club. A special fan club night at the Cavern not only allowed the Beatles to fine tune their music, but it was also an occasion for a racous party. During the fan club night, Bob Wooler spent an inordinate amount of time listening to John Lennon's future plans for the Beatles. There was no doubt that Lennon was the group's leader, and Wooler noticed that John's songwriting was also becoming more commercial and pop-oriented. It was Paul McCartney's middle-of-the-road, commercial influence which brought a new maturity to John's talents. Wooler realized that the Beatles were ready for rock music fame and fortune. The only question was: "When would success come?"

As the Beatles flew to Hamburg, Stu Sutcliffe, their original bass player, died of a brain tumor. The death of John Lennon's closest friend was a tragedy, but Stu's death reinforced Lennon's resolve to become a major rock star. One night in Hamburg, John confided to Horst Fascher that he and Stu had made a pact that if something happened to one of them, the other would pursue a career in either art or music. John told Horst that Stu's death was a sign that the Beatles would achieve international stardom. Fascher was impressed by John's zealous attitude toward his music after Stu's death. After returning from Hamburg the Beatles were informed that Parlophone Records was going to audition the group. After three successful stints in Hamburg the Beatles were prepared to make one final attempt to find a suitable recording contract.

On June 6, 1962, the Beatles auditioned for Parlophone Records in EMI's Studio 3 in London. After the session George Martin informed Brian Epstein that the Beatles Drummer, Pete Best, was an inadequate studio drummer. The controversy over Best's drumming ability brought out internal conflicts that had been smoldering beneath the surface for years. Paul McCartney allegedly demanded that the Beatles replace Best with a new drummer. John Lennon was not opposed to Best remaining with the group. However, the Beatles believed that their music had progressed to a point where they were ready to record a commercially appealing record. The Pete Best incident focused attention upon the Beatles' music, and when Ringo Starr became their drummer, the sensational publicity helped the Beatles' career.

The Pete Best controversy also involved Bob Wooler. For two years Bob had been friendly with Mona Best, and he was helpful in publicizing her Casbah Club. Bob also believed that Pete Best was an integral part of the Beatles' music. In a number of *Mersey Beat* articles, Wooler described Pete as a rock and roll version of American movie star Jeff Chandler. Pete's sensuous good looks prompted many to view him as an English James Dean. In Bob Wooler's view the Pete Best controversy resulted from differences between Best and Paul McCartney. Wooler urged the Beatles to ignore their petty differences, and he suggested that the group could be torn apart by the rift. What Wooler didn't realize is that the demonstrations staged by Best's fans had encouraged other record companies and promoters to consider signing the Beatles' to contracts. There was no doubt in Wooler's mind that Best was an excellent drummer. "I am quite sure it was not because Pete was not good enough. Remember all that time in Germany...It was more likely a personality clash with Paul McCartney," Wooler reflected.

Joe Flannery, a close friend of Brian Epstein and John Lennon, recommended that Pete Best join Lee Curtis and the All Stars. At this point in the Liverpool music scene, there was no indication that the Beatles would become superstars. Many record companies looked upon Lee Curtis as England's next major rock star, and Pete Best's fame with the Beatles was a potential asset in the career of Lee Curtis and the All Stars. But Best's career was doomed to failure, and he soon faded from the music business. He married a girl who worked at a candy counter in a local department store and settled down near his doting mother.

When the Beatles achieved stardom, Pete Best was brought to America to appear on talk shows, and he was in constant demand to answer questions about his role in the group. In 1965 PF Records in New York released an album entitled: MY THREE YEARS AS A BEATLE. This bizarre LP consisted of a series of interviews examining the reasons for Best's problems with the Beatles. It was

The Beatles at the New Brighton Tower

released to capitalize on the Beatles's enormous popularity, but the album failed to sell. In 1980 Best cooperated with a London writer, Patrick Doncaster, on a book of reminiscences entitled *Beatle*. In 1984 it was published in England but also failed to sell well. It is tragic that Pete Best's post Beatle career is one which has concentrated upon tales of the Beatles' past. He became so depressed that it was rumoured that Pete attempted to commit suicide in 1983. His mother screened his calls and refused to allow the press to talk to her son.

But in 1962 as the Pete Best incident flared, Bob Wooler continued his policies of strongly supporting the Beatles, and he also acted as a surrogate father for John Lennon. Before concerts at the Cavern, Bob and John would spend hours in the Grapes Pub talking about music and the changes in the Beatles' career. Sam Leach, a young man who promoted local dances, was also an avid supporter of the Beatles career, and he frequently asked Bob Wooler about the possibility of the Beatles becoming a mainstream British rock act. Leach was so busy staging concerts that he soon forgot about the Beatles, but he was a knowledgeable figure who encouraged the Beatles' ambitions.

From 1960 to 1967 Wooler's activity at the Cavern and assorted Liverpool clubs helped to form much of the popularity of the Merseyside sound. During the early 1960s it was the Beatles that Wooler enthusiastically plugged, and when they became major English rock music stars in early 1963, it was as much due to Wooler's support as it was to Brian Epstein's careful marketing.

The lessons which Bob Wooler taught the Beatles were significant ones, and there are many incidents which reveal his sensitivity to public taste in music. Wooler was quick to point out that groups who could not duplicate their sound on stage had brief careers. He pointed to an obscure American act, B. Bumble and the Stingers, as an example of how sloppy stage presence and poor musicianship could destroy a group's appeal.

As the Beatles honed their musical act, Bob Wooler analyzed the individual personalities of the Beatles. It was their differences, Wooler suggested, which made the Liverpool group so fascinating to their fans. George Harrison was "a worrier," John Lennon, "a pessimist," and Paul McCartney was a "confident but diffident" young man. Wooler suggested that the individual differences in the Beatles' personalities created a different fantasy for each fan. They also made excellent copy for newspaper stories. No rock music group had ever possessed such a combination of music and personality like the Beatles.

Many of the books on the Beatles' early years suggest that John Lennon was the group's leader. However, Wooler believes that Paul McCartney was an equally important force in the Beatles' music. It was McCartney who possessed the knack for writing commercially appealing musical material. Paul was also very influential in selecting clothing, hair and stage styles. Unlike the other Beatles he was a middle class, somewhat establishment, young man who found it difficult to write outrageous songs. McCartney maintained the balance and the chemistry which brought the Beatles into the commercial mainstream of the rock music business. "He watched the other Beatles like a mother hen," Wooler recalled, "And Paul often thought of himself as being above the group." What Wooler feared would happen was that moving to London would change the Beatles musical chemistry. Fortunately, the Beatles' music continued to reflect a strong commercial appeal. The Beatles individually underwent a number of personality changes as they withdrew into the cloistered world of musical superstardom. It was the only way to deal with the excessive pressures of the music business, Wooler maintained, and they were no longer the happy-go-lucky, convivial spirits from Liverpool. This loss of innocence made it very difficult for Beatle unity to remain strong and it contributed greatly to their 1970 breakup.

Had it not been for Brian Epstein's management, Wooler suggested, the Beatles would not have been a worldwide entertainment phenomena. It was Epstein who brought them firm personal and musical discipline. "They were unmanageable," Wooler stated. "Brian made them control their excesses." This helped to transform their raw, often unintelligible, music into the mainstream of British rock and roll. "The Beatles were a law unto themselves," Wooler remarked, and "Brian changed their headstrong ways."

In a 1961 issue of *Mersey Beat,* Wooler asked the question: "Why do you think the Beatles are so popular?" Although this column appealed to pubescent teens, Wooler's essay shrewdly pointed out the Beatles' reason for success. They had listened to the records of American rock pioneers, notably, Little Richard, Chuck Berry, Eddie Cochran, Gene Vincent and Carl Perkins, and from these artists' influences they created a totally British form of rock music. They didn't perform cover versions of American tunes, but they provided an entirely new interpretation for American rock music songs. In addition, Lennon and McCartney's original tunes were the cement which held the group together. Rather than copying the pop sounds of Bobby Vee, Del Shannon, and Frankie Avalon, the Beatles were forging a new musical direction.

In the spring of 1962 another of Wooler's columns in the *Mersey Beat* presented a reappraisal of the Beatles short but significant career. This column was used from 1962 through 1963 to argue that the Beatles were singlehandedly responsible for the popularity of Liverpool bands in Hamburg and London. Wooler suggested that the Beatles had elevated Liverpool music to great popularity, and he was sure the Beatles would soon leave Liverpool for London. Almost everyone ignored the *Mersey Beat* column, most people believed it was simply Wooler's means of continuing to support the Beatles. The column was written just before the Beatles left from the Manchester Airport to fly to Hamburg to fulfill a seven week engagement at the Top Ten Club. When Wooler suggested that the Beatles were changing the direction of English and European rock music, no one paid any attention to his ideas. "If it is possible for a Rock 'n' Roll group to become a status symbol," Wooler wrote, "then the Beatles have made it.

The Beatles in Liverpool

During 1962 a number of American rock stars were an important influence upon the Beatles' musical development. On June 21, 1962, for example, Bruce Channel appeared at the Tower Ballroom, New Brighton. Channel's record "Hey Baby" reached number 2 on the U.K. charts in 1962, and he brought a country, rockabilly type band to Liverpool. One of Channel's back up musicians was Delbert McClinton, a superb harmonica player. It was McClinton's musical roots which John Lennon found intriguing. As he grew up near Fort Worth, Texas, McClinton absorbed a type of Tex-Mex musical sound which mixed rhythm and blues with honky tonk music. Much like Doug Sahm, McClinton fused nontraditional black, Cajun and Southwestern music into his own unique sound.

After performing with Bruce Channel, John Lennon invited McClinton for some drinks at one of Liverpool's afterhours clubs. As they sat in the corner of a dreary, afterhours club and watched Lord Woodbine throw darts, McClinton taught Lennon a harmonica riff. After several practice runs, John learned the brief harmonica solo which was included in "Love Me Do." Bob Wooler sat nearby and watched this curious lesson. The next day Wooler reminded John Lennon that McClinton was one of the finest, if unrecognized, harmonica stylists in the world. The lesson that McClinton gave John prompted the Beatles to include more harmonica solos in their stage show. But McClinton was only one of many American musicians to influence the Beatles.

A number of American rock stars were attempting to revive their sagging careers by performing in England. Gene Vincent, whose fame rested in America largely on the hit record, "Be Bop A Lula," was typical of the fading Americans who delighted English and European audiences with his performances in the early 1960s. It was not just Vincent's energetic stage act but his dress and musical energy which helped many fledgling rock stars launch their English careers. Rod Stewart's first few years of performing, for example, were ones in which he was virtually a carbon copy of Vincent.

As the Beatles were developing their musical talents, Gene Vincent momentarily crossed their path in 1962, and he influenced the direction and content of their music. Since 1960 Vincent had used the U.K. as a means of making a living, and he recorded a series of excellent songs in London. As the demand for Vincent's records increased in the U.K., he went into the studio to record a number of new and old tunes. In 1962, for example, a session at the EMI studio in St. John's Wood produced by Bob Barratt included a rerecording of his million selling hit retitled: Be Bop A Lula, 62." This was Gene Vincent's last Capitol Records session and it revived his career momentarily in England and on the European Continent. The British magazine, *Hit Parade* featured an article entitled: "Gene Vincent—Citizen of Britain," and this in-depth analysis pointed out that the English considered Vincent one of their own.

On July 1, 1962, Gene Vincent appeared at the Cavern and his set included such old rock standards as Little Richard's "Tutti Frutti," and "Lucille," Ray Charles, "What'd I Say," as well as Vincent's own hits. The Beatles performed at this show with Gene Vincent, and John Lennon struck up an immediate friendship with the American rocker. John informed Vincent that much of his early music was modeled on "Be Bop A Lula." Offstage Vincent was a quiet almost reflective individual, and he talked about his own roller coaster ride on the musical charts. Gene Vincent gave John Lennon a good piece of advice when he suggested that rock music was a difficult and unpredictable way to make a living. It was also, Vincent suggested, the only lifestyle that he could accept. John Lennon left Vincent unconcerned about the monetary gains from rock music. If Gene Vincent could survive on small gigs and a well earned reputation in the late 1950s, then John Lennon believed he could play for the love of rock music.

After the engagement with Gene Vincent, John Lennon spent an extraordinary amount of time telling Bob Wooler about his impressions of the American rocker. There was no doubt that Lennon was smitten by the stage mannerisms and thoughtful pesonal concern that Vincent showed over Lennon's songwriting. A few months later, in November, 1962, Lennon and Vincent met again when Gene played a two week engagement in Hamburg at the Star Club. The Beatles and Tony Sheridan backed Gene Vincent, and Horst Fascher and his brother Freddy showed up to cheer on this dynamic musical aggregation. From November 1-14, 1962 the Star Club did an incredible amount of business, and the demand was so great for the music that Gene Vincent and John Lennon quietly snuck off to the Blockhutte one night. This small German bar with a country-western motif was originally discovered by Paul McCartney, and it offered a quiet place away from the bustle of the Grosse Freiheit to discuss music. It was during these discussions that Vincent gave Lennon some advice on studio recording techniques which led to the unique sound of "Please Please Me." It was Gene Vincent's opinion that the Beatles needed to attempt spontaneous versions of their songs, and this convinced John to cut down the number of studio takes. This prompted John to demand that the Beatles practice their original songs daily and develop a style which could be carried into the studio.

While performing in Hamburg, Gene Vincent's behavior became so bizarre that he began pulling guns randomly on people. John Lennon was scared to death one night when Vincent began shooting at an empty warehouse. Yet, John was heavily influenced by Vincent and in 1975 Lennon's rock and roll album produced by Phil Spector contained a tribute version of "Be Bop A Lula."

It was not only Vincent's music which impressed Lennon. His lifestyle was an alluring one to young John Lennon, and he listened intently to Vincent's stories for long hours. During his Hamburg engagement, Vincent confided to Lennon that he was unhappy with his musical backup bands. As a result of this conversation, Vincent decided to hire a Liverpool band to back him while on tour. By 1964 the Shouts, a nondescript musical group featuring a wild organ, toured with Vincent. It was not a pleasant musical match as the Shouts had a Motown soul sound, and they found it difficult to back Vincent's rockabilly oriented rock music. When John Lennon heard

Bob Wooler, 1983

that the Shouts' were backing Gene Vincent, he shuttered at this musical collision. Not all Liverpool bands were musically sound and Gene Vincent paid a heavy price for hiring this group.

Once "Love Me Do" was released by Parlophone, Bob Wooler's influence with the Beatles declined. It was not so much due to their feelings for Bob's advice as it was due to the increased touring and recording. Although the Beatles performed at the Cavern Club 292 times, the last show on Saturday, August 3, 1963 was not really their farewell performance. Beginning in early 1963 Beatlemania overtook England and the Beatles were lost to Liverpool.

In his association with the Beatles, Bob Wooler's most controversial incident took place on June 18, 1963 at Paul McCartney's 21st birthday party. The Beatles had been on tour with Roy Orbison, and Paul's Aunt Jinny scheduled a party at her house in Huyton. Billy J. Kramer and The Fourmost were among the musical guests. As the party progressed there was a great deal of drinking, and this led to tales of sexual conquest among the young musicians. In a moment of jest, John Lennon remarked that Wooler "called me a queer." Lennon allegedly hit Wooler in the face with a shovel and then proceeded to kick him in the ribs repeatedly. Bob was ready to sue but a $500 out of court settlement ended the threatened legal action. Yet, Wooler remained friendly to the Beatles and continued to promote their music.

As the Beatles grew in musical stature they became even more popular than Wooler originally had envisioned. When the Beatles made their last appearance at the Cavern on Saturday, August 3, 1963 Wooler simply announced: "It's the Beatles!" As he went back through his records Wooler was able to document 292 Beatle performances at the Cavern. Although Wooler remained Cavern owner Ray Mc Fall's right hand man until 1967, the magic of the Merseyside sound faded after the Beatles moved to London.

Bob Wooler managed a band known as the Carolls in the 1960s, and he was married for a brief time to Beryl Adams. She had been Brian Epstein's secretary at the Whitechapel NEMS store. For a period in the 1970s Wooler was a bingo caller at the Locarno Ballroom. Although he engaged in business dealing with Allan Williams, Wooler never regained the successes of the Beatle days.

In the 1980s Bob Wooler continues to influence the history of the Beatles by speaking at conventions and cooperating with historians and journalists. He has never asked for anything for himself, and he is a reminder of the spirit of rock and roll music. Although Wooler was offered a position in the Beatles' organization when NEMS Enterprises moved to London, he preferred to remain in Liverpool. In 1983 Wooler was helping a local band, Mojo Filter, much the same way he had publicized the Beatles. It was almost like a dream watching young girls dance in a single line in front of Mojo Filter in a Liverpool bar in 1983 as they sang a Monkees' song. As Bob Wooler pointed out: "Liverpool is still the best city in England for original rock bands." Bob was more than right as Ace Records immediately signed Mojo Filter to a recording contract. The ghost of the Beatles can be seen as these four talented young men carry on the Liverpool musical tradition.

CLIVE AND BRIAN EPSTEIN

Clive and Brian Epstein: The Beatles' Legacy

Brian Epstein's fame as the Beatles' manager is a well-documented facet of his career. There is a great deal written about Brian's relationship with his family, his business practices and his personal life. This essay will examine Brian's relationship with his younger brother Clive, and the manner in which his family contributed to his successes and failures in the entertainment business. Since Brian Epstein was a complex and often difficult person to understand, rock historians have failed to analyze all facets of his brilliant career. A number of Beatle books have suggested that Brian was a poor businessman. This conclusion is one which is easily sustained by pointing out that Brian literally gave away a number of lucrative merchandising contracts for Beatles memorabilia in America. However, this argument fails to note that merchandising rock music products was an entirely new business. In order to understand Brian Epstein's business genius it is necessary to examine his brother's influence upon Brian's business activity.

Clive John Epstein is little more than a footnote in the early history of the Beatles. This is due to the fact that Beatle biographers have focused their attention upon Brian's life. Philip Norman's excellent book, *Shout: The Beatles In Their Generation* suggests that "Clive was good at exams...." and Peter Brown's, *The Love*

The Beatles on BBC-TV

You Make: An Insider's View of the Beatles argues that Clive did not
have "the same fascination as Brian" for his mother. Either Clive is
dismissed as an important influence as Philip Norman's book has
done, or he is cast into a secondary role as Peter Brown's study
suggests. In reality, Clive was very close to his mother, and he was
important in molding Brian's character. The notion of parental
favoritism is one of the strongest myths associated with Brian and
Clive's formative years. Like most parents, Harry and Queenie
Epstein proudly displayed their family to friends and relatives.
Queenie raised the boys strictly and they appeared well adjusted.
There were pressures in the Epstein family, however, which were
important in shaping Brian and Clive's character. During the
course of his famous older brother's relationship with the Beatles,
Clive was primarily in the background of his brother's
entreprenurial activity. As a result few people recognized how
important he was in advising Brian on business matters.

Although a year younger than Brian, Clive was also an
important figure in the Beatles' career. Since he was a notoriously
private person Clive did not seek the publicity that Brian thrived
upon in the 1960s. Yet, Clive often acted as close personal counsel to

his brother and helped make many of the decisions in the Beatles' career. The wisdom of Clive's advice was the result of his family background. The Epstein's were an upper-class, mercantile Jewish family with a well earned reputation for business success. Clive and Brian's parents, Harry and Queenie Epstein built the family furniture business into one of the most successful in Northern England. The lessons in commerce and business management which Harry Epstein instilled in his boys had a lasting effect upon their lives. But before the boys could enter the family business, it was necessary to provide for their education. It was a combination of this exclusive English public school training and family business expertise which helped Brian and Clive to develop into exceptional businessmen. It is ironic that Clive Epstein became a central figure in the Beatles' musical career, because he had little interest in the rock music business. As a trusted confidant to Brian and an insightful businessman, Clive became an integral, if unrecognized, part of the Beatles' success.

In order to fully understand Brian and Clive, it is necessary to analyze how the Epstein family history shaped the personalities of the two men who would guide the Beatles to fame and fortune. In 1933 when Malka Hyman, an 18-year-old daughter of a Jewish furniture baron, married Harry Epstein, it united two families who had distinguished themselves in the furniture business. There were no entertainment figures in either family and their only concerns were business ones. Like many well-to-do English families, the Epsteins viewed their sons as inheritors of the furniture business. Malka's father owned the Sheffield Cabinet Company, and the Epstein's operated Liverpool's most profitable furniture store. There was a non-nonsense business tradition in both families which precluded any interest in show business. Yet, the Epstein's unwittingly sparked the entertainment bug in Brian when Harry purchased the North End Music Store (NEMS), because it was an ideal business location adjacent to the Epstein furniture store in Liverpool's business section on Walton Road. Harry Epstein believed that NEMS was a music retailing business which was an excellent companion enterprise alongside the family furniture store. The North End Music Store placed a great deal of pressure upon Brian Epstein early in his life, but he was able to live up to his father's expectations by making NEMS a profitable record store. In his autobiography, *A Cellarful of Noise,* Brian stated: "I am an elder son—a hallowed position in a Jewish family—and much was to be expected of me."

From 1934 to 1940 there were many pleasant experiences for the young Epstein boys. Brian's carefully decorated nursery revealed not only a conscientious mother's touch but signs of affluence. Peter Brown suggests that Brian was "a spoiled, moody, anxious child, his mother's little darling and the incarnation of Little Lord Fauntleroy." A more objective description is that Brian was much like any upper-middle class Liverpool youngster. In fact, close family friends remarked that he was no more or no less spoiled than other boys in his immediate social-economic class.

It was during World War II that the Epstein family experienced significant problems. The German bombings of Liverpool forced Harry and Queenie Epstein to move the boys to Southport on the West Lancashire coast in 1940. While attending Southport College, six-year old Brian developed an artistic temperament and displayed a penchant for reading. It was obvious to his schoolmasters that Brian had an aptitude for intellectual pursuits. Although he was absent from his family, Brian thrived academically at the Southport College. During World War II, Harry and Queenie Epstein nurtured the belief that their boys were destined for distinguished business careers. This feeling not only created a strong bond between the boys and the family, but it placed extraordinary pressure upon Brian and Clive to distinguish themselves in school. Initially, there was little to separate the boys from one another during their early years. They were both bright, well-mannered and exceptionally well-bred young men whom nearly everyone liked.

When Brian was nine years old, an unsettling pattern developed in his educational pursuits. In 1944, Brian was expelled from the exclusive Liverpool College because he had completed an allegedly "lewd" drawing in his mathematics class. This was the third of eight schools that Brian attended during what became an increasingly turbulent academic career. The strict unbending rules of the Liverpool College were demonstrated when Queenie Epstein was informed that Brian was expelled for designing a theater program displaying scantily-clad dancing girls. Because there was evidence of latent anti-semitism at Liverpool College, Queenie Epstein searched for a new educational outlet. She wisely sent both Brian and Clive to Beaconsfield School in Kent which actively recruited Jewish students. But Brian's academic performance did not improve, and he failed the entrance exams for the better British public schools. After Rugby, Repton and Clifton turned down Brian's application for admission, Harry and Queenie Epstein

The Beatles: An Early Breakfast

realized that it was going to be difficult to secure Brian a place in one of the better public schools. As a result, Brian's parents searched for a special school and decided upon Clayesmoore, a nondescript public school in Dorset. At Clayesmoore, Brian played rugby, studied art and blossomed into a serious drama student. Harry Epstein, however, was horrified by his son's penchant for the theatrical world. At Clayesmoore, Brian worked very diligently because he disliked the students, the academic setting and the local citizens. His record at Clayesmoore was considerably better than at previous schools. However, Brian was still considered a problem child by the British public schools, because he refused to conform to the strict standards and the appropriate behavior required by these prestigious institutions. Brian thought, acted and carried himself differently from the other students at Clayesmoore and the faculty labeled him a loner with a penchant for bizarre behavior. In sum, Brian Epstein was a rebel.

However, the Epstein family decided that Brian must attend a more prestigious public school. Clive advised his parents of such an institution, Wrekin College in Shropshire. Wrekin College was a well-known public school with a reputation for producing business executives and government leaders. Although it was not on the same level as Eton or Harrow, nonetheless, it was a fine public school. In England the public schools are much like America's better private colleges, and Wrekin is one of the U.K.'s best schools. Although Clive distinguished himself at Wrekin, Brian hated the institution and remarked, "I am going there only because my parents want me to...." Brian's admission to Wrekin College was largely due to Clive's persistent badgering of the school administration, and it was difficult for Brian to accept his brother's help. Although he loved Clive, Brian was sensitive to excessive family aid, and he badly wanted to achieve his own success.

When Brian was accepted as a student at Wrekin College, Clive had already received excellent academic marks. Wrekin was Brian's eighth school, and he was admitted despite his past academic record. Brian remained for two years at Wrekin College, but his educational achievements there were not solid ones. Brian continued to nurture his acting interests, and he performed a small part in a play about Christopher Columbus. As Brian developed his acting avocation, he was also increasingly intrigued by fashion and dress design. This was hardly the type of career direction which made Harry Epstein happy, and he urged his son to consider business opportunities. Wrekin was noted for turning out businessmen, but the commercial world seemed to have little importance in Brian's life. Recalling his days at Wrekin College, Brian commented in *A Cellarful of Noise:* "I didn't like it (Wrekin) nor it me..." It was this rebel type of demeanor which prompted many people to wonder about Brian's future.

Although Brian Epstein grew up in a well-adjusted and loving family, he suffered from comparisons with his brother Clive. A quiet, reserved individual, Clive did not promote any sense of sibling rivalry, nonetheless, family and friends often remarked that Clive seemed to be heading toward a successful business career. Brian did not receive such laudatory comments concerning his vocational progress. Clive had a reserved, almost detached personality, and he often appeared distant and lacking in warmth. A shrewd businessman, Clive had entreprenurial skills and connections in the manufacturing industry. In the family furniture business he quickly eclipsed Brian's performance, and this caused Brian to consider finding another way to achieve his own successes. Unwittingly, it was the psychological reaction to this business rivalry with his brother which prompted Brian to enter the rock music management business. He saw in the Beatles not only a chance to make a fortune, but he realized that there was fame and power in a rock entrepreneur's career.

As is often the case with brothers, Clive played the role of the disciplined, unemotional sibling to balance Brian's behavior. To this day, no one has been able to discover how Clive reacted to his brother's brief career at the Royal Academy of Dramatic Arts in London. Clive simply remarks, "No comment," on questions about Brian's show business career. He will speak about "the problems we had with Brian's education," but he has remained noncommital on many of the important events surrounding his brother's life. The career directions which Brian Epstein explored were ones that his family felt uncomfortable with, and the Epstein's concern was heightened by Brian's dilettantish business and personal interests.

Although he may have silently disapproved of his brother's attitudes, lifestyle and penchant for nonconformity, Clive helped Brian with many of his problems. A good example of Clive's willingness to aid Brian occurred when he urged Brian to enter the family business. Clive made a strong point of the training, business connections and experience in his father's store. So it was largely due to Clive that Brian entered the Liverpool furniture and record business. It was also Clive who urged Brian to consider examining the business side of the music industry. Brian once remarked that his brother defined show business as two words with the emphasis on the last word. As Brian began his business career his brother Clive was an extraordinarily strong influence.

In September, 1950 Brian left school to begin work as a salesman at the Epstein's Walton Road furniture store. It was while working in the family business that Brian discovered his talent for sales. He had seriously contemplated a career as a dress designer, an actor or an artist. However, once he entered the furniture business Brian was swept away with his success as a salesman. It gave him a feeling of power and a sense of accomplishment that he had not previously experienced. In addition, Brian's salary allowed him to dress in the most fashionable clothes. Brian's tastes included expensive restaurants, fine wines and lavish entertainment. By Liverpool standards, young Brian was a smashing success, but he still harbored hidden show business career desires.

As Brian established himself as a local businessman, a letter arrived from the British government. On December 9, 1952, the Royal Army Service Corps instructed Brian to report for a physical examination. After a quick physical, Brian was inducted and instructed to report to the RASC depot in London. Soon he settled into army life as a clerk. In less than a year, however, Brian was discharged from the British army. When he was not selected to become an officer, Brian allegedly impersonated an officer one night, and this resulted in months of psychiatric evaluation. After consulting with four army doctors, Brian remarked that he was discharged because "I was a compulsive civilian and quite unfit for military service." Despite his troubles with the army, Brian received an honorable discharge and his personnel file described him as "sober, conscientious and trustworthy." The army experience lurked in the back of Brian's mind for years, and his dissatisfaction with the military was demonstrated when he remembered that after his discharge: "I ran like a hare to Euston train after handing in my hideous uniform." Back in Liverpool, young Brian resumed his career in the family store in Walton Road. There is one important aspect of Brian's military career which has generally gone unnoticed. During his army service he discovered a new found penchant for detail and organization. Although he was a meticulous young man, Brian became an organizational genius in the army. Once he assumed the Beatles management they were given a detailed itinerary for each day. This is a habit that Brian developed during his brief stint in the Royal Army Service Corps.

There was another important change in Brian's life during his military career. He discovered the theater district in London's West End. For many years Brian had attended plays at Liverpool's two professional theaters the Playhouse and the Royal Court. However, the London theater district, particularly the Covent Garden area, caused Brian to romanticize the theater and to consider a career as an actor. Soon Brian informed his friends that he would study to become an actor. Brian Bedford, a close friend at the Liverpool Playhouse, was an important influence upon Brian Epstein. As he watched his friend perform Shakespearean drama, Brian was obsessed with the notion of becoming an actor. Bedford had studied acting at the Royal Academy of Dramatic Art, and he urged Brian to audition for a position in the next RADA class. After a night of drinking at Liverpool's Basnett pub, a young rising British actress, Helen Lindsay, also urged Brian to audition for RADA.

At the moment Brian Epstein considered becoming an actor, he described himself as middle-aged to a close friend. "I'm a doomed middle-aged businessman," Brian remarked. This observation is an interesting insight into Brian's character, because he was only 22 years old. After meeting with London's RADA director, John Fernald, Brian was accepted as an acting student. Like his past

The Beatles: The Mid-1960s

academic experiences, Brian's tenure at RADA was less than distinguished. It was a brief experience which lasted for three terms, and suddenly in 1957 Brian returned to the family business. Few people realized that the organizational skills acquired in the army combined with Brian's acting school lessons to produce an interest in show business management.

By the late 1950s, Brian and Clive were firmly established in the family business, and they were well-known figures in Liverpool. In this period, Brian and Clive's adult personalities began to take shape. Although he lived in constant fear that his homosexuality would be discovered, Brian appeared to be relaxed and at ease in social situations. Clive, on the other hand, was well adjusted, but he often appeared aggressive and overbearing socially. It was during this period that Clive developed the business training and insights which served him well when he began managing the Beatles' assets after Brian's untimely death. In order to understand Clive Epstein's impact upon the Beatles, it is necessary to examine his career with Brian and the Beatles.

For many years, Brian Epstein had developed a strong interest in classical music. There were few people in Liverpool who were as knowledgeable as Brian, he was able to build the family department store into one of the most influential music stores in Northern England. As Lonnie Donegan's skiffle music, Cliff Richard's English brand of rock and roll and the early American rockers like Gene Vincent made their appearance on the English charts, Brian Epstein curiously followed the course of rock music's development. He displayed little, if any, serious interest in rock music. However, Brian's quiet outer attitudes were designed to hide his curiosity about the rock music world. By 1961, it was obvious to many of Brian's close friends that he had a strong interest in rock music.

In the late 1950s, Brian transformed the family music department into Northern England's most profitable record enterprise. In fact, Anthony Newley opened the NEMS second record department at the city center shop in Whitechapel. The Great Charlotte Street NEMS store was not only a profitable business venture, but it convinced Brian that hit records could be manufactured by promotion and carefully planned publicity. This was a lesson not lost on Brian when he became the Beatles' manager. By 1960 Brian used the slogan "The Finest Record Selection in Northern England" to advertise NEMS. Brian boasted that no customers request would go unnoticed and soon the word spread that NEMS could secure any record in the world. Now in his mid-twenties, Brian was a confident, somewhat aggressive, businessman who was able to think about new entreprenurial activity. One of Harry Epstein's maxims was that the boys should continually reassess their career directions. This lecture prompted Brian to reconsider his show business intent.

As a result when Raymond Jones, an 18 year old boy from Huyton, walked into NEMS on Saturday October 28, 1961, and asked for the Beatles' "My Bonnie," Brian was unwittingly drawn into the burgeoning English rock music business. Since Brian was behind the counter when Jones walked into NEMS, he was intrigued by the young man's request. After some casual conversation Brian began to search for the Beatles' "My Bonnie." In characteristic fashion, Brian's search turned into virtually an obsession, and he discovered the world of rock and roll music. In order to learn about rock music, Brian needed a knowledgeable source.

As a result, Brian cultivated the friendship of Bob Wooler, the resident disc jockey/compere at the Cavern Club on Mathews Street. Not only did Wooler inform Epstein about the local beat groups, but he was also instrumental in convincing Brian to educate his brother and family. Soon Clive was engaging in knowledgeable discussions about Buddy Holly, Gene Vincent and Eddie Cochran with his family and friends. In local Liverpool clubs like the Cavern there was a musical explosion which was to very shortly bring new singers, songwriters and bands into the mainstream of the British music industry. Brian Epstein recognized these changes, and he became interested in managing a local Liverpool rock group. But Brian's family, Clive included, attempted to dissuade him from a musical management career. It was not until Brian discussed his interests in music with the family lawyer, E. Rex Makin, that the seriousness of Brian's new career direction became apparent.

It was not surprising that Brian should consider a career as the manager of a rock music group. By 1961, he had built NEMS into the major record store in Northern England. Long before he went to the Cavern on November 9, 1961, Brian had surveyed the rock music scene. Although in later years, Brian commented that the Cavern was "dark and damp and smelly, and I regretted my decision to come," nonetheless, the Beatles lunchtime performance impressed Brian. In his autobiography, *A Cellarful of Noise,* Brian remarked that the first time he saw the Beatles "...they gave a captivating and honest show and they had very considerable magnetism." After the show, George Harrison remarked: "What brings Mr. Epstein here?" This led to a lengthy discussion with the group about their musical future.

On December 3, 1961, the Beatles were asked to come to Mr. Epstein's office at 4:30 p.m. to discuss a possible management deal. Although Brian Epstein states in his memoirs that management was not "yet formed in my mind," John Lennon told Bob Wooler that he was certain that Mr. Epstein was going to offer the Beatles a contract. John requested that Bob Wooler come along, and they stopped at four pubs on the way to the Whitechapel office. They arrived quite late and John introduced Bob as "me father." Brian Epstein smiled at this pun, and Brian offered a management deal to the boys. For a month Brian had carefully investigated the rock music business, and he believed that the Beatles were an excellent business venture. The books which suggest that Brian managed the Beatles because he was in love with John Lennon fail to mention Brian's extensive investigation into the profitability of the Beatles. They were more than just a leather-jacketed rock music phenomena to Brian, and he believed that they were the next wave of English musical talent. In particular, Brian was struck by the manner in

The Beatles' Achievements, 1962

which the young girls responded to the Beatles, and he saw a way of encroaching upon Cliff Richard's musical domain.

One Liverpool acquaintance of Brian Epstein believed that music management was a natural outlet for Brian's creative talents. Since his days as a student at the Royal Academy of Dramatic Arts, Brian had displayed strong interest in avant garde entertainment ideas. In 1961, the leather-jacketed Beatles were among the most interesting and unique phenomena in Liverpool, and once Brian discovered the group, he was smitten with their musical talents.

Before he signed the Beatles, there is no record of what Brian and E. Rex Makin discussed, it was apparent that the long and frequent discussions about music management indicated that Brian had a strong interest in managing a rock music group. These meetings also suggest the high level of professional business organization inherent in Brian's approach to his new venture. Due to their close relationship, Clive heard a great deal about the local Liverpool music scene from his brother, and Brian often expressed his reservations about managing a rock group to Clive and local disc jockey/compere Bob Wooler. The projected financial returns from a group such as the Beatles did not appear lucrative in the early 1960s. Yet Brian retained a nagging suspicion that the Beatles were potential superstar rock musicians. Although Brian remarked that they were vulgar, uncultured, and raw, the Beatles had the appeal of early American rock artists like Gene Vincent and Eddie Cochran.

Most books analyzing Brian Epstein's interest in the Beatles focus upon his alleged homosexual attraction to John Lennon. This theory is titillating but it has obscured more significant aspects of Epstein's career. The major source of this rumor is Hunter Davies authorized Beatle biography. John Lennon allegedly confessed an affair with Brian, but he asked Davies' not to use this incident in this book. The most recent statement of a Lennon-Epstein affair is in Peter Brown's *The Love You Make: An Insider's Story of the Beatles.* Brown describes Brian Epstein as "light headed and giddy" around John Lennon and mentions the vacation they took to Spain in 1963 as an example of the attraction. While there may or may not be some truth to this story, it ignores the systematic and businesslike manner in which Brian organized the management of the Beatles. A number of Liverpool observers who were at the Cavern and in the bars and small clubs the Beatles frequently remarked that Brian and John often seemed unfriendly or disinterested in each other's opinions. The infatuation that Brian allegedly had with John Lennon is something that most Liverpool residents believe to be the product of over-analysis and speculation.

In order to understand Brian's business skills, and the corporate legacy he left to his brother Clive, it is necessary to analyze some of Brian's early business activities. "The early Beatle promotions were originally designed to build Brian's reputation and increase NEMS's record sales," Clive remarked. The Beatles were a business tool by which Brian would not only increase NEMS' record profits, but also attract customers who might shop elsewhere. Brian realized that he did not fully understand the mechanism of the rock music business since his own musical interests were classical. He sought out two knowledgeable figures in the Liverpool music scene, Bob Wooler and Allan Williams, to teach him the inside tricks of the business.

Although they were close personal friends, Williams and Wooler were completely different in personality, temperament, and knowledge concerning Liverpool's music scene. Allan Williams was a volatile Irishman who dropped out of school at an early age. Although he lacked cultural refinement, Williams possessed a primitive charm, but he was prone to irrational personal outbursts. Many of the myths associated with the Beatles were created by Williams' lucid examples and descriptions of their performances in his Liverpool clubs. Despite their musical skill, the Beatles were often at odds with Williams, and he told Brian Epstein not to manage them, because they were "an uncontrollable, no-good lot." A version closer to the truth suggests that Williams was furious that Epstein moved in and signed the Beatles without consulting him. In sum, Allan Williams' mistakes with the Beatles served to reinforce Brian's decision to manage them. Yet, long before he signed the Beatles, Brian listened for long hours to Williams' tirades and occasional lucid comments about the Liverpool music scene. It was a tough way to get an education because Williams was difficult to socialize with for more than five minutes. However, Brian learned very quickly what made groups like the Bluegenes, Rory Storm and the Hurricanes, Kingsize Taylor and the Dominoes, and the Beatles so popular among Liverpool music aficinados.

Perhaps Allan Williams' strongest asset was his ability to set up popular night clubs. His Jacaranda and Blue Angel clubs introduced many of England's premier rock groups to live audiences. The disc jockey/compere who assisted Williams, Bob Wooler, was one of the first Liverpool rock music experts to recognize the Beatles' enormous talent. Wooler, unlike Williams, was a mild, charming and well-educated Englishman who was a father figure to many local rock musicians. In addition to his massive record collection, Wooler was also an accurate barometer of future musical trends. More than one fledgling British musician sought out Wooler for his advice. Brian Epstein found Wooler to be a very reliable person, and they became good friends. In his quiet, ingratiating manner Wooler quickly educated Epstein to the dangers and pitfalls of the rock music audience.

In 1961, Wooler and Epstein made the rounds of the various clubs and small pubs which housed the burgeoning Liverpool musical explosion. The sight of the two refined, highly intellectual personalities going from one club to another, surprised many people. No one could believe that Brian Epstein was intent upon signing a local band and Wooler was as encouraging as Williams was discouraging. It was Wooler who convinced Brian Epstein of the Beatles enormous musical skills.

An important aspect of Brian Epstein's education at the hands of Wooler and Williams was their continual references to the hollering and screaming by young women in the audience. Cliff Richard had been something of a teen idol for three years in England, but he lacked the raw sexual magnetism of American rock stars. Soon Brian Epstein realized that the charismatic Beatles were an act similar to Elvis Presley. As Brian Epstein watched Allan Williams make one mistake after another in presenting the Beatles, he realized that packaging was the key to the Beatles' future success. It was Allan Williams' inability to delegate authority and control the activities of his bouncers and employees that prompted Brian to develop a well-organized management program. Once he became the Beatles' manager, Epstein carefully typed out careful and detailed daily instructions to the group, because Brian believed that discipline was necessary in the Beatles' musical life.

Although Brian Epstein became the Beatles' manager, he continued to work in the family department store, NEMS. As Clive Epstein remarked: "The suggestion that Brian gave everything up and was trying to get the Beatles a record deal is absurd. Brian had a responsible and demanding position at NEMS." The Beatles were simply one of Brian's relatively insignificant business diversions. Clive views the Beatles as an extension of Brian's dilettantish nature. He would flirt with a business idea, then quickly abandon it

The Beatles: Decca Audition Bootleg L.P.

and move in a new direction. The Epstein family believed that the Beatles were another of Brian's experiments in a new area.

Brian formed a company called NEMS to promote the Beatles, naming it after the family business. Because of his close, brotherly relationship (as well as Clive's business skills) Brian selected Clive as one of the main partners. In 1962, NEMS was formally incorporated with 10,000 shares of stock. Brian owned 7,000, Clive owned 2,000, and the Beatles held the remaining 1,000 shares. With 90% of NEMS stock in the Epstein family, Brian and Clive ran the business end of the Beatles' musical careers. NEMS served as an agent to collect royalties paid to the Beatles from record sales and merchandising rights. When Brian and the Beatles formally agreed to a revised management contract on October 2, 1962, Clive was present and helped iron out the legal difficulties which had made the first contract invalid. For the next half dozen years, Clive was a silent witness to one of the most phenomenal revolutions in rock music history. There were many spectacular and intriguing experiences awaiting Clive in his years with the Beatles.

Once NEMS was formed, Brian sent off a number of letters on an impressive new letterhead, and he urged Tony Barrow of the

Liverpool Evening Echo to mention the Beatles' music in his popular column. In an effort to bolster his view that the Beatles were Liverpool's most popular rock group, Brian sent Barrow copies of Bill Harry's *Mersey Beat* newspaper poll which showed the Beatles to be the most popular local music group. Barrow informed Brian Epstein that he would not mention the Beatles because they had not recorded in England and suggested that Brian contact someone at Decca about a possible record audition for the group. When Decca heard that NEMS, the largest retail record store in Northern England, had a rock band they were more than interested in doing business. For Brian Epstein was already something of a legend among British recording companies because of his ability to market large numbers of records. As a result, a young assistant A and R man, Mike Smith, was sent to Liverpool to hear the Beatles perform. Smith liked what he heard and because of his persistent badgering, Decca eventually auditioned the Beatles.

When the Beatles arrived at Decca's West Hampstead Studio on New Year's day, 1962, they were prepared to record for someone like Mike Smith. Unfortunately, the Beatles were assigned to Dick Rowe, Decca's head of A and R. It was not surprising that Rowe found the Beatles dreadful. Brian Epstein had a tremendous musical knowledge, but the Decca audition revealed that he was woefully inadequate at selecting rock songs for the Beatles to perform. Of the 14 songs prepared for the Decca audition, only three were Lennon-McCartney originals, and they were among the weakest songs in the Beatles' repertoire. The remaining songs they performed were old standards like "Besame Mucho" and "Sheik of Araby."

It was a blessing in disguise when the Beatles were not signed to a recording contract after the Decca audition. Brian called his brother Clive in, and they discussed the reasons for Decca's reluctance to sign the Beatles. Brian believed that Lennon-McCartney songs needed more emphasis, and he met shortly after the audition with John and Paul to convey his strong support about their songwriting. As a result of Brian's encouragement, Lennon and McCartney's productivity reached new heights. Even though Pye, Phillips, Columbia and HMV, all subsequently rejected Beatle tapes, Brian was convinced that the group could still parlay its unique sound and brilliant original songs into a recording contract.

After a great deal of negotiation, Brian Epstein convinced the executives at EMI to sign the Beatles to their Parlophone label. In 1962, Parlophone was a small part of EMI's musical empire and best known for comedy records featuring Peter Sellers. For some years the head of A and R at Parlophone, George Martin, had attempted to persuade EMI to broaden its scope. When Martin agreed to record the Beatles, he not only saw something new in their music, but he believed that Parlophone's business structure was right for rock records. On September 4, 1962 the Beatles traveled to London and registered at a hotel in Chelsea. They reported to EMI's Studio 2 in St. John's Wood to record "Love Me Do." After 17 takes, the record was finished, and its release changed the course of rock music history. This began a whirlwind career for the Beatles which intermittenly involved Clive in a key role.

A good example of Clive's importance in the Beatles show business affairs took place in August, 1965, when the Beatles second movie *Help* opened in Liverpool. After three years of British superstardom and almost two years of international renown, the Beatles were not prepared for an incident in Liverpool. As a gigantic civil reception took place at the town hall, which is just around the corner from the Cavern Club on Mathews Street, a man suddenly appeared carrying leaflets accusing Paul McCartney of fathering his daughter's illegitimate child. Not only was the leaflet in poor taste, but the allegations were false. However, Brian and Clive wisely chose to settle the problem with the distraught father without further publicity. What settlement was reached no one will reveal, but the incident illustrates the care and skill which the Epstein brothers used in handling the Beatles' affairs. Not only were Beatle management problems complex, but they involved making quick, often expensive, decisions. Almost everyone associated with NEMS Enterprises realized that Beatle record sales depended upon a scandal-free atmosphere. So such nuisance suits were settled immediately to protect the group's image.

During the first few years at NEMS Enterprises, Clive recalls that Brian was infatuated with the American record-buying market. It was after "She Loves You" spent eight weeks on the British charts in August, 1963, that Brian envisioned a possible Beatle American concert tour. Yet Brian confessed to his younger brother that he had no idea how to go about promoting such an American tour. In August, 1963, Brian traveled to New York with a few names and addresses of booking agents, but he was soon lost in the midst of New York's entertainment jungle. Accompanied by singer Billy J. Kramer, Brian was able to meet a friendly American businessman, Sid Bernstein, who had the vision to see a future in the Beatles' music. Bernstein had vacationed in London earlier in

The Beatles: Posed Elegance

1963 and had been amazed by the frenetic zeal of Beatle fans. But it was not the Beatles themselves who impressed Sid Bernstein as much as Brian Epstein's business skills and promotional ideas. Bernstein saw in Brian Epstein the making of an entreprenurial genius, so he signed a contract with Brian for the Beatles to perform in New York's famed Carnegie Hall. Bernstein selected February 12, 1964, President Abraham Lincoln's birthday as the concert date because he believed that it would be much easier to fill Carnegie Hall for a holiday concert.

It was almost by accident that Sid Bernstein was able to book the Beatles. Clive Epstein recalls that Bernstein called his mother in August, 1963 inquiring about the Beatles' availability for New York bookings. Since Brian wasn't home, Queenie jotted his number down for future reference. When Brian left for New York in late 1963, Bernstein's number was in his address book. It was not long before Sid Bernstein promoted the Beatles American concerts.

From 1964 to 1967, the Beatles were the most sought after rock group in the world. As millions of dollars were earned by the Beatles in concerts, record sales and peripheral merchandise, they were so busy that it became impossible to enjoy the fruits of their labors. In

1967, the Beatles formed the Apple Corporation to reinvest their sizeable earnings in developing new talent. In the midst of organizing this altruistic effort, Brian Epstein died.

The Beatles erroneously assumed that once Brian died, he no longer had a claim to their musical profits. To their dismay, the Beatles discovered that Brian Epstein's 25% commission was paid directly to NEMS. A subtle, almost technical, clause in the management contract suddenly made Clive Epstein the director of NEMS business activities. Pete Shotton, John Lennon's boyhood friend, had just become a director of the Apple Corporation, and he attended the first board meeting after Brian's death. It was a strange and perplexing affair as Shotton was greeted by a roomful of businessmen who had no idea that the Apple Corporation intended not only to merchandise the Beatles but to promote new talent.

One of the problems with the Apple Corporation was that a dozen subsidiary companies were established to avoid the British tax collector. John Lennon jokingly dubbed Apple Enterprises an attempt to evade taxes and have a "smashing time" doing it. The lack of a business framework at Apple bothered Clive Epstein. He believed that the Beatles should expand their horizons and write books, and little greeting cards as well as molding their music in a highly commercial manner. In many respects, the Apple Corporation Ltd. conflicted with Brian Epstein's NEMS Enterprises. It was Brian's network of interlocking companies which included publishing, retail, film and night club rights which made it difficult to unravel the NEMS business picture. Much to his chagrin, Clive Epstein discovered that his brother Brian even owned a quarter share in a Spanish bullfighter. Although many groups attempted to purchase the Beatles's rights, Clive was surprised to discover a $20 million dollar offer in 1966 from a wealthy American investor for the outright purchase of NEMS Enterprises. But the establishment of the Apple Corporation Ltd. complicated Clive Epstein's business problems.

When the Beatles announced the formation of Apple in 1967, they suggested that the company would finance the careers of many new recording artists, film makers, and literary figures. The Beatles invested two million dollars in Apple's five divisions: records, films, electronics, retailing and publishing. Paul McCartney was the first Beatle to take an active role in promoting and producing the new Apple talent. Soon the other Beatles followed suit, and the Apple Corporation seemed a hipster's dream in 1967-1968. The summer of love in San Francisco's Haight-Ashbury in 1967 and the prominence of the love generation induced the Beatles to launch a corporate structure which made artistic sense and had a counter culture type of business leadership. Clive Epstein and many NEMS employees were horrified by the hippie party atmosphere at Apple. When the Beatles' clothing store, the Apple Boutique, opened, one critic called it a psychedelic Woolworth's. Apple's ideas were good but it was the Beatles' money which was spent and no one was accountable for the product. Disaster was imminent.

Few people realized how difficult it was to analyze the Beatles' financial structure, because of the early success of the Apple Corporation Ltd. The Beatles' Apple venture was a business which was artistically and commercially unique. The Apple headquarters at 95 Wigmore Street in London was a bizarre office building with a psychedelic exterior which caught the general public's eye. Apple Scruffs, as the Beatle fans who stood outside the building were known, often were invited inside to glimpse a new product. When George Harrison recorded his tribute to the fans, they were invited into the recording studio to hear Harrison's version of "Apple Scruffs." This was hardly the type of behavior most entertainment figures employed with their fans. After Brian Epstein's death, the business atmosphere at Apple was described by one employee as "a continual cocktail party." Perhaps Peter Brown put it best when he suggested that controlling spending at Apple was "like riding the back of a tiger." The Beatles were involved with the Maharishi Mahesh Yogi when they learned of Brian's death, and the Maharishi advised the Beatles to smile because Brian Epstein's death was not an important event. Peter McCabe and Robert D. Schonfeld's book, *Apple To the Core: the Unmaking of the Beatles,* reported the Maharishi's comment and wondered aloud why the Beatles followed the Maharishi's dictates. There is little doubt that the Beatles were confused and uncertain about their direction and the Maharishi's suggestion was a calming one.

But the Beatles could not replace Brian Epstein. Their attempt to make the movie, *Magical Mystery Tour,* was an unqualified failure, and the general public was bored with a psychedelic bus ride through the English countryside. When *Magical Mystery Tour* was broadcast over British television in Christmas, 1967, the critics wondered if the Beatles' creativity was still intact. Had Clive Epstein been a part of this project, the Beatles might have received better artistic and business advice. A good example of the need for

The Beatles: A Bootleg Album Cover

sound advice occurred when the Beatles began the filming of *Magical Mystery Tour* on September 11, 1967. Brian opposed the film because it lacked commercial potential. They ignored his warnings, and when Brian died on August 27, 1967 the Beatles went on with the project. The pressures and tensions of their business and professional careers made the *Magical Mystery Tour* movie an unmitigated disaster.

What hurt the Beatles' career and prevented Clive Epstein from reorganizing the Beatles' business problems was a major reorganization of NEMS Enterprises. Only a few hours after Brian's death, Peter Brown moved to succeed Epstein. Since the early 1960s Brown was a trusted aide, and in August, 1967 he was Brian's right hand man. Brown politely informed the Beatles that he was assuming their management. Clive Epstein could not believe Brown's gall. Not only had Brian trained Brown, but he had delegated increasingly complex business dealings to Brown. Rather than supporting NEMS Enterprises, Brown appeared to be solidifying his own power. In Peter Brown's book, *The Love You Make: An Insider's View of the Beatles,* Brown complains that many of the Beatles employees would not cooperate with him. Although the chaos within NEMS could not be blamed entirely on Brown nonetheless, it was Clive Epstein's business expertise which brought stability to NEMS after Brian's death.

Just before Brian Epstein died, he entertained the idea of selling NEMS. The Beatles were shocked to learn that Robert Stigwood and David Shaw were attempting to take over the board of directors of NEMS Enterprises. To forestall a nasty public fight, Clive Epstein arranged for a deal by which Robert Stigwood took his office furniture, the Bee Gees, Cream, and Jimi Hendrix to found his own company. Some critics have suggested that Clive gave away the bank, but in September, 1967, these acts were not the multimillion-dollar talent of later years. Furthermore, the Beatles were personally upset with efforts to sell NEMS because they had little knowledge of Stigwood's abilities. John Lennon complained that the Beatles were being treated like cattle, and Clive Epstein helped to calm John's fears.

In the tumultuous days after Brian's death, Clive nervously anticipated that he would succeed his brother as the director of NEMS Enterprises. A brilliant businessman in his own right, Clive was much too sophisticated and intellectual to market rock music products. He felt uncomfortable among the menagerie of jugglers, dancers, huskers, singers and small time hustlers who plagued the Apple Record offices. The open use of alcohol and drugs, the lack of artistic and corporate discipline, and the chaotic nature of the Apple product made it an unattractive business proposition for Clive. He longed for the quiet serenity of lunch at Liverpool's Adelphi Hotel or the sophistication of the Liverpool countryside.

Yet, four days after Brian's death, Clive Epstein was appointed chairman of NEMS Enterprises. Peter Brown's book failed to mention that Clive prevented Brown from taking over the reins of the Beatles' career. A number of people close to the Beatles' career were highly critical of Clive's inability to understand the Beatles' business affairs. This criticism is an inaccurate portrayal of Clive's abilities, and it is the result of the McCabe and Schonfeld book, *Apple to the Core: The Unmaking of the Beatles.* McCabe and Schonfeld suggest that Clive was described by Paul McCartney as a "provincial furniture salesman." This quotation is a curious one because McCartney has maintained a close and personal friendship with Clive for two decades. In fact, once Clive was named director of NEMS Enterprises, the Beatles arranged for a business meeting and they wore conservative dark suits as the limousines drove them to Brian's Chapel Street house in London. Clive and Queenie

Epstein sat nervously sipping tea and discussing the Beatles'
future. It was a lengthy and frank meeting, and neither Clive
Epstein nor the Beatles knew how they should replace Brian's
leadership. It was a strange meeting as the Beatles had been
studying with the Maharashi, and they were developing an interest
in meditation, mysticism and Indian music. These new directions
hardly seemed to fit the Beatles' current situation, and they were
confused about their own future. This meeting, however, revealed
the deep respect that the Beatles maintained for Brian after his
death. They also discussed Clive's business ideas, and suggested
that he play a more vigorous role in Beatle affairs. In the aftermath
of Brian's death the Beatles and Clive Epstein clung to one another
as business reorganization altered the structure of England's most
popular and profitable rock music group.

The Beatles did everything they could to comfort Clive and
Queenie Epstein. Yet it was their respect for Brian's business skills
which served to make them momentarily cooperative. In October,
1968, when the Beatles contract with NEMS expired, it appeared
that they would seek new management. To facilitate future Beatle
business activity a company, Nemperor Holdings, was formed to
provide new business directions. As the Beatles' attempted to direct
their musical careers internal disputes threatened to destroy their
success. Due to these problems Nemperor Holdings persuaded
Robert Stigwood to accept a half a million pound settlement, and
resign as a NEMS director. This deal was quickly negotiated by
Clive Epstein, and he demonstrated a more than adequate
knowledge of the rock music business. But the Beatles still missed
Brian Epstein's firm business hand. The Beatles were not able to
properly assess the degree of talent within their Apple Corporation.

Despite this cooperation there were also serious differences
between Clive Epstein and the Beatles. Epstein's conservative
demeanor and cautious approach to business expansion prompted
the Beatles to resist many of his ideas. The Beatles were now eager
to direct their own careers. Because of their deep respect for Brian
Epstein, the Beatles allowed Clive Epstein's NEMS Enterprises to
market their film *Magical Mystery Tour.* John Lennon reflected the
Beatles disappointment when he remarked that he was horrified
that every major television network refused to screen the film.

After a number of inept marketing attempts, NEMS sold a color
print of *Magical Mystery Tour* to BBC-TV, who screened it in black
and white. There was no advance publicity and the Beatles *Magical
Mystery Tour* was a commercial disaster. The Beatles were

incensed that Clive Epstein was unable to adequately promote their product. In fairness to Epstein, it is obvious that *Magical Mystery Tour* lacked immediate mass commercial appeal. It was the Beatles' first attempt at movie making, and although Paul McCartney's idea for *Magical Mystery Tour* was a brilliant one, the film was too advanced for its time. *Magical Mystery Tour* was an improvisational film which depended upon unrehearsed spontaneity rather than a carefully crafted script. Once filming began on September 11, 1967, the Beatles and a bevy of camera men took off for two weeks to ride the *Magical Mystery Tour* bus through the south of England. After six weeks of editing hundreds of hours of footage, the movie was mixed with Beatle music. Eventually, the sound and film were crafted to 64 minutes of total spontaneity which the critics labeled as "senseless garbage" and which failed to excite English and American audiences. Since 1967 *Magical Mystery Tour* has developed a cult following, and it helped to influence a new school of experimental filmmakers in the 1970s and 1980s.

On December 17, 1967, *Magical Mystery Tour* was previewed for a party of specially invited guests at London's Lancaster Hotel. Linda Eastman, an American photographer, attended the party, and the following day took a series of photos of Paul McCartney. Clive Epstein's troubles with the Beatles began once Paul McCartney met his future wife Linda Eastman. When Linda's father, Lee Eastman, and her brother, John, who offered Paul some intelligent and constructive advice about the Beatles' finances, met Paul he began to consider some new business ventures. On Eastman's advice, Paul purchased several thousand stock shares in the Beatles songwriting company, Northern Songs. When John Lennon found out about these purchases he confronted Paul angrily with the accusation that he was not cooperating with the other Beatles. Unwittingly, Clive Epstein was caught in the middle of this squabble, and this was one of the main reasons that Clive decided to sell NEMS, now known as Nemperor Holdings. An equally important influence in Clive's decision to sell the company was the back taxes owed to British tax officials. Once the complicated tangle of Brian Epstein's estate was unraveled, there were large sums of money owed not only to the tax officials but to many other individuals and companies. The sale of NEMS Enterprises was one of the means of meeting these bothersome expenses.

Once Clive Epstein made public his decision to sell NEMS, the Triumph Investment Trust Bank of England, headed by Leonard Richenberg, was the first serious bidder. In an aggressive business

Paul McCartney: What Is Apple's Future?

move, Richenberg offered one million pounds for Nemperor's business assets. After lengthy negotiations and a series of discussions with the Beatles, Clive demonstrated his loyalty to the Liverpool four by agreeing to sell NEMS to the Beatles' Apple Corporation. At Apple, Lee Eastman representing Paul McCartney, and Allen Klein, representing the remaining Beatles, were involved in an intricate power struggle. The problems between Eastman and Klein threatened to delay the sale of Nemperor Holdings. The Beatles had difficulty raising the money to purchase the Nemperor Holdings Company outright. In a desperate move, the Beatles asked for a meeting with the Chairman of EMI, Sir Joseph Lockwood. After some small talk and a glass of sherry, John Eastman, who attended the meeting at Paul McCartney's insistence, blurted out that the Beatles needed a one million, two hundred and fifty thousand pound advance to purchase the Nemperor Holdings Company. After this discussion, Sir Joseph Lockwood informed the Beatles that he would consider the proposition. It appears that Lockwood had made up his mind to help the Beatles because it was an excellent business proposition. The large loan would guarantee the Beatles' future productivity and there would be an immense amount of interest. From EMI's corporate viewpoint the loan would guarantee that the Beatles would produce music and other forms of revenue to pay off the loan.

It was the shrewd New Yorker, Allen Klein, who then entered the picture to complicate the sale of Nemperor Holdings. In Klein's opinion, the loan was an unwise business move, and he shrewdly pointed out that an audit of the books might bring about the acquisition of Nemperor Holdings with little or no money involved. John, George and Ringo were impressed with Klein's knowledgeable explanation of the Beatles' financial problems, and he was granted the authority to pursue a fiscal solution.

An American businessman, Klein was a legendary figure in the entertainment industry. In the late 1950s and early 1960s, he was an accounting Svengali to Bobby Darin as well as Steve Lawrence and Eydie Gorme, and for a brief period Klein was Sam Cooke's manager. His sharp mind and judicious accounting skills prompted the Rolling Stones to hire Klein as their American representative. When the Beatles' financial problems became public knowledge, Klein was determined to manage their financial resources.

In 1965, Klein had negotiated a $1.25 million record advance for the Rolling Stones. The Beatles were in awe of Klein's ability, but Paul McCartney quickly soured on the American businessman. It seemed that McCartney found Klein's personality difficult to accept. A shrewd person, Klein realized that he had much in common with John Lennon. Both were parentless. They were also aggressive, creative individuals with a different view of business and culture. In a rapid fire, spellbinding manner, Klein convinced John Lennon that he could solve the Beatles' financial woes. He also assured Yoko Ono that her films would be distributed by United Artists. It was a wise move for John Lennon to appoint Klein to handle his affairs, because an uncompromising professional is what the Beatles needed to cut out the deadwood and bring the Beatles' business management back into an organized state of affairs. John Lennon then informed Sir Joseph Lockwood at EMI that the Beatles would not need the loan, and that Klein would handle all future business dealings.

After Klein was empowered to handle Lennon's assets, a split with Paul McCartney followed. In an attempt to straighten out the complicated question of who really handled the Beatles' finances, a meeting was arranged between Allan Klein and John Eastman. It was a tense affair as Klein aggressively stated John Lennon's financial needs and John Eastman delicately stated Paul

The Beatles on BBC-TV, 1963

McCartney's financial goals. When Klein called Eastman a fool for wanting to purchase the Nemperor Holding Company, Eastman left the room disgusted. After Eastman left, Klein found himself in the room with Ringo Starr and George Harrison. He sat down and informed the remaining two Beatles how he could protect their finances. The result was that, after the meeting, Klein represented three of the four Beatles.

On February 14, 1969, Clive Epstein received a letter from Klein requesting a meeting. The letter angered Clive because it questioned "the propriety" of his contract with the Beatles. Klein had completed an audit of the Beatles' books, and he believed that he could persuade Nemperor Holdings to sell its interest in the Beatles. Lee Eastman traveled from New York to London to meet with Klein, Clive Epstein and the Beatles. A raucous shouting match took place between Klein and Eastman, and everyone left disgusted.

With British tax officials persistently badgering Clive Epstein for his late brother's taxes, Clive reopened negotiations with Leonard Richenberg of the Triumph Investment Trust Bank. By February 17, 1969, all of the details were worked out and Triumph became the owners of 70% of Nemperor Holdings. The Beatles were upset that Clive sold his interest to a British bank. They instructed EMI records to forward their royalties to the Apple Corporation. Triumph sued the Beatles and suddenly all record royalties were deposited in a bank by a British court pending the outcome of the lawsuit. Eventually, John, George and Ringo's representative Allan Klein worked out a compromise with the Triumph Investment Trust Bank which allowed the bank to collect 700,000 pounds plus 25% of the Beatles royalties. It was this agreement which allowed the Beatles to finally spend some of their money. In addition the Beatles agreed to pay Triumph 5% of their royalties from 1972 to 1976, and the Beatles also sold the remaining 10% of their interest in NEMS to Triumph. These concessions persuaded Triumph to drop legal action against the Beatles.

Clive Epstein's years with the Beatles were interesting and eventful ones. He had a genuine affection for the boys, and he represented their interests to the best of his abilities. However, he never fit into the flamboyant and controversial life of the rock star business manager as his brother Brian Epstein so skillfully had. Although Clive excelled in school, eclipsed his brother in the family business, and was considered the better adjusted of the Epstein boys, he was unable to match Brian's sensational business feats in the rock music world. As a result, Clive left the Beatles' business activities to a new group of entrepreneurs and slipped quietly back into the obscurity of Liverpool life.

Bo Diddley

JOE FLANNERY

Joe Flannery: The Invisible Beatle

In 1961 Joe Flannery emerged as an important figure in the Liverpool music scene. As the manager and promoter of Lee Curtis and the All Stars, Flannery established his reputation as a rock music entrepreneur. Initially, Flannery's younger brother, Pete, played rock music in local Liverpool clubs billed simply as Pete Flannery. His stage name not only proved to be unappealing but his ability to package his music was just as noncommercial. As a result, Joe Flannery entered the picture and restructured his brother's music and appearance. In early 1961 as Joe Flannery was sitting in his Liverpool home listening to the record by the American performer Curtis Lee, "Pretty Little Angel Eyes," he decided to change his brother's stage name to Lee Curtis. At this time Flannery presented Lee Curtis' music so that it had a Phil Spector type of rock music sound. Flannery believed that Lee Curtis and the All Stars could make a positive transition to commercially appealing music like Spector's Wall of Sound in America.

There were a number of important show business experiences in Flannery's background which made him an excellent music promoter. He had performed extensively in small clubs and theaters as a young man. Flannery toured England and Europe as part of a night club act known as Joe and Ken. Young Flannery teamed with English comedian Ken Dodd as a promising cabaret act. Not only

Joe Flannery in His Liverpool Office, 1982

was Flannery a smooth vocalist, but he also had a singing style reminiscent of American crooner Frank Sinatra. Eventually, Flannery tired of the show business grind, returned to Liverpool to pursue his business interests. Ken Dodd went on to become one of England's finest comedians and an international star. While Flannery was making his fortune in the wholesale grocery business, he could not escape the urge to promote local Liverpool music groups. As Joe Flannery watched inexperienced musical promoters like Sam Leach break into the beat music field, he reassessed his career direction and decided to enter the show business management field.

Although Flannery's musical interests were shaped by Eddie Fisher, Nat King Cole and Perry Como, nonetheless, he was an extraordinary judge of musical talent. One of Flannery's obsessions was collecting American rock and roll records. The Phil Spector sound, Motown records and obscure rhythm and blues performers like Arthur Alexander were an integral part of Flannery's record collection. Soon John Lennon, Lee Curtis and Rory Storm among others were seeking Flannery's musical advice. When Pete

Flannery formed his rock group, Joe persuaded his brother to follow the American rock music format.

For a brief period of time a group known as Lee Curtis and the Detours performed around Liverpool, but this musical aggregation didn't jell in local clubs. Consequently, Flannery changed the back up musicians and promoted Curtis' good looks and dynamic performing style. Flannery also highlighted the group's visual appearance by adhering to current fashion design and creating a smooth stage presentation. In many respects, Flannery was a year ahead of Brian Epstein in shaping a rock music act which reflected the Merseyside sound. Soon the popularity of Lee Curtis and the All Stars attracted attention from other musical artists.

As Lee Curtis and the All Stars became a popular act, John Lennon was intrigued by their stage show. Therefore, he observed Curtis' performances regularly. Few people believed that there was a special reason for Lennon's interest in Curtis' stage style. Since Joe Flannery was a close friend of Lennon's and both artists were from Liverpool, everyone naturally assumed that John went to see Lee Curtis perform as a courtesy. Nothing was further from the truth. Lennon modeled his early stage presence in 1961-1962 upon Curtis' act. The reason that Lennon was so heavily influenced by Lee Curtis was due to Joe Flannery's presence. John believed that Flannery had unique commercial insights into the Liverpool music scene. Once Joe Flannery became an integral part of the Merseyside music environment, he was an inspirational influence upon John Lennon.

From 1961 to 1963 Lee Curtis was one of Liverpool's most popular performers, and he appeared destined for show business stardom. Joe Flannery was quietly in the background orchestrating Curtis' musical career. In polls by local Liverpool newspapers and small music magazines, Lee Curtis and the All Stars were listed regularly as the second most popular act in the Merseyside area. The Beatles were the dominant group. In October, 1962, *Mersey Beat,* the main music newspaper in Liverpool, reported that Lee Curtis and the All Stars were the resident Friday night band at the Majestic Ballroom, Birkenhead. They were receiving a great deal of publicity for a song entitled "Barberock," which was based on the tune "Finiculi, Finiculi" from *The Barber of Seville.* In addition to the popularity of this song, Lee Curtis and the All Stars were buoyed by the addition of ex-Beatle Pete Best on the drums. Even though the publicity generated by Lee Curtis' musical skill would have brought most rock musicians immediate commercial success,

Lee Curtis, 1964

his lack of hit record sales was due to the fact that his music was too smooth and too sophisticated for English rock audiences. Despite Curtis' good looks and Pete Best's teen idol sneer, the group faded into musical obscurity. However, Joe Flannery's role was an important one in the evolving Liverpool music scene.

An example of Flannery's promotional skills occurred the first time he booked Lee Curtis and the All Stars into Hamburg's Star-Club. Because Curtis was an unknown act to Hamburg audiences, Flannery phoned Horst Fascher at the Star-Club and negotiated a unique booking arrangement. "If you take Lee Curtis I will guarantee three days of shows without pay," Flannery informed the startled Fascher. After the trial period, Fascher booked Lee Curtis and the All Stars for a lengthy run. In fact, Curtis' performances were so dynamic that Star-Club Records inquired about signing him to a contract. German fans were so enthralled with Curtis that Star-Club Records hoped to release immediately a single. Flannery, however, wanted his brother to sign with a major British record label, but he wisely informed Star-Club Records that they could broach a record deal in the future. It was Flannery's gracious, but highly business-like nature, which impressed most Hamburg and Liverpool observers.

As a number of record companies showed an interest in signing Lee Curtis and the All Stars in 1961, Joe Flannery demonstrated his professional background and extensive years of training in the entertainment business by rejecting these offers. Flannery did not have his brother sign a contract immediately, because he preferred to analyze the commercial direction of British rock music. Many Liverpool observers commented that Flannery was destined to become one of England's most significant entertainment entrepreneurs. The skills of the well-known British promoter, Larry Parnes, were often compared with Flannery's, and a number of night club owners and concert promoters predicted a great future for Flannery's acts.

It was not long before many Liverpool singers and beat groups were approaching Flannery as a management consultant. Not only was Flannery an astute businessman, but he had a clear understanding of English rock music. During his years as a successful grocery merchant, Flannery realized the necessity of careful planning and precise marketing. This is one of the tragic ironies of show business that these skills did not allow Lee Curtis and the All Stars to become a major recording act. Yet, Flannery was significant in the Liverpool music story, and this chapter will examine his relationship with Brian Epstein and the Beatles.

It was due to the developing Merseyside music scene that Flannery spent a great deal of time with Epstein and Lennon. As Lee Curtis refined his musical talent, young John Lennon and the more reserved Brian Epstein were in close contact with Joe Flannery. Although Flannery initially knew Lennon and Epstein as personal friends, he soon became their musical guru. This was due partially to the popularity of Lee Curtis' music. John Lennon often wondered why Joe Flannery selected a particular song for Curtis to perform and why the stage show changed so dramatically every few weeks. Soon Lennon realized that Joe Flannery had a highly professional means of altering Lee Curtis' act to make it appear as a new innovation. By 1962 Curtis was one of Hamburg's most popular performers at the Top Ten, Star Club and the Kaiserkeller Club. Joe Flannery not only managed Lee Curtis and the All Stars, but he became intimately involved with the Beatles' musical career. Some critics have suggested that Flannery created the rift between Pete Best and the Beatles so that he could add Best's drumming skills to Lee Curtis and the All Stars. This theory is the result of the intense publicity surrounding Best's sudden departure from the Beatles. What is frequently ignored is the fact that there was every chance that Lee Curtis and the All Stars would be more popular than the Beatles. In a 1962 *Mersey Beat* poll, Curtis' group finished second to the Beatles, but many casual observers believed that Flannery's group was destined for superstardom.

When he was not promoting Lee Curtis' career, Flannery spent many hours with John Lennon and Brian Epstein educating them concerning the entertainment business. Flannery talked for hours about selecting the proper songs and stage attire which made new performers stand out as professional entertainers. These lectures were not lost on Brian and John, because they increasingly analyzed the Merseyside music scene for helpful commercial hints.

John Lennon often sat around Flannery's house playing an inexpensive guitar and singing Elvis Presley and Del Shannon songs. It was Flannery, for example, who first played Little Willie John's "Leave My Kitten Alone" for John Lennon, and they talked for hours about the female back up singers used by Little Willie John in the original song. Flannery pointed out that background harmonizing was an essential part of rock music and he believed that the Beatles' could employ this musical technique. It was not long before three part harmony was a strong aspect of the Beatles' stage show. By 1962 "Leave My Kitten Alone" was an integral part of the Beatles' live show. Another important musical contribution occurred when Flannery emphasized the importance of proper record production and a commercially aggressive label. Flannery suggested that Ahmet Ertegun's Atlantic Record company and Berry Gordy, Jr.'s, Motown label were excellent examples of American record companies. As a result Lennon paid more attention to the music of Ray Charles, the Coasters, the Marvelettes and Barrett Strong. Soon songs by these artists were featured prominently in the Beatles' act. It was strange to Lennon that Flannery, who carried himself like a college professor, was so knowledgable about the music business. John confessed one day to Flannery: "I want to live in New York and be an American." It was natural for John to make this remark to Flannery, because Joe's friends often jokingly referred to him as "the American." This prophetic statement was an indication of how strongly American musical influences shaped the Beatles early career. As the music scene evolved in Liverpool from a jazz to a rock and roll format, Flannery recognized the cataclysmic changes in English rock music. As a result he provided indispensible management for his

Lee Curtis and the All Stars

brother's group, Lee Curtis and the All Stars. Because of his extensive background in the music business, Flannery realized that packaging, promotion and an intangible ability to generate publicity were important factors in promoting Curtis' career. John Lennon immediately sought out Flannery's advice and often took the bus to Joe's house for encouragement. While educating young John Lennon and booking Lee Curtis, Joe Flannery reacquainted himself with Brian Epstein.

In 1940 young Joe Flannery and Brian Epstein socialized in Epstein's beautiful home. Joe Flannery's father, Chris, was a cabinet maker who specialized in a type of merchandise that Harry Epstein sold in his Walton Road furniture store. On more than one occasion the Flannerys and the Epsteins gathered for a combination of business and social pleasures. On these memorable gatherings, Joe and Brian romped through the house, shared toys and played together. Two decades later they met in a Liverpool pub, and the two grown men laughed as they reminisced about their childhood friendship. Both Flannery and Epstein were imbued with show business ambitions, and they talked for hours about forming businesses to promote different types of musical acts.

Joe Flannery was the first to concentrate upon show business management by opening the Carlton-Brooke Agency. Eventually, Flannery managed Beryl Marsden, Liverpool's most promising female pop singer, and Lee Curtis and the All Stars. Since Flannery was active in the show business management milieu, he spent an inordinate amount of time in and around the Liverpool rock music clubs. It was during this time he was intensely promoting Lee Curtis in 1961 and 1962 that Joe Flannery had his most significant contacts with the Beatles and Brian Epstein.

Among his many early experiences with the Beatles, one of Joe Flannery's most interesting moments occurred on July 7, 1961, when the Beatles and Lee Curtis and the All Stars shared the bill at the Iron Door Club on Temple Street in Liverpool. Flannery had seen the Beatles play a number of times, but he was very curious about the rumors that they had blossomed into a top Beat group. The Beatles had already made their first trip to Hamburg, and the response to their music from local crowds was overwhelming. Allan Williams, who often booked the Beatles, was a detriment to their reputation, because he had nothing positive to say about their music. However, local fans and a number of Germans who were on vacation heard the Beatles in and around Liverpool. As Joe Flannery watched the Beatles perform that night in the dank, smelly Iron Door Club, he realized that they were becoming a local phenomena. Since they had played at the Indra and the Kaiserkeller clubs in Hamburg, the Beatles had returned to Liverpool to even greater local popularity. Many accounts of the first Beatle trip to Hamburg suggest that they came back disenchanted with the music business. Most Liverpool observers remember that the Beatles were elated with their chance to play long musical sets in Germany. Joe Flannery went to the Cavern Club on Mathews Street for a welcome home night for the Beatles after they had made their first trip to Germany. As the Beatles appeared with Johnny Sandon and the Searchers, it was obvious to Flannery that they were already an accomplished musical group. Not only did the Beatles' play most of the songs that Flannery had spun on his record player for John Lennon over the years, but they gave a special flavor to these tunes. It was the Beatles' ability to cover another artist's record in their own way, Flannery realized, which made them destined for the English record charts.

After Brian Epstein watched the Beatles' perform at the Cavern Club, he contacted Joe Flannery and they met for some drinks at the Beehive Pub on Paradise Street. In a burst of enthusiasm, Epstein blurted out that he not only wanted to manage the Beatles, but he believed that they were the musical wave of the future. Although Joe Flannery was a close personal friend of Brian Epstein's, he realized that there was a certain amount of trepidation in Brian's manner. They both agreed that the Beatles' possessed an enormous original talent, but could this musical skill be promoted effectively in a mass market?

As they discussed the Beatles' future, Brian Epstein confessed that he was having second thoughts about signing the boys to a management contract. Brian remarked that in late November, 1961, he had mentioned the possibility of managing the Beatles' to his parents at the dinner table. They laughed at the thought of four young men from Liverpool making a type of music that the world would pay to hear and see. This depressed Brian and he had serious misgivings about a management contract with the Beatles. Joe Flannery soothed Brian's feelings and pointed out how versatile and skilled the Beatles were as songwriters, performers and even as comedy artists. Brian Epstein complained that the Beatles were too difficult to control and they were too independent for almost any manager. Flannery countered that this was not only a sign of their talent, but it was an example of a unique type of creativity.

As Brian Epstein sat in the Beehive Pub with Joe Flannery, he was in the process of deciding whether or not to manage the Beatles. Although his family objected to a management contract with the Beatles, Brian laid out a careful plan to merchandise and promote their records through the family owned NEMS record department. Brian also confessed that he found it repugnant to go into the type of pubs that the Beatles played, and he wondered whether Joe Flannery might assist him in this area. Another problem was that Brian was ill-informed about the management end of the music business. He had a great deal of knowledge of musical tastes from managing NEMS record department, but this was not the same experience that musical entrepreneurs used to succeed. As a result, Brian learned all that he could from Joe Flannery. The promotion and packaging of a rock music act was Flannery's speciality, and he willingly shared his knowledge and ideas with Brian Epstein. In sum, they formed a quasi-partnership to promote local Liverpool acts. The two men were good personal friends, and they never considered signing a formal management contract; they simply based their partnership upon a handshake. From December, 1961 until November, 1963 Joe Flannery was an integral part of the Beatles' success story. Since he was a quiet, unassuming young man, Flannery did not stand out when Beatlemania took over England. As one of John Lennon's friends remarked in the Ye Crack Pub: "Joe Flannery is the invisible Beatle." Yet, Flannery's skills in many respects helped to foment the English rock music revolution.

After spending a great deal of time with Brian Epstein, Flannery realized that his boyhood friend was very serious about the rock music business. In December, 1961, after Epstein signed the Beatles to a management contract, he became very secretive about many of his plans. It appears that Brian had read a great deal about Elvis Presley's manager, Colonel Tom Parker, and he modeled his personal management style upon the Colonel's. This secrecy led to the charge that Epstein was acting strangely. To counter these rumors, Joe invited Brian to his home for some drinks and casual conversation. During the course of the evening, Joe asked Brian some tough questions about his plans to secure the Beatles a recording contract. In addition, Flannery believed that the group often worked for booking fees which were too low. As a result of these questions, Brian told a series of grandiose stories about his future plans for the Beatles. Not all of Brian's exaggerations were insignificant ones. He was able to create one preposterous legend which helped publicize the Beatles' early career. This occurred when he faked a phone call from Colonel Tom Parker in America inquiring about the Beatles' music. Philip Norman's book, *Shout: The Beatles In Their Generation,* devotes an entire section of his excellent study to this tale. What it demonstrated was Brian Epstein's ability to publicize the Beatles on a grand scale. Joe Flannery chuckled as he remembered Brian convincing most of Liverpool that American recording executives were watching the Beatles' progress. It was not long before fiction became fact.

One of Flannery's special qualities was his ability to promote American and British entertainers in the same show. When Brian Epstein arranged for the Beatles to appear with Little Richard on October 12, 1962 at the Majestic Ballroom, Birkenhead the Beatles were ecstatic. Brian informed Little Richard: "My boys idolize you." This comment flattered the American entertainer and that evening he posed for pictures with the Beatles. Little Richard remarked after the show: "I never thought that they would make it." Yet, despite these early misgivings Little Richard recognized that the Beatles had a unique crowd appeal. After he watched the Beatles perform a second time, Little Richard changed his mind about their music. Joe Flannery was largely responsible for convincing Little Richard that the Beatles had possibilities as recording artists.

Joe Flannery and Tony Sheridan, Hamburg, 1962

Flannery played some live tapes for the American entertainer, and the songs included some of Little Richard's tunes. He was impressed with the original manner in which the Beatles could perform other people's material. As a result, Little Richard changed his attitude about their music.

After thinking about the Beatles strong crowd appeal, Little Richard called Art Rupe at Specialty Records. The Los Angeles-based rhythm and blues label had moved into the mainstream of rock and roll music with artists like Little Richard and Lloyd Price. One of the most significant songwriters and producers of the 1950s, Bumps Blackwell, went to work for Speciality while studying classical music at UCLA, and he was soon responsible for a burst of hit records. Neither Rupe nor Blackwell were interested in an English rock music act. British rock and roll had never been marketed effectively in America and Speciality Records declined an offer to listen to an audition tape. A few days later Little Richard called the Chicago-based Vee Jay label and extolled the Beatles' musical virtues. Vee Jay executives were intrigued by the strong fan following that the Beatles had generated, and they watched the progress of the Beatles' first single "Love Me Do." In 1963, as a result of Little Richard's call, Vee Jay released the first Beatle record in the United States.

The intensity with which Little Richard promoted the Beatles' music was due to a concert he had attended on October 28, 1962. This event was billed as the Little Richard Show and it was held at the Empire Theater in Liverpool. In addition to Little Richard, Jet Harris and the Jetblacks, the Sounds Inc. and the Beatles performed before a sold out crowd. In the intimate setting of the Empire Theater, Little Richard was enthralled with the Beatles performance. Not only did they receive a better crowd response than the other acts, but they were able to present a show which was as professional as Little Richard's. As the Beatles and Little Richard performed together in late 1962, Joe Flannery hovered in the wings offering advice and encouragement. Many people did not recognize the changes in rock performing styles, but it was Flannery who encouraged the Beatles to learn from the American entertainers who passed through Liverpool. Consequently, many people ridiculed the entertainers for clothing or personal appearance mannerisms, and Flannery always defended the Beatles and other rock acts against these anti-intellectual barbs. Many times Joe Flannery pointed out the importance of Little Richard's unique style to John Lennon, and this led the chief Beatle to consider changes in their act.

When the Beatles performed with Little Richard at the Star-Club in Hamburg in 1962-1963, they spent an inordinate amount of time with the American entertainer. In particular, Paul McCartney learned all that he could from Little Richard's vast songwriting repertoire. It was a golden opportunity for McCartney to craft his songs in the presence of a musical genius, and they went over many of McCartney's lyrical tunes for hours. John Lennon, however, reacted violently to Little Richard. Not only was Lennon abusive, but he often made fun of Little Richard's stage presence. As a result Little Richard and John Lennon had a number of personal and artistic differences, and the American found John temperamental and overly aggressive. Yet, this was still a time of learning for both Lennon and McCartney and there is no doubt that Little Richard influenced their songwriting.

An interesting movie which details Little Richard's influence upon the Beatles' music is a British television program entitled: "Don't Knock The Rock." When it was screened on the British independent television network in May, 1964, "Don't Knock The Rock" was billed as "Little Richard's Farewell Performance in

England." This strange 38-minute British television show was so popular in the U.K. that it was rebroadcast twice after more than 50,000 letters were written to ATV. This was an indication of how popular original American rock music was in England. Many of Little Richard's early recordings were in Joe Flannery's collection, and John Lennon continued to request songs from Flannery to update the Beatles act. As a tribute to Little Richard the Beatles included "Long Tall Sally" in virtually all of their early performances. Many of the bootleg albums documenting the Beatles' early career contain excellent versions of Little Richard's "Long Tall Sally," and the Beatles frequently spoke of his influence from the stage. The Beatles paid tribute to Little Richard when their fifth British EP was entitled: *Long Tall Sally*. When Paul McCartney sang the lead and played piano solo on "Long Tall Sally," he was simply recreating the song in a manner the Beatles' had done many times before the Hamburg Clubs. The *Long Tall Sally* EP was an enormous commercial success, and it was the only EP on the British Top 30 album charts in the summer of 1964. The following year the *Long Tall Sally* EP had sold over a million records in the world and over 250,000 copies in the United Kingdom. It was a fine tribute to Little Richard to have this EP launch the Beatles' most spectacular period of worldwide commercial success. It was also ironic that as the Beatles became show business superstars, Little Richard began having second thoughts about his musical future. As Little Richard contemplated returning to his first love, gospel music and lay preaching, he watched the Beatles enter the vortex of show business success. He silently hoped that they could survive the coming ordeal.

Like many American entertainers, Little Richard began having problems drawing crowds to his concerts in the mid-1960s. As the Beatles, the Animals, Van Morrison and Them, the Kinks, Manfred Mann and the Rolling Stones inaugurated a new type of British rock music, Little Richard found it increasingly more difficult to sell out his shows. It is one of the tragic ironies of show business that the Beatles were unwittingly responsible for one of the poorest attended Little Richard shows in his lengthy career. On Sunday, October 13, 1963, the Odeon Theater in Liverpool presented Little Richard, the Everly Brothers, Bo Diddley, Julie Grant and the Rolling Stones in concert. The show was a dismal failure as the Odeon Theater was only half filled, because the Beatles were performing that night on an ATV variety show entitled: "Sunday Night At the London Palladium." Virtually all of Liverpool was

Lee Curtis in Concert, 1964

home watching the Beatles. The crowd was generally a mean one composed of a great number of Teddy boys. In their leather jackets and greasy hair they stood out in the Odeon Theater and they threw lighted cigarettes on the stage and an occasional beer bottle on stage. There were also hoots and rude remarks about Little Richard's make up. Joe Flannery's liberal attitude was demonstrated when he defended Little Richard in front of a number of smirking backstage guests. It was apparent that Little Richard's use of make up and his flamboyant clothing titillated the normally staid English audiences. Little Richard not only wore lipstick, mascara and pancake makeup but he used sequined blouses to highlight his stage presence. Mick Jagger of the Rolling Stones was so angered by the crowd that he asked Joe Flannery how Little Richard applied his makeup. In a moment, Flannery produced a make up kit and accentuated the mouth and eyes of young Jagger. As Mick looked in the mirror he was pleased with his new appearance. Bo Diddley sat in a nearby corner chuckling at this little escapade and he could not help but wonder how some of the Chess Record acts might react to these changes in the rock music business. What this story demonstrates is how helpful Flannery was to local musicians and how accessible most of the talent was during this early stage of the English rock revolution.

The ease with which Joe Flannery moved in rock music circles astounded many Liverpool observers. Not only was Flannery an important influence upon the beat groups, but his opinions were sought out by managers, club owners and record executives. However, he was always the invisible man on the Merseyside music scene. Despite his show business career, there was a shyness and a deft avoidance of publicity in Flannery's personal life. He was willing to share his knowledge with people, but he retained a highly private personal life. Like Bob Wooler, Flannery was a show business professional who avoided publicity.

From 1961 to 1963 Joe Flannery was an important agent for Brian Epstein and the Beatles. Because Brian was so heavily involved in the family business, Flannery often helped to arrange concerts in Wales, Ireland, Scotland and Germany. Not only was Joe Flannery a consummate show business professional, but he was honest and trustworthy. These were traits that Brian Epstein soon discovered were difficult to find in the rock music business. It was a time of learning and growth for both Brian Epstein and Joe Flannery and they were an important influence upon each other as well as the Merseyside music scene. In many respects, Flannery's willingness to help the Beatles took time away from promoting Lee Curtis and the All Stars. Yet, as I sat with him in his home in Liverpool in May, 1983, Joe Flannery had only the highest praise for the Beatles and Brian Epstein. He also talked a great deal about his successes and failures promoting Lee Curtis and the All Stars.

By 1962 Lee Curtis and the All Stars and the Beatles were an equally popular rock group in Liverpool and Hamburg, Germany. Curtis' brooding good looks and American style rock and roll voice prompted a number of London booking agents to inquire about his availability. Soon English record companies auditioned Lee Curtis and the All Stars. Almost every major English record label analyzed Lee Curtis' music, and there was a great deal of interest in his brand of rock and roll music. Unwittingly, Brian Epstein stymied Curtis' career by so effectively publicizing the Beatles' music. Initially, many Liverpool observers believed that Lee Curtis and the All Stars were, in fact, more popular than the Beatles. Despite these comparisons the relationship between the Beatles and Lee Curtis remained a friendly one.

The reason for the good feelings between Curtis and the Beatles can be traced back to a March 16, 1961 appearance at the

Iron Door Club on Temple Street in Liverpool. Curtis's group and the Beatles shared the bill, and Curtis' bass player forgot his instrument. As the Beatles entered this Iron Door Club on a wet, dreary Thursday evening they were unusually nervous. Each member of the group carried a little bag with a clean change of clothes. As Joe Flannery wandered into the dank, smelly third floor dressing room he saw John Lennon. He walked over and shook John's hand. "What's the matter, John," Flannery inquired. John confessed that the Beatles were nervous about their upcoming debut at the Cavern Club on Mathews Street. During the evening Flannery built up Lennon's confidence and encouraged the other Beatles. Flannery also introduced himself to Paul McCartney and they became good friends. Over the years McCartney has remained in touch with Flannery, and they still laugh and reminisce about the early days.

One of the more interesting stories involving Paul McCartney occurred when he heard Lee Curtis and the All Stars perform "I'll Remember You." McCartney loved the song, and he built it into the Beatles act. Because of his friendship with Joe Flannery and Lee Curtis, McCartney formally requested permission to use the song in the Beatles act. Once he did there were inevitable comparisons between the two singers. Curtis told McCartney to do the song in his way, and Curtis would continue to perform his version. This indicates McCartney's humble nature in the years prior to the Beatles' international stardom. When Lee Curtis appeared at the Tower Ballroom in New Brighton, Little Richard heard about the controversy between McCartney and Curtis over "I'll Remember You," and the veteran American rock performer sang the song with his own twist. It was all good fun and there was a sense of support and comaraderie among the musicians.

Once the Beatles hit the British charts the relationship between Brian Epstein and Joe Flannery cooled. In early 1963 Epstein began to reap the fruits of his promotional activity, and the phenomena soon to be known as Beatlemania began to build in the English countryside. As the Beatles' popularity soared, Brian Epstein was concerned that Lee Curtis and the All Stars might rival his group's popularity. This led to petty arguments between Flannery and Epstein and some differences about the music. Eventually, Brian informed Joe that John Lennon and Paul McCartney did not want dual bookings with Lee Curtis, because the female fans screamed too loudly when Curtis took the stage. It is unlikely that either Lennon or McCartney made such a request; it was obvious that Epstein was obsessed with his campaign to make the Beatles a superstar group. His fanaticism was slowly destroying his friendship with Joe Flannery.

As a result of this mild disagreement, Brian Epstein and Joe Flannery discontinued their business relationship. They remained on friendly social terms, and they often had dinner together. Joe Flannery suddenly realized that he had spent too much time with the Beatles and Brian Epstein, and he turned to vigorously promoting Lee Curtis and the All Stars. Although he had effectively structured Curtis' act, Flannery now believed that a recording contract was a requirement for final stardom. In order to promote his brother's music, Joe Flannery spent an inordinate amount of time researching American record tastes in order to guarantee a commercial sound. Dick Rowe was one of the first record executives that Flannery approached regarding a recording contract. Since the Beatles had failed their audition with Rowe and then gone on to great success, Decca was signing virtually every act that came through the door. Flannery argued that Lee Curtis and the All Stars were one of the few unsigned British rock groups with both experience and a unique sound. He believed that Curtis could provide Decca hit making records.

When Lee Curtis and the All Stars auditioned for Decca Records they not only impressed the company executives, but they were recognized as a group which could record both pop and rock songs. Eventually, this wide ranging musical talent worked against Lee Curtis and the All Stars, because they failed to score in either market. After they signed a contract with Decca, Peter Sullivan was assigned as the A and R person for Curtis' group. This was a mistake because Sullivan believed that heavily orchestrated songs replete with strings and complicated background sounds was the future of English rock music. Decca, England's largest classical record label, had little understanding of the rock music market. When Decca released "The Stomp" by Lee Curtis and the All Stars they failed to adequately promote the song and it faded into obscurity. In many respects Curtis' "The Stomp" was very similar to Chubby Checker's "The Twist," but Decca could not capitalize on the dance craze mania of the early 1960s.

The failure of Lee Curtis and the All Stars is an important commentary upon the British rock and roll scene. Peter Sullivan tried desperately to break Lee Curtis as an American modeled rock act, but he was unable to provide the production techniques necessary for a hit record. Sullivan pointed to acts like Lulu, Tom

Joe Flannery, Dick Rowe and Lee Curtis: The Decca Audition

Jones and Englebert Humperdinck as the type of English singers that American's embraced. Lulu's version of Ernie Maraseca's tune "Shout" was typical of Decca Records' disastrous attempt to promote their artists in the United States. This attitude stiffled the raw spontaneity and original sound of Lee Curtis and the All Stars. "I think Dick Rowe and Decca were trying to cater to the rock music trend for heavy orchestration," Joe Flannery remarked, "and they had neither the feel to produce a marketable rock record nor the knowledge to merchandise it." Rowe, a family man in his mid-40s, had not moved beyond Perry Como's music. Consequently, it was not coincidental that Como's song "Temptation" was picked as Lee Curtis' first 45 single release.

    Although Lee Curtis and the All Stars did not succeed as a major rock and roll record act, there were a number of excellent recordings released by Curtis. After signing with Decca, three singles were marketed in the United Kingdom. None of these 45s made the British charts, but the records old very well in Northern England. In the Liverpool area all of Lee Curtis' singles sold close to 10,000 copies each, but Decca Records was unable to promote Curtis' music in a broader market. Since Curtis was such a popular

Lee Curtis: An Acoustic Set, 1964

local artist, the Phillips record label signed his group after their Decca contract expired. When Phillips Records released Lee Curtis and the All Stars version of "Ecstacy," they scheduled a rigorous promotion tour to popularize the record. It was Phillips' marketing of "Ecstacy" which prevented it from becoming a hit. The promotional activity centered around a predominantly teenage audience, when in fact Curtis' song was a middle of the road, adult oriented rock tune. In the early and mid-1960s there were no AOR English radio outlets, and this hurt Lee Curtis and the All Stars commercial potential. The English record buying audience was never able to fully appreciate Curtis' music, because many of his best songs were not released by Decca and Phillips.

Eventually, the Hamburg, Germany Star-Club label produced two albums and three singles featuring Lee Curtis and the All Stars. When Star-Club Records released two anthology albums of the best performances at the Star-Club, they included Lee Curtis' "Shot of Rhythm and Blues," from a 1964 recording session and an excellent version of Carl Perkins' "Boppin The Blues." These songs are examples of Curtis' musical diversity, because he was able to perform either rhythm and blues or rockabilly music.

By 1963 Lee Curtis and the All Stars were a popular club act in England and Germany. Although Curtis' recording future was uncertain, Brian Epstein expressed interest in signing him. "Brian and I met in 1963 at his office and I agreed to act as the booking agent for NEMS. Brian also indicated that he would sign Lee Curtis to a management contract," Flannery remarked. When Epstein mentioned to the Beatles that he was about to sign Lee Curtis and the All Stars they protested that their old drummer, Pete Best, would be brought back into their presence and this made them uncomfortable. John Lennon speculated that Lee Curtis might try to upstage the Beatles in concerts. Paul McCartney pointed out that Curtis' version of "I'll Remember You" was received much better than the Beatles performance of the same song. As a result Brian Epstein informed Joe Flannery that he would not sign Lee Curtis and the All Stars. Although this ended the business relationship between Epstein and Flannery, they remained social friends.

After the Beatles achieved superstar status, Lee Curtis and the All Stars continued to play in England and Germany. In January, 1964, as the Beatles were preparing to leave for America, Lee Curtis played a concert at the Pavilion in Torquay with the Searchers. The concert was headlined by the Searchers because their hit, "Needles and Pins," was rising on the British charts. It was destined for the number 1 position, but the Searchers were not yet a dynamic stage act. The result was that Lee Curtis and the All Stars stole the show. Both Curtis and Alma Coogan, a pop singer, were called back for encores, but the crowd only politely acknowledged the Searchers' music. What this story suggests is that neither Decca nor Phillips records were able to properly merchandise Curtis' act. An interesting sidelight to this concert is that Alma Coogan fell in love with Lee Curtis and trailed him to Germany. Coogan who eventually recorded the Beatles' "Help" and "Eight Days A Week," was romantically linked to Brian Epstein, and there were rumors that they would marry. There is no doubt that Coogan's infatuation with Lee Curtis was another problem in Joe Flannery and Brian Epstein's business relationship.

Eventually, after a serious auto accident almost ended his career in 1967, Lee Curtis married and began a family. He worked for a time managing a beat club in Manchester and Curtis was also an employee of a London casino. When these positions did not work out he returned to Liverpool to pursue a successful career as an interior decorator. Curtis has five children and divides his time between his family, his business, and his continued performance as a rock musician.

Lee Curtis, 1966

As Joe Flannery reminisced about his relationship with Brian Epstein, he clarified many myths surrounding the Beatles' career. Flannery believes that Epstein was an excellent businessman. "No one associated with Brian Epstein ever had money problems," Flannery reflected. "Brian trained his acts in business management." Another interesting development in Brian's career, according to Flannery, was his desire to take the Beatles in new commercial directions. Unfortunately, Epstein informed Flannery of this "new direction" only a few weeks before his death. So the secret remains shrouded in history.

In 1984 Lee Curtis headlined an English tour billed as the "Merseyside Sound: Twenty Years Later." The success of Curtis' music was revealed as every theater was sold out to hear a legend in the English rock music world. It was almost prophetic as I sat in Joe Flannery's house in 1983, because he believed that it was not too late for Lee Curtis. The success of the "Merseyside Sound: Twenty Years Later" tour suggests that there is still a market for Liverpool music. Had it not been for the charisma and energy of the Invisible Beatle, Joe Flannery, there would not have been as energetic and as exciting music as the Merseyside sound produced. Almost no one realizes Flannery's importance to the fame of Brian Epstein and the Beatles.

PART II
JOHN LENNON: THE MAKING OF AN ARTIST

John Lennon: The Making of an Artist

The intellectual achievements of John Lennon are well known. He was a pioneer rock music songwriter, an exceptional poet, a lyricist and an individual with a penchant for insightful prose. After Lennon's celebrated songwriting career with Paul McCartney, he became a solo artist in the 1970s who wrote about feminism, psychotherapy, politics and the general themes of change in American life. The impact of John Lennon's revolutionary mind was demonstrated when Jon Wiener, a Professor of History at the University of California, Irvine, sued the Federal Bureau of Investigation under the Freedom of Information Act to obtain copies of F.B.I. surveillance reports. When the twenty-six pounds of documents arrived, Weiner found that J. Edgar Hoover, the Director of the F.B.I., ordered an around the clock documentation of Lennon's life. Hoover was acting directly on the orders of American President Richard Nixon. For years the politically sensitive Nixon had been looking for the source of his political problems. That Nixon found John Lennon a threat to American democracy is a ludicrous comment on American politics. What is important, however, is the degree of hostility to John Lennon's ideas. This section of *The Beatles: Untold Tales* employs two essays to demonstrate why Lennon's artistry was so politically explosive to an American President.

What influenced the Internal Revenue Service, the United States Department of Justice and the Federal Bureau of Investigation to conduct a witch hunt against John Lennon is not clear. The attempt to deport Lennon for drug convictions was an indictment of youth culture which was very popular with voters in the late 1960s and early 1970s. John Lennon was a literary-musical symbol of the 1960s. Because of Lennon's identification with youthful rebellion, Attorney General John Mitchell believed that the Republican party would benefit from a campaign of harrassment and intimidation. Had it not been for John's well developed intellect, the F.B.I. and the Justice Department might have looked for another target. In the essay: "John Lennon's Pubs," three pubs which John frequented provided much of the inspiration and raw material for his prose, poems and songs. In the Grapes and Ye Crack in Liverpool and the Blockhutte in Hamburg, Germany, John came of age as a writer. What is amazing about these pubs is that many of the regulars still carry around miniature sketches by John Lennon and recall his prose and free verse poems with great admiration. There is no doubt that John Lennon had a unique and bizarre intellectual capacity. He was a young writer who carefully catalogued his thoughts in small notebooks and read them willingly to strangers and friends alike. From 1960 to 1963 Lennon grew into a literary giant and the pubs provided the perfect atmosphere for this creative transformation.

As John Lennon matured in the late 1950s and early 1960s, Tony Sheridan, an Irish musician transplanted to Hamburg, and Charlie Lennon, John's Uncle, had a great deal of contact with and influence upon young John. In an article entitled: "Remembering John: Tony Sheridan and Charlie Lennon," the formation of Lennon's personality and the influence of his family is dissected by two of his closest friends. The result is that a well-rounded picture of Lennon emerges from the pubs, the schoolyard and the small clubs which formed the back drop for the rock and roll musical revolution of the early 1960s.

JOHN LENNON

John Lennon's Pubs: An Artist's Inspiration

In John Lennon's formative years three pubs were important in developing his literary and songwriting talents. These working class bars provided inspiration, insight and ideas which John translated into songs, poems and short stories. Two of the pubs, Ye Crack and the Grapes, were located in Liverpool. The third drinking establishment, the Blockhutte, was a country-western bar a block from the Kaiserkeller and Indra night clubs on the Grosse Freiheit Street in Hamburg's famed Reeperbahn section. In the late 1950s and early 1960s, John Lennon's intellectual growth progressed in the carefree atmosphere permeating these bars. Many of the characters who inhabited these clubs found their stories and personal experiences reflected in a Beatle song or some of Lennon's literary works. Standing on a table or stool in one of these smoke-filled drinking spots John read his works, and soon the lyrical magic which made the Beatles so successful emerged.

The criticism by the patrons of Ye Crack, the Blockhutte and the Grapes helped Lennon's literary growth. As John expressed his ideas to the casual costumer, he became aware of themes which interested the average person. One of the reasons that the Beatles' music was so successful was its ability to mirror the triumphs and frustrations of the working class. There was also a timeliness to Lennon's songs which appealed to diverse age, occupational and educational groups. Had it not been for these pubs, John Lennon might not have written so inspirationally about a wide variety of subjects. The pubs provided Lennon a family feeling, and he believed that his ideas were critiqued honestly by the working class patrons. These quaint drinking spots served as the inspiration for songs, poems, drawings and prose.

In 1964, the Beatles became American rock music superstars, and many Lennon-McCartney songs recreated experiences in Ye Crack, the Bluckhutte and the Grapes. When John emerged in 1964 as a critically acclaimed author with two books on the best seller lists, *A Spaniard In The Works* and *In His Own Write*, it was due to the force and influence of these pubs. In order to fully understand how the pubs shaped John Lennon's writings, it is necessary to examine each bar's contributions to the thematic qualities of his literary works.

The location of the three pubs was an important part of their appeal to young John. Since the pubs were all close to either the Art College of the Liverpool Institute or local music venues that John frequented, they were convenient escapes where he could pursue serious writing. Ye Crack was a typical working class English pub a short walk down a small alley near the Liverpool Institute. For students at the Art College, it was simply the closest place to drink beer and was extremely popular with the bohemian and intellectual crowd. The Grapes, located a few hundred yards from the Cavern Club on Mathews Street, was a popular pub with two small drinking rooms adjacent to the bar area. The wide-ranging conversations and varied clientele made its atmosphere very creative. The Blockhutte, John's most obscure pub, was near Bruno Koschmider's clubs on the Reeperbahn in Hamburg. It had a unique visual ambience due to a pseudo-cowboy motif. The Blockhutte had all the characteristics of an existential pub. One night in the Blockhutte a young German student expressed his feelings about the existential life to John. It was the ability to make your own decisions and direct your own life, the German student lectured, which separated those who succeeded in life from those who failed. Tony Sheridan sat next to John drinking beer as the student continued to tell the two musicians that they should make a personal commitment to the lifestyle they felt most productive. This lecture had a lasting impact upon John as he subsequently pursued a professional music career.

The Grapes, John's favorite bar in 1961 and 1962, was one in which his writing talents matured considerably. At the Grapes

young professionals who worked in the banks, law offices and small shops in downtown Liverpool helped John to understand the middle class, and his contact with dock workers and the unemployed was equally important. The Grapes was a meeting place for all classes and types of people, and John discovered parts of the English character that he had never experienced. It was in the Grapes that John first met theater people, local homosexuals, and common working class types. This mix of characters inspired John to sketch out the little dramas which unfolded each day. The last bar to influence John, the Blockhutte, was a typical German bar in that it had a bizarre, often unpredictable, atmosphere which was totally alien to Lennon's Liverpool background. As a result, some of John's best ideas were developed in the midst of this German drinking spot. The Blockhutte's country-western motif was also very significant because it struck a creative chord in John's mind. He could respond to the pseudo-cowboy atmosphere with imaginative discourses on the human condition. The Blockhutte's proximity to the Indra and Kaiserkeller clubs in Hamburg prompted John to visit the bar regularly. As he walked into the Blockhutte John was often greeted with the remark: "Hello pardner." John would laugh loudly at the friendly German uttering, and he would often talk about the American West with a bewildered German.

The Blockhutte and Ye Crack encouraged John to build his experiences literarily, musically and artistically. These bars provided the freedom for John to experiment with different ideas and to see what did and what did not appeal to people. In effect, the pubs were a training ground not only for John's writings but for his innovative songwriting skills. It was John's ability to point out the intellectual differences in the individuals who patronized these pubs which made him a unique writer. John was intrigued by some obvious similarities between the patrons in these drinking establishments. In Ye Crack, for example, the majority of the drinkers were students, whereas the Grapes attracted a more cosmopolitan crowd. Yet, John found that his ideas for songs were received very well in each bar. John once remarked to Bob Wooler that his music appealed to a wide variety of age, occupational and educational groups. John's literary experiments were turned into songs, and he used the reactions of patrons at Ye Crack and the Grapes to finalize many of these new tunes.

An example of John's ability to draw ideas from these pubs occurred on March 21, 1961 when Lennon walked into the Grapes on Mathews Street after the Beatles played their first engagement

The Blockhutte

at the Cavern. John remarked to Bob Wooler that the Grapes clientele was intriguing because the crowd was so diverse. As he talked to the patrons John remarked that they all seemed to like his songs, poems and short stories. A good example of how a song was written occurred when John began to sing lyrics similar to the Beatles song, "Do You Want To Know a Secret," and the Grapes crowd roared its approval when John confessed that the song resulted from watching two Walt Disney movies, "Fantasia" and "Cinderella." But the Grapes crowd did not like all of Lennon's songs, and they criticized tunes like "Hello Little Girl." One of John's close friends called this song "an abomination." John remarked: "You are right about me song." It was John's openness to criticism, his eagerness for new ideas, and his willingness to take risks which established him as an important writer. Although rock music lyrics were not taken seriously as a cultural form until the late 1960s, John Lennon's writing provides a capsule history of the forces shaping counterculture values.

Like many great writers much of John Lennon's literary contribution was completed in rough form by the time he was 21 years old. His ideas crystallized at an early age, and his skills were at their peak during his studies at the Art College of the Liverpool Institute. By the time the Beatles were playing at the Kaiserkeller and Top Ten Clubs in Hamburg and the Cavern Club in Liverpool, Lennon's catalog of hit songs and literary masterpieces were safely tucked in his spiral notebooks. Not only did Lennon establish his musical identity in the early 1960s, but he also began a serious writing career. By 1964 when *A Spaniard In the Works* and *In His Own Write* became best sellers, John had crafted many of the songs which carried the Beatles to international stardom. Lennon was particularly proud of his two books, because these works were not the product of a cooperative writing venture with Paul McCartney. Rather they were John's own imaginative efforts. The rough drafts of these books were completed in Ye Crack, the Blockhutte, and the Grapes long before Lennon became a music superstar. John Lennon habitually carried a notebook which he filled with writings and drawings, and his books were taken from these simple spiral notebook binders. One critic, John Wain, writing in the *New Republic* suggested that Lennon was determined to communicate "almost exclusively in puns..." The contribution of Lennon's writing, according to Wain, was "in putting the young nonreader in touch with a central strand in the litarary tradition of the last thirty years in every English-speaking country."

An important study analyzing John Lennon's writings argues that the ability to communicate through the use of puns developed while attending Dovedale Primary school. James Sauceda's *The Literary Lennon*, published by Pierian Press in 1983, brilliantly characterizes Lennon's penchant for using puns. At the age of seven John bound together a collection of stories he entitled *Sport and Speed Illustrated*. These childhood yarns revealed a serious writing talent. This small booklet contained hundreds of words with altered spellings and ironic intonations. It was obvious that the writings of Lewis Carroll and James Joyce influenced John's literary style, since he was able to employ farce, irony and a non-traditional narrative style to make serious points.

Much like Dylan Thomas and William Faulkner, Lennon came from a storytelling tradition. For centuries there was an oral tradition in Liverpool which passed folk history down from one generation to the next, and a great deal of John's formative intellectual ideas resulted from this history. In Lennon's Irish subculture the story predominated over the written novel. There was also a strong feeling against established intellectual forms, and this notion influenced Lennon to develop non-traditional intellectual patterns. Lennon lacked discipline in his writing but in many respects this was a strength. Much of what John Lennon wrote reflected youthful anarchy. This was a significant factor in Lennon's development as a writer because it allowed him to reflect randomly on his environment. John had many experiences to communicate, but he usually structured his personal stories in obtuse, complicated little poems or stories. It was difficult for John to reveal his own pain, and these stories allowed him a psychological means of reliving and coping with personal anxieties. In essence, Lennon's writings were a form of therapeutic soul cleansing, and a means of coping with an increasingly complex world.

John's writing provided another significant outlet. He was able to criticize the lifestyles and the conventional morality forced upon him by Aunt Mimi. Growing up in a stable, middle class suburban Liverpool home appeared to be idyllic. Just the opposite can be deduced from Lennon's life. Aunt Mimi and Uncle George obviously loved John, but they were too critical when they described John's parents. They also restricted John's intellectual growth, because the Smith's believed he might turn out like his parents. Since Mimi Smith raised John from the time he was five years old, she had an inordinate influence upon his character. The first outward signs of John's intellectual rebellion did not occur until his mother died. Many of John's stories reflected a cynic who withdrew into a shell.

In 1952 John entered the Quarry Bank Grammar School, and his writing efforts intensified due to a television program—the Goon Show. This BBC TV series masterminded by Peter Sellers attracted a cult following similar to that of Monty Python in the 1970s and 1980s. The Goon Show presented sketches of British life which were irreverant and critical of establishment values. From 1952 to 1956 Peter Sellers brilliantly wrote and produced vignettes which mirrored the frustrations of many English citizens. As a result of the Goon Show, John was encouraged to write his unique prose, intensify his drawing activity, and to share his accomplishments with his classmates. Once writing became an important part of John's life, he never lost his zeal for the creative process. In 1961 he wrote sporadic columns for Billy Harry's *Mersey Beat* magazine, and his early publications further whetted John's appetite to publish his work. On February 27, 1964, two of Lennon's most popular works—"The Tales of Hermit Fred" and "The Land of the Lunapots"—graced *Mersey Beat's* pages, and these stories illustrated Lennon's ability to employ nonsensical prose to make more serious points. John's early stories were varied, but they were an important indication of the success which John would experience in a few years as a writer.

The San Francisco beat poets also were an important influence upon John Lennon. In particular Allen Ginsberg's epic poem, *Howl*, served as an example for Lennon's poetry, but he also read Lawrence Ferlinghetti and Gregory Corso's work. John frequently requested the Cunard Yanks to bring in any books published by San Francisco's City Lights book company. During the Beatles' early years John produced a book entitled *The Daily Howl*. Much of *The Daily Howl* was written in the early 1960s, and it was completed in Hamburg's Blockhutte bar in 1960. In 1963-1964 a number of people close to the Beatles stated that *The Daily Howl* was John's way of presenting his serious ideas. The book's title was inspired by a line from Ginsberg's poem *Howl* in which the San Francisco poet complained that the best minds of his generation were being destroyed by conformity and middle-class values. Lennon identified strongly with the beat writers because of their preoccupation with anti-establishment themes. The creative energy behind the early drafts of *The Daily Howl* prompted the faculty of the Liverpool Art College to pass it around the instructors' lounge. *The Daily Howl* was written during a time the Beatles were experiencing a great deal of difficulty breaking into the music business. As a result, *The Daily Howl* was a form of intellectual catharsis which John Lennon needed to cope with the problems of the music industry.

It was as a result of this type of writing that John first began to shape his intellectual ideas. Part of the reason for John's literary drive was a change in his surroundings. When he began frequenting Ye Crack, John discovered a meeting place to entertain his friends, and he also met his first serious girlfriend, Cynthia Twist. This began a lengthy courtship which resulted in their marriage. The romance with Cynthia Twist also coincided with some important changes in John's lifestyle.

One of the most creative periods in John Lennon's life occurred in the Fall of 1959 when he moved into a flat on Gambier Terrace. Stu Sutcliffe and John rented a large apartment just across the street from the Anglican Cathedral. Bill Harry lived a few hundred yards away at 69 Parliament Street, and the Gambier Terrace flat was just a few blocks away from the Liverpool Institute and Ye Crack. John's art teacher, Arthur Ballard, had secured a scholarship for young Lennon to begin work on a National Diploma course. John used the extra money from the scholarship to provide

Liverpool's Ye Crack

his first solitary living arrangement. Although John had roommates there was a sense of freedom to the new apartment. One of the students who shared the rest at the Gambier Terrace flat, Rod Murray, eventually was given one of John's notebooks. It contained drawings and stories and in September, 1984 Murray auctioned off this valuable property. The Gambier Terrace apartment was one of John Lennon's most important early intellectual influences, because he had the peace and solitude necessary to work on his art and writing.

During 1959-1960 England was concerned with the Beatnik influences. As a result, the *Sunday People*, a national newspaper, did an expose on Liverpool's beatniks. Allan Williams came to Lennon's Gambier Terrace flat and asked to use it. Williams then proceeded to mess up the rooms and create an "arranged beatnik" atmosphere. The *Sunday People* completed an article entitled: "Beatnik Horror." Allan Williams and Stu Sutcliffe were in the photo used by the newspaper to illustrate the beatnik influence.

By 1961 Lennon was caught up in the Beatnik idea. He also began to read poetry, as well as the beat writers and he attempted to use these influences in his music. The English beat poet, Royston

Ellis, visited the Gambier Terrace apartment and later that night turned up at the Jacaranda to hear the Beatles play. It was Royston Ellis, according to Bill Harry, who first introduced the Beatles to soft drugs. Purple hearts, a pharmaceutical pill, and the benzedrine strip from the inside of a Vick's inhaler were often used to get high. When the Beatles departed to play in Hamburg in August, 1960, Rod Murray was left with the rent bills, and he also acquired some of John Lennon's possessions by default. The prize that Rod Murray acquired was John's book *The Daily Howl*, which recorded some of Lennon's earliest and most innovative intellectual exercises.

The significance of the Gambier Terrace flat is that it provided John Lennon one of his more creative outlets. Although Ye Crack was an excellent pub for testing his ideas out with people, John found the solitude of the Gambier Terrace flat conducive to his writing. It was a highly productive period for John as he wrote songs, poems and short stories.

During his studies at the Liverpool Institute, John evolved into an original thinker. He no longer accepted the trite ideas and conformist mentality of Aunt Mimi's Mendips suburban mentality. John's old boyhood friends like Pete Shotton noticed that he was a much different person after attending the Art College of the Liverpool Institute. This was due to meeting new people, operating independently as a student, and coming to grips with books and ideas which revolutionized John's thought processes.

In January, 1959 Ye Crack was the scene of one of John's most significant meetings. One day Lennon's art teacher, Arthur Ballard, brought his prize student, Stu Sutcliffe, to Ye Crack for a beer. John discovered that Stu was virtually an intellectual brother. They shared the same tastes in books, poetry, music, art, and food, and once they discussed politics John and Stu realized that they also shared the same iconoclastic views about English society. During their first meeting Stu and John left Ye Crack at closing time and talked until the wee hours of the morning at Stu's flat. It was a time of intellectual awakening for young John Lennon.

What attracted John to Stu Sutcliffe was the brooding intellectual nature of this young art student. Not only did Stu's clothes cause him to stand out, but he talked impressively about Vincent Van Gogh and the French impressionist painters. In fact, it was Stu who first introduced John to the wonders of the bohemian life as Stu's dark glasses, menacing scowl and impressive use of literary quotes became role models for John. The friendship blossomed and Stu joined John and Pete Shotton in a band known as

Johnny and the Moondogs. Pete Shotton soon left the band to become a policeman, but he continued his friendship with John Lennon. After later resigning from the police force, Shotton managed the old Dutch Cafe near Penny Lane. One night John and Paul McCartney came into the cafe for a bit to eat after playing a local dance. At this point John informed Pete that the group was known as the Beatles. The group's name, John remarked, was due to Stu Sutcliffe's clever takeoff on the American band Buddy Holly and the Crickets. Many years later John paid tribute to Stu's early influence in the Beatle song, "In My Life." During his years at the Liverpool Art Institute Stu Sutcliffe was an important influence upon John Lennon's artistic and literary development. There were other local Liverpool friends who also acted as a catalyst to many of John's creative projects.

One of John's most significant friends, Bill Harry, a student in the Commercial Design program, was an aspiring journalist with a clear, understanding influence on John Lennon's early literary ambitions. Bill Harry introduced John to a number of new literary ideas. Harry also convinced John to pursue journalism as a potential career, and he led John to the type of literature which prompted Lennon's prose to reflect a professional quality. One night in a drunken rage in Stu Sutcliffe's basement studio on Percy Street, the boys took turns reading from Lewis Carroll's *Alice in Wonderland*. The reading amazed John because Stu made a number of creative changes in Carroll's prose. It was a type of intellectual experimentation which intrigued John, and he intensified his efforts to write similar poems. In a few years these poems became two best-selling books and were widely acclaimed in leading literary circles. But at this point Lennon lacked the confidence to publicly articulate his ideas. Only his close friends were allowed to look at John's writings, but they could see the promise in these early stories.

After listening to Stu and Bill use mockery as a literary device, John was inspired to sit down and write a poem about a group of mystical toys who wondered if a sleeping boy were alive. In this allegorical work, John Lennon's poetry juxtaposed two contradictory images of the world to suggest the absurdity of 20th century life. In December, 1965, this brief poem "The Toy Boy," appeared in *McCall's* magazine without fanfare or advertisement. John Lennon's instructions to *McCall's* specified that it appear without publicity about his Beatle career. Although he was an international music superstar in 1965, nevertheless, John still longed for recognition as a creative writer. Strangely enough this poem was virtually ignored by the media, and John was crushed that one of his better efforts passed largely unnoticed. What "The Toy Boy" demonstrates is the high level of Lennon's talent during the early years of his writing career.

"The Toy Boy" was originally written while John was drinking in Ye Crack many years earlier. This was just one of many Lennon works to use nonsensical limericks, misspelled words and unique artistic sketches to establish John Lennon's personal identification as an artist-writer. Although he had written in his small notebooks for some time, John did not expect anyone to take these writings seriously. However, he found that the clientele at Ye Crack responded positively to John's ideas, and they listened intently to his whimsical stories.

It was also at Ye Crack that John Lennon and Paul McCartney formed the intellectual friendship which resulted in their long-lasting songwriting fame. When Paul and John first met at the St. Peter's Church on June 15th, 1956, they were brought together by a common interest in rock and roll music. The similarities between the two young Liverpool lads were apparent to their close friends. They were avid readers, interested in art, and both possessed journalistic skills. But John and Paul were also quite different from one another. McCartney was highly disciplined, whereas Lennon was unstructured and lacked elementary organization. Paul could turn out a song in a few hours, but John needed weeks to come up with a tune. McCartney's lyrics rhymed and had a pop flair, while Lennon's lyrics were obtuse and often confused. Once Lennon and McCartney came together as a songwriting team, however, their strengths and weaknesses meshed into one of the most prolific song teams in history, but John and Paul were not close friends until they attended school at the Liverpool Institute.

It was Paul McCartney who added not only a touch of discipline to Lennon's work, but Paul was also influential as an academic role model. Paul, training to become a teacher, had a strong scholastic record, and his work was highly respected by faculty members at the Liverpool Institute Grammar School. McCartney was a shy, serious student who impressed his teachers with his dedication to classroom work. Once he met John Lennon, Stu Sutcliffe, Pete Shotton and other students at the Liverpool Art College, McCartney's interests shifted to rock music. Suddenly the world of scholarship and teaching was replaced by music and songwriting interests. Paul was not content with the notion of becoming a

John Lennon's Gambier Terrace Flat

teacher and settling into a predictably dull and dreary academic life. In England once an instructor was established in a school, that remained his or her lifetime employment, and there was a sense of intellectual death among many of McCartney's teachers. He could see that they longed for more creative outlets and that the educational system dulled their talents. Paul vowed that he would not be caught up in the middle-class conformity which English education foisted upon students.

In school McCartney was not only a strong academic student, but he had extraordinary creative energy. Rock and roll music did not change his academic nature, but it allowed McCartney new outlets and an alternative direction for his talents. The myth has grown up that Paul McCartney's academic demise began when he began drinking beer at Ye Crack. This notion is largely the result of comments made by McCartney's English instructor "Dusty" Durband to Philip Norman. In Norman's painstakingly researched book, *Shout: The Beatles In Their Generation*, John Lennon is blamed for McCartney's frequent absences from class. In reality, McCartney simply tired of the dull, dreary school life, and he made the decision to pursue a career in the world of rock music. It not only

Paul McCartney and John Lennon : Mid-1960s

altered Lennon and McCartney's lives, but changed the course of musical history. Paul's classroom work remained solid, and he was still interested in school. However, McCartney made the decision to spend more time writing songs with John. From his earliest collaboration with Lennon, McCartney enjoyed being part of a rock music group. It is in these early musical groups who eventually became the Beatles that the seeds of a professional music career were nurtured for Lennon and McCartney.

In the early months of 1958 John Lennon and Paul McCartney were known as the Quarrymen. The name was taken from John's Quarry Bank High School. John gleefully informed Stu Sutcliffe that it was a great way of repaying his old school for showing faith in his talent. William Pobjoy, the headmaster of Quarry Bank, had personally supported John's application for admission to the art college of the Liverpool Institute. Even though John failed to pass his exams, Headmaster Pobjoy recognized that John's "enormous creative talents" were reason enough for admission to the art college. While attending art college and performing and writing with Paul, John began to envision a career as a professional entertainer. One night in 1959 at Ye Crack the regulars were surprised when John started singing "It Won't Be Long." At the time no one realized that in November, 1963, this song would be included on the *With the Beatles* LP. This story is an indication of how many Beatles songs were written and ready to record long before the Beatles signed a recording contract.

The Beatles' musical artistry is usually pinpointed as a recognizable force by 1962. However, as early as 1959, the Quarrymen's reputation was solid in and around Liverpool. They were a suburban rock band with a strong following, and the Lennon-McCartney led group were noted for long, enthusiastic musical sets. Many studies of the Beatles suggest that their lack of discipline on stage, their strange dress and their problems securing stable bookings reflected the need for professional help. In time Brian Epstein provided a refurbishing of their image, but this line of reasoning ignores the impact which the Beatles had upon their audiences in their early years.

Once the Beatles attracted a dedicated following, they also searched out new musical and performing possibilities. One of John and Paul's favorite early television programs was Carroll Levis' "Discoveries" show. This show, broadcast over Grenada television, featured the best local amateur talent in Northern England. A wide variety of strange and sometimes dull acts were presented in a weekly format. In order to appear on the "Discoveries" show it was necessary to fill out an application form. When John Lennon sent in the request for an audition he listed the group as Johnny and the Moondogs. Lennon reasoned that the name was similar to those used by American groups, and this would appeal to the selection board. Much to their surprise in June, 1959 Johnny and the Moondogs received a letter that they could audition for Carroll Levis' "Discoveries" program. The immediate problem was that no one had train fare to Manchester for the audition. This obstacle was solved when Colin Hanton offered money he had saved for the fare. Hanton was also a drummer and he persuaded the group to let him play the drums at the audition.

The short trip to Manchester was an inspirational one as the boys talked about their future. They also discovered that they had almost ten pounds between them. After getting off the bus they went directly to the railroad station to purchase the quicker and more comfortable railroad tickets home. The bus was much cheaper than the railroad, and the realization that they had more money prompted the Beatles to purchase the train tickets. After a lunch of bangers and mash in a local pub, John stood up and toasted "Johnny and the Moondogs." When they arrived at the Grenada television studios, the Beatles performed Eddie Cochran's "Twenty Flight Rock," and Chuck Berry's "Johnny B. Goode." George Harrison remarked after the audition that the judges displayed virtually no emotion. John Lennon countered by suggesting that Carroll Levis' selection panel had little understanding of rock music, and this did not bode well for the future. Graham Nash, soon to become a major rock music personality with the Hollies, attended the audition, and he was impressed with Johnny and the Moondogs. Although their performance earned them a second or final audition, John decided that they must take the final train home. If they stayed for the ten o'clock audition, John pointed out, they would have to sleep in the park. It was the lack of hotel money which kept the Beatles from appearing on Carroll Levis' "Discoveries" program. During the train ride home John and Paul wrote "I'll Be On My Way" as a tribute to this frustrating experience in the music business.

As Johnny and the Moondogs descended from the railway station, they were depressed by the experience in Manchester. John called Cynthia and asked her to go to a dance. He badly needed ego-reinforcement, and Cynthia readily agreed to spend some time alone with John. The Carroll Levis experience prompted John to spend hours in Ye Crack writing songs and experimenting with lyrical and musical ideas. Rather than discouraging Lennon, the Manchester trip served to fuel his desire for a show business career.

After returning from the Carroll Levis' "Discoveries" audition, John's writing patterns were so disciplined that his friends were startled. Each afternoon when the local pubs closed, John wandered down to one of the quaint nearby coffee shops to fill his notebook with songs, poems, short stories and drawings. A great deal of this material eventually found its way into Beatle albums, and many of the ideas were later instrumental in John's solo career.

The patrons who sat around Ye Crack and the nearby small coffee houses did not realize how many Beatle songs germinated in these obscure surroundings. One of John's earliest compositions "Hello Little Girl" was completed in 1959, and in 1962 the Beatles used this song for their Decca audition. The idea for "Hello Little Girl" was an interesting one centering around Cynthia Twist's youthfulness. Another important song from the Ye Crack was "I Call Your Name." This tune appeared on the Beatles fifth British EP "Long Tall Sally," and it was the B side of Billy J. Kramer's hit "Bad To Me." These songs were examples of the importance of Ye Crack in developing John's earliest songwriting talent. Had he not been a bored student with a passion for words, John might not have spent his free time writing these tunes. Ye Crack was essential in providing the freedom for John's creative energies to reach their natural limits.

John Lennon's dependence upon Ye Crack's atmosphere was demonstrated one night when he screamed: "Me freedom, me freedom." John then blurted out that it was difficult for him to write and read his work in other places. He was particularly critical of the anti-intellectual atmosphere in Mona Best's Casbah Coffee Club. The Casbah had a reputation as a gathering spot for Liverpool's young intellectuals. This bothered John because he believed that Mona Best catered to a pseudo-intellectual crowd who had little knowledge of either music or culture. This small teenage dance hangout located in the quiet West Darby section was primarily a vehicle to promote Mona's sons musical career. Although Pete Best formally joined the Beatles as their drummer in August, 1960 when they left to play their first Hamburg engagement, he was never really an integral part of the Beatles music. Pete's group, the Blackjacks, often played the Casbah with the Beatles, and he was only asked to join Lennon's group when they were without a drummer for their first Hamburg engagement at the Indra Club. Best's drumming lacked the skill necessary for success in the music world. He was a good-looking, moody young man who fit the angry rebel image nicely, but lacked talent and personality. He had a tedious musical style which excited few people, and his mother's continuing presence caused a great deal of resentment. Mona Best was an intelligent, attractive woman, and she hoped that her son would become a rock music star. Since 1958 she had attempted to push Pete into one musical group after another, and her obedient, almost docile, son followed his mother's every wish.

Mona Best invited bands without drummers to play on weekends at the Casbah Club with Pete supplying the drums. One of the problems with the Mersey Beat sound was that very few musicians could afford the expensive drum set necessary in making rock music. Makeshift guitars, tambourines, harmonicas and saxophones were easier to acquire for a reasonable price. The sign of ones own drum set was one of affluence. Since the Best's were a prosperous middle-class family, young Pete had his own drum kit, and the Casbah Club opened in the basement of the Best's home to showcase his musical talents. He was a reclusive young man with a musical ability which few people respected, and John Lennon once remarked that Pete's mystique was greater than his talent. Yet, due

George Harrison, Pete Best and John Lennon

to his mother's indefatigible drive, Pete Best was for a brief moment a member of the Beatles. The Casbah Club provided the forum for Pete and the Beatles began their short, but turbulent, musical partnership.

John Lennon's views on the Casbah experience were hostile ones. He complained that Mona Best interfered with everything, and John read a special poem aloud in the Casbah ridiculing the amateur nature of the club and the clandestine efforts to make Pete a rock music star. One night in Ye Crack, John stood up somewhat tipsy and blurted out a silly little lymerick entitled: "An Ode to Mona." Using Lewis Carroll inspired language, Lennon startled the patrons by spinning an allegorical tale of a deceitful mother who manipulated her offspring into situations he could not control. In the final moments of John's story the young man attempts to commit suicide but failed. John was suggesting that Pete Best could not succeed in completing even the simplest task. This was unfair of Lennon, but it illustrates the depths of John's hatred toward Pete. This silly little poem had a tragic sense of irony as years later, Best did allegedly attempt a suicide which failed.

In John's discussions in Ye Crack and the Grapes there was mention of Colin Hanton's role in the Casbah Club. On a number of occasions Hanton was the Beatles' drummer. One night he appeared ill, and Mona insisted that Pete sit in on the drums. John and Paul did not like the manner in which Mona foisted Pete upon the Beatles, and it became a long standing bone of contention. Since Mona owned the Casbah Club and paid the bands their small wage, she had tremendous control over the groups. Paul McCartney was particularly critical of Mona's James Dean image building for her son. But Mona made it very clear that if the Beatles hoped to play in the Casbah, they would have to accept Pete as their drummer. So it was less the lack of available drummers, as most books have suggested, and more likely due to Mona's insistence that Pete and the Beatles joined forces. Pete Best was the last person to realize that he was the middleman in a tug of war between his mother and John Lennon. This drama was unimportant because neither the Beatles nor Pete Best realized that million-dollar musical success was on the horizon. In fact, once the Beatles emerged as superstars, the almost forgotten Pete Best suddenly became a momentary celebrity. The protests when Pete was fired as the Beatles' drummer have been romanticized by the press. There was very little in Best's drumming to recommend him, and many professional musicians who witnessed this little drama snickered as young girls raised a hue and cry over the loss of Pete. One Liverpool musician suggested, "Pete's departure was regretted for non-musical reasons."

It was during the period of controversy with Mona Best and the unsavory experience at the Casbah Club that John Lennon turned increasingly to the Beatnik poet Allen Ginsberg to shape his thoughts. For some time John was intrigued by Ginsberg's epic poem "Howl." As a result, Lennon attempted to write a number of poems and some songs about the problems of middle-class conformity and meddling parents. Whether or not he had Mona Best in mind is difficult to assess, but John spent an inordinate amount of time writing about personal conflict which affected the human intellect. In Ye Crack and the Grapes, John read Ginsberg's poetry and adapted it to criticize those around him who did not understand his intellectual pursuits. It was Ginsberg's poetry which helped John to survive artistically during the low points in the Beatles early days. In 1958-1959 Beatnik poetry prompted John to talk about moving to San Francisco. In reality, John was lost in the late 1950s. He was unsure of what name to use for his band and what songs to select when they played local dances. It was a time of growth and experimentation, and it is important to analyze the problems which Lennon faced in this period.

From 1958 to 1960 the Silver Beatles, as the Quarrymen were sometimes known, continued to play small halls without apparent success. Yet, to seasoned observers like Bob Wooler, there were signs of the Beatles' growing musical appeal. Everywhere the band played, the same crowd turned out to hear their music. Wooler remarked that the Beatles were a phenomena, and it was too bad that someone could not expose their music to the rest of England. In the late 1950s John informed Wooler that his writing was improving, and he often signed his songs Long John Silver. In 1960 there were a number of poems and drawings attributed to the Legendary Long John Silver. This was Lennon's way of using an alter-ego to suggest that his talents were multi-dimensional ones. After the Beatles became international superstars, John Lennon denied using the name Long John Silver. In fact, Lennon personally wrote Roy Carr and Tony Tyler a lengthy letter suggesting that this reference be deleted from a revised edition of their book, *The Beatles: An Illustrated Record*. The reason for John Lennon disavowing the use of the name Long John Silver remains an unsolved Beatle mystery. John was probably embarrassed to admit that in a moment of alcoholic inspiration a number of nights at Ye Crack, he took on the personality of an imaginary individual. In reality, Long John Silver was a creative means for John to promote many of his best ideas, and it always brought applause and unroarious laughter at Ye Crack when John announced: "Now for me Long John poems."

The ambiance of Ye Crack was obviously a formidable influence upon many of Lennon's ideas. When one of his old friends began studying for an advanced degree in history, John made fun of him as a "Nowhere Man." This term suggests that John, like many members of his generation, was hostile to historical forces. He was a blue collar poet who believed that he was making his own history. It was this curious means of criticizing the traditional historical process which made John one of England's more astute social critics. He often remarked that colleges were a closed club for a select few, and those individuals who graduated from the more prestigious English universities no longer recognized the real direction of English life.

Another important source of inspiration for John Lennon's writings was Allan Williams. An entrepreneur with a mercurial temperament, Williams had a penchant for developing bizarre ideas. He also possessed an excellent knowledge of the rock music scene, and he was able to recognize the type of clubs in Liverpool which became immensely popular. But Allan Williams had virtually no business skills, and his erratic personal behavior frightened away potential investors. John Lennon once remarked that he listened to everything Allan said and then did exactly the opposite. John jokingly remarked that Williams was the man who gave away everything he had. Williams blanched at John's intemperate remarks, but in later years Williams resurrected many of John's saying when he spoke to Beatle conventions. In his own way, Williams was an important influence upon John because of his bigger-than-life plans and minimal success. To Lennon, Williams was an actor playing out a script that he neither understood nor could perform. John referred to Williams as a "walking disaster" who could educate anyone to the joys of failure.

In 1960 the Silver Beatles played Williams' New Cabaret Artists Club. Willie Woodbine, who was born in Trinidad, was Williams' right-hand man at the club, and he became very friendly with the musical acts. In fact, his nickname "Lord" resulted from a particularly cheap brand of English cigarettes known as Lords. A tall, slender man prone to erratic behavior, Woodbine was the perfect foil for Williams. Woodbine lived the music, established an immediate rapport with the bands, and he was one of the few employees that Williams could trust. In addition Williams strange personality blended well with Woodbine's bizarre behavior. They were the perfect odd couple in the Liverpool music scene. After he left the New Cabaret Artists Club, Woodbine sold liquor to sailors and watched local prostitutes mingle in his afterhours club. The Liverpool authorities soon discovered that Lord Woodbine's club was no more than an abandoned attic in an old house and it was closed by the Constable. John Lennon was amazed at Willie Woodbine's charisma, and he described Woodbine as the most bizarre person he had ever encountered. Unlike Allan Williams, Woodbine was a likeable character and became something of a minor role model for young John.

It was not long before the Beatles' association with Allan Williams and Lord Woodbine led to their first engagement at the Indra Club in the famous Reeperbahn night club section of Hamburg, Germany. Prior to the Beatles' engagement Allan Williams claims to have made a visit to the Kaiserkeller Club in Hamburg and arranged the Beatles' German booking. This is a story that no one in Hamburg has verified. The reason for the Beatles' first contract in Hamburg was nothing more than pure

Lord Woodbine's Second Hand Store, Liverpool, 1983

luck. Each day Allan Willams allowed the Beatles to practice in his Jacaranda Club. When Williams arrived at the club about 4:30 in the afternoon to set up the bar for the evening's business, he would tell the Beatles to quit practicing. One day Derry Willkie of Derry and the Seniors came into the club to hear the Beatles practice and Willkie began weaving tales of the Reeperbahn's delights. In a spur of the moment decision, Paul McCartney picked up the telephone and called the Kaiserkeller in Hamburg. Much to his astonishment Bruno Koschmider, the owner of the Kaiserkeller, answered the phone. Although Koschmider's English was atrocious, nonetheless, he recognized that he could obtain the services of a Liverpool band inexpensively. Rory Storm and the Hurricanes and Derry and the Seniors had already joined Tony Sheridan as English musicians who were supplying profitable acts for Koschmider's clubs. Koschmider liked the spunk of the young boys, and in his barely literate English he promised to call them back with a firm booking offer. After the Beatles left the club, Williams was setting up the bar when he received a call from Koschmider. Sensing an adventure, Williams confronted John Lennon about the phone call to Hamburg. Williams demanded that the Beatles pay a commission, and he offered his van to transport the Beatles to Hamburg. No one was happy with Williams' bullying behavior, but the Beatles did not have an alternative. John Lennon began drawing cartoons and writing little poems about the incident, and he labelled Williams "Allan the Hun." It was a few drunken weeks on the Reeperbahn, not business, which prompted Williams to go to Hamburg. Williams had just turned 30, and he was ready to eat, drink and be merry at someone else's expense.

As John Lennon watched this drama unfold he continued to write incisive lyrical poems. His notebooks were filled with James Joyce influenced allegorical tales of travel and adventure in foreign lands. The colorful behavior of Allan Williams and Lord Woodbine offered new adventures, and John Lennon remarked that he felt like a character in a Franz Kafka novel. After John read Kafka's *Metamorphosis* he commented that his life seemed to fit into Kafkaesque mold. It was during his visits to Hamburg in the early 1960s that Lennon discovered a pub, the Blockhutte, which served as an important inspiration for much of his future work.

On August 18, 1960, the Beatles arrived in Hamburg and immediately transported their musical equipment to the famed Reeperbahn. The Beatles did not realize that Bruno Koschmider had just changed the Indra Club from a strip joint into a rock music venue. They were surprised at the boisterous audiences, but the Beatles were an immediate hit in this dark, smelly basement club. As they sat on one end of the club playing their instruments, there was an immediate acceptance of the Beatles' music. As a result of their success, Koschmider quickly moved the Beatles into his larger Kaiserkeller Club at Grosse Freiheit 36. Each night the Beatles played 4 1/2 hours of music with musicians such as Tony Sheridan, Rory Storm and the Hurricanes and Kingsize Taylor and the Dominoes. The pay was about $12 a night, and the Beatles lived in a number of different small rooms provided by Koschmider.

John Lennon's writings took a new twist in Hamburg. He often attempted science fiction stories, only to crumble up the sheets and throw them away. As he tossed in his bed at night in the room above Bambi Kino movie theater, John's mind was dominated by new thoughts and images. Often the second-rate American western movies provided dialogue which inspired silly little poems. Generally, however, John was lonely and in need of reassurance. The small, windowless room above the Bambi Kino was a depressing place. Consequently, John searched for a pub where he could express his ideas and drink a beer. It was some time before

John Lennon discovered the Blockhutte. It was Paul McCartney who first had discovered this surrealistic drinking spot when the owner's daughter, Corey, invited him down for a drink. The Blockhutte was a block away from the main bars on Grosse Freiheit, and few tourists wandered down to it. It had a country-western motif and each night a German dressed as a cowboy sang songs about the American West. There was a strange feeling in the club and it was packed with Germans eager to listen to country western music. The Blockhutte became one of John Lennon's hidden spots where he could go to read his books, write his poems and shout out his ideas to the astonished audiences.

Before he settled down to write his poems and draw hundreds of cartoons in the Blockhutte, John Lennon was determined to see the "other" side of Hamburg. One of his roommates in the small flat above the Bambi Kino was young Tony Sheridan, an Irish-born rock singer who had become the Elvis Presley of Hamburg. Tony promised John that he would see all of the sights in and around the Reeperbahn.

After a period of getting acquainted, Tony Sheridan and John Lennon wandered up to the Herbertstrasse. This was a block-long section of houses with women selling themselves from small windows. The Herbertstrasse prostitutes, dressed in a grotesque manner, struck a responsive chord in John's consciousness. He was attracted to the unique and bizarre nature of Hamburg life. They provided a frightening glimpse into the German character and offered vices not freely available in Liverpool. In particular, John was struck by the raw atmosphere and free thought on the Reeperbahn. As transvestites walked virtually unnoticed on Hamburg's streets, the local police ignored drugs, fights and odd behavior. John Lennon was mesmerized by his new surroundings.

Once John discovered the charms of the Herbertstrasse, he attempted to relate his feelings to Pete Best and Stu Sutcliffe. Pete was not impressed with the Herbertstrasse, and he chided John Lennon for his low-level, thrill-seeking mentality. Pete jokingly referred to the Herbertstrasse as a place for the misfits, and he felt it was Lennon's favorite haunt. Stu Sutcliffe had a much different view of the Herbertstrasse. There was a sense of artistic inspiration for Sutcliffe in these strange surroundings, and soon Stu's art reflected the sexually bizarre nature of the Herbertstrasse. Stu was fond of the term "human gargoyles," and he employed this phrase to describe the prostitutes, pimps and street characters in the Reeperbahn. Because they spent so much time around the

Herbertstrasse, John and Stu were stopped by a number of undercover policemen for questioning. It appeared that their dress, notably leather jackets, and their greasy hair stood out in Hamburg. The humor of this contradiction in the German character did not pass John unnoticed. After this adventure John and Stu promptly walked down to a sausage stand and ate two bratwursts and a big plate of french fries. After three beers and a few giggles they wandered home to consider Hamburg's other intriguing sights.

It was while playing at the Indra Club and the Kaiserkeller from August 18, 1960 through December 16, 1960, that John wandered down to the Blockhutte. Since Corey, the owner's daughter, had first invited Paul McCartney there, the bar had been visited by most of the English musicians. They relished the cornball country music, and Corey and her Dutch father provided an unusually warm reception for the musicians. Often, John, Paul and George drank in the Blockhutte until 6 in the morning. They frequently stumbled out of the Blockhutte as people began to straggle into St. Joseph's Church for the morning mass. Once John was relieving himself next to the church as a priest strolled by muttering: "Bless you, son." What intrigued John Lennon about the Blockhutte was not just the pseudo-western decor but the friendly atmosphere. Cowboy hats, six-guns, and western memorabilia often made the Blockhutte the perfect refuge from the pill-crazed musical atmosphere surrounding the Reeperbahn. Customers wandered in from the street dressed in expensive western clothes and would mumble in halting English, "Howdy, pardner." John Lennon fell on the floor laughing one day when a 4 foot 11 inch cowboy walked in and hit his head on the bottom of the bar.

Many of these incidents were recreated in John Lennon's notebook. He often wandered to the Furscharften bar, where he composed long letters and reorganized his ideas for songs. John was surprised by the tolerant attitude of Germans living around the Reeperbahn, and he soon developed a fond feeling for the locals. As John sat at the corner of DavidstraBe and Bernard-Nocht-StraBe overlooking the Hamburg harbor, he was impressed with the average German worker. Not only did they ignore the tourists, but the conversations were serious ones. The idea for Lennon's song "Working Class Hero" was born in this obscure bar in Hamburg, and he spoke of the song for many years. It was not until the 1970s when the song "Working Class Hero" appeared on *The John Lennon Plastic One Band* L.P. that the Furscharften bars patrons were immortalized in song.

It was the atmosphere in the Blockhutte which filled John's notebook with interesting stories, but the Furscharften bar provided a writing atmosphere. It was impossible to write in the Blockhutte because he was so well known, but the Furscharften was a spot where no one recognized John as an English musician working in one of the small clubs. As local Germans talked quietly, American soldiers drank a few beers, and an occasional prostitute wandered in to rest her feet, this Hamburg bar provided another type of education for John Lennon, one that helped him further develop his writing talents. As a result of the Blockhutte and other German bars like the Furscharften, Lennon's writings began to display stronger social themes. John Lennon was still in the formative stages of his literary career, and he continued to grow as a writer due to the freedom of these German bars.

Of all the bars which influenced John Lennon the Grapes in Liverpool was the seminal one. It was at the Grapes that John's ideas came together in their final form, and his most important writing took place. Since his early days at the Ye Crack near the Liverpool Institute, John had developed a passion for writing in notebooks. The Blockhutte experiences helped to fill these journals with interesting tales and colorful anecdotes, but it was not until he began writing in the Grapes that John's work emerged as polished.

It was while listening to wide variety of Liverpool characters as he rummaged through his notebooks at the Grapes that John crystallized his thoughts about music and literature. The reason that the Grapes was the last pub to significantly influence John was that the Beatles did not begin playing at the Cavern until late March, 1961. Since the Grapes pub was only a few hundred feet from the Cavern, it became John's last hangout before Beatles fans made him a virtual recluse. On a cold, rainy Tuesday night on March 21, 1961, the Beatles made their debut at the Cavern as the guests of the Bluegenes, later known as the Swinging Bluegenes.

A few hours before the performance, John sat with Bob Wooler in the Grapes reading aloud from his notebooks and discussing the music that the Beatles would perform that night. After the Beatles' brief set, Lennon and Wooler strolled down Mathews Street for a quick drink and some conversation just before the Grapes closed. John informed a startled Wooler that his career ambition was to become a serious writer, and he talked at length about his experiences in Ye Crack and the Blockhutte. It was the barroom atmosphere, John maintained, which brought out the best in his writings, and he felt a special creative urge in the pubs. John was excited as he talked about his future, and he showed Wooler a number of ideas for songs which he had picked up in the various pubs. The Hamburg experience, in particular, had inspired John to intensify his writing efforts, and when he returned to Liverpool, John spent hours in the Grapes recounting tales of Hamburg's intellectual and personal vices.

In April, 1961, shortly after their debut at the Cavern Club in Liverpool the Beatles returned to play at the Top Ten Club in Hamburg. Although John lived with the other Beatles in a small apartment above the Top Ten Club, nonetheless, he continued to spend two or three nights a week drinking beer and writing at the Blockhutte. Sitting at a corner table, John wrote for two or three hours many nights. He began to develop subjects which became the core of his Beatle song-writing experiences. When John recorded "Ain't She Sweet" at Polydor Records with Tony Sheridan, he took his copy to the Blockhutte to play it before his friends.

The Blockhutte was also the inspiration for some of John's best drawings. When his book, *John Lennon: In His Own Write* was published in 1964, it contained many of the drawings that he had completed in the Blockhutte.

When *In His Own Write* reached the number 1 spot on the *London Times Literary Supplement,* John was honored by Foyles

The Beatles: Mid-1960s

book shop with a special luncheon. During the Foyles luncheon John was mentioned in the same breath with Shakespeare, and this comparison shocked the normally stoic Lennon. He smiled as he recalled the boisterous Germans at the Blockhutte, and he shuddered as he looked out at the condescending English audience. It was an uncomfortable feeling for John Lennon to be publicly compared to writers like James Joyce and Lewis Carroll. After the long, dull literary luncheon, John walked two blocks to a local pub to unwind and ended up toasting the Blockhutte as staid English patrons looked on in horror. The reason for John's bizarre reaction to the Foyles literary luncheon is that acclaim as a serious author suddenly led to a deepening depression and the development of a serious writer's block. No longer did John write free form verse or draw public sketches. Suddenly much of his creative energy dried up. "I screamed out one night that they were eating me up," John informed Brian Epstein. The demand for new literary works and the pressure to promote his books drove John increasingly to drug use. The result was that his talents dissipated quickly, and his prose suffered.

Although John continued to write songs with Paul McCartney, his creative talents no longer had the fiery drive of the Ye Crack, the Grapes and the Blockhutte days. It is difficult to analyze the reasons for John's changing attitude toward his writing. Perhaps fame had intruded so that John was no longer able to be alone with his thoughts. The interference from fans, business interests, and music publishers created a perpetual writing block for John, and he was never able to retain the creativity of the years from 1958 through 1964.

Although a severe depression racked John Lennon's soul shortly after the Foyle's literary luncheon, he was still able to write a number of important songs. In fact, after penning "Help" Lennon confided to a friend that he was having trouble with his confidence level and self-image. It was difficult for anyone to beleive that half of the world's most famous songwriting team was unsure of his talents. There were many incidents in the mid-1960s which reflected Lennon's depression. One Sunday in 1965, for example, he appeared in Hyde Park wearing a fake beard and a hat. After wandering around for some time, Lennon listened to speakers decry British Imperialism, and he marveled at a bearded black man who pungently attacked Britain's subtle form of racism. John was stimulated by these speeches, and he went into a heavily wooded area of Hyde Park to talk to the trees and the squirrels. He was crying out for help, but no one could believe that the chief Beatle might need a moment of rest. During the early 1960s the three pubs that John Lennon frequented provided the inspiration and security he lacked during his years as a rock music superstar. By the mid-1960s the harried life of a Beatle was virtually destroying Lennon's sanity. He looked back upon Ye Crack, the Blockhutte and the Grapes with fond memories. As John met the press in the 1960s and 1970s he often alluded to these pubs or images which were developed in their warm and friendly confines. Much of Lennon's creativity is traced to these drinking spots, and they provided some interesting insights into how a rock songwriter created the music which made him a legend.

Chuck Berry: John Lennon's Favorite Artist

JOHN LENNON

Remembering John: Tony Sheridan and Charlie Lennon

John Lennon's life has intrigued chroniclers of rock music since his untimely death on December 8, 1980. As a result of Lennon's assassination a number of kiss-and-tell books were published by major New York houses. These rememberances offer very few significant insights into Lennon's life and were quickly relegated to the discount shelf at local bookstores. The best examples of these works are May Pang's, *Loving John: The Untold Story* and John Green's, *Dakota Days*. Neither book is a substantial biography of Lennon. Pang's story is one which examines her "lost weekend" in 1973 when John and May lived together for eighteen months in Los Angeles. It was a very creative period in Lennon's life, and it was also a time in which he restructured his life. May Pang was not only John's mistress, but she also received production co-ordinator credits on the *Walls and Bridges* and *Rock and Roll* albums. During the recording of these L.P.s, Pang was in a position to offer important historical information about John's life by examining his work with Phil Spector and Harry Nilsson, among others. However, *Loving John* fails to provide any real degree of insight into Lennon's life.

The problem with May Pang's view of John Lennon is that it involved little analysis. Phil Spector and John fought incessantly over a collection of old songs which eventually were issued in

Lennon's *Rock and Roll* album. One person close to Lennon remarked that there was a soap opera quality to the Spector-Lennon relationship, and the petty fighting and constant bickering offered important insights into both artist's temperament. As May Pang watched this scenario develop, she failed to record the best moments in this artistic struggle.

The Harry Nilsson-John Lennon drinking bouts were legendary ones in Los Angleles. For years Nilsson was a close friend to each of the Beatles, and he scored a major hit record with a song written by Apple recording artists, Badfinger. This tune, "Without You," helped to bring Nilsson into the vortex of Beatle activity. Soon Harry and John Lennon were fast friends. In the 1970s John produced Nilsson's "Pussy Cats" album, and they often engaged in marathon musical and drinking bouts. Harry Nilsson appealed to a warm, compassionate side of Lennon and was able to bring John out of his dreary shell. May Pang fails to point out the extraordinary impact that Nilsson had upon Lennon's mental health. It is unfortunate that *Loving John* is advertised as a close, personal encounter with John Lennon.

Another book in a similar vein is John Green's, *Dakota Days*. Green, a professional tarot card reader, was hired in 1975 by Yoko Ono to help John break a long-standing writing block. *Dakota Days* is advertised as a "professional encounter" with John Lennon, and it is replete with tales of witch craft, all-night parties and close intellectual encounters of a strange kind. Green's publisher, St. Martin's Press, boldly proclaims on the book's dust jacket that it is: "The True Story of John Lennon's Final Years."

Unfortunately, the boring story which follows is little more than a cat-and-mouse game between the two men. Eventually John Lennon has the last laugh by using the author's name during a vacation. *Dakota Days* is a highly suspect book because Green is able to recall intimate and lengthy conversations in great detail. Yet, when he arrived in Lennon's Dakota apartment complex, Green often had trouble remembering why he was there or what they were supposed to discuss. Despite these drawbacks there are some interesting tales and hilarious anecdotes in *Dakota Days*. While Pang and White have written self-serving tomes which reveal very little about John Lennon, nonetheless, *Loving John* and *Dakota Days* are important books. They are examples of one method of analyzing Lennon's life. The observations and remembrances of close friends are important to cultural historians. There are a number of people who were close to John Lennon during his formative years who offer

Charlie Lennon: The 1980s

important insights into his character development. By examining these sources it is possible to analyze the complex nature of Lennon's personality and to suggest how weak May Pang's and John Green's observations were during a critical period in John's brief life.

This essay will analyze the reminiscences of Charlie Lennon and Tony Sheridan, both of whom were very close to John from 1943 to 1963. In this twenty-year period Charlie Lennon, John's uncle, watched him grow to maturity while Tony Sheridan taught John the intricacies of rock music some years later in Hamburg. Charlie Lennon is an undiscovered source, because he is a historical figure who has not attempted to cash-in on Lennon mania. Tony Sheridan is equally important, because he refuses to talk to most journalists. Uncle Charlie and Tony are wary of the Lennon hucksters, and they agreed to tell their stories to provide another view of John, a complex and contradictory individual who was inordinately troubled about his family background. In time this frustration led to extensive therapy sessions with Arthur Janov, the author of *The Primal Scream, Primal Therapy: The Cure for Neurosis.* Had it not been for Lennon's preoccupation with his family history, he would not have completed Janov's therapy sessions. During these clinically controlled experiments, John was forced to relive some of his most painful early experiences. The rationale for Lennon's 1970 therapy can be traced to events in his life from the mid-1940s through the early 1960s. It was a significant crisis period in John's life. When Charlie Lennon talks about John's development, the problems of these early years seep into the conversation.

After the dream therapy sessions in which John was forced to relive the traumatic horrors of his childhood, he wrote a haunting song entitled "Mother." During the early 1960s, Charlie Lennon remembers lyrical poems very similar to this type of music, and there was a poetic sense in Lennon's writings which reflected this attempt to "mirror" his personal tragedies. The songs on John's first solo album, *John Lennon/Plastic Ono Band*, were important reflections of many of the ideas which matured during young John's long walks with Charlie Lennon. The therapy sessions with Janov helped Lennon to come to grips with his bitter feelings about his collaborations with Paul McCartney. In July, 1971 John recorded a blistering attack upon McCartney in a song entitled: "How Do You Sleep." Lennon was intellectually so unsure of himself that he could not vent his anger toward McCartney until after he had completed the Janov therapy program. Despite the fact that John had crafted hundreds of hit songs, he was apprehensive about his writing talent.

John Lennon's complicated intellectual makeup made him very dependent upon Liverpool's backward oral tradition. Much like Dylan Thomas and William Faulkner, Lennon's writings reflected the folk culture of his surroundings. This tradition helped to shape John's writing style, and it also made him an adept story teller. One of the strengths of the Lennon-McCartney songwriting collaboration was the ability to relate a simple story in a powerful literary manner. Malcolm Doney's book, *Lennon and McCartney*, suggests the importance of their songwriting collaboration: "Lennon and McCartney were unique in that their time coincided with a period of intense youth ferment—a new generation establishing itself in an era when social values and attitudes were under reassessment." It is John's differences with McCartney which continue to intrigue historians of pop culture. A clue to understanding Lennon's differences with McCartney is to realize that John used these personality tiffs to criticize McCartney's pop music direction. However, in critiquing Paul's music, John often was personally insulting and ended up alienating McCartney. Over the years hard feelings developed and soon the most famous songwriting team in history was no longer talking. Eventually, Lennon's criticism of McCartney's character turned into personally abusive comments on Paul's lifestyle. It is unfortunate that John and Paul were not able to iron out these differences before Lennon's tragic assassination. There is no doubt that they loved each other, but the strain of fame and fortune destroyed an early boyhood friendship.

The best examples of John's self-destructive behavior occurred in Hamburg's Top Ten Club. After a violent argument with his new manager, Brian Epstein, John for no apparent reason poured a glass of beer over Brian's head. This story has been used time and time again to suggest that John was a difficult, often impossible, person. The truth is that John was protesting Epstein's decision to force the Beatles to sing mainstream pop songs like "Besame Mucho." Thus, it was not an impulsive attack upon Brian Epstein. Often John Lennon's way of displaying his unhappiness was to make a direct, inflammatory, personal statement. As a result of his behavior, John often found it difficult to maintain long-term friendships.

The most perceptive comments about John's personality quirks during his early years were made by Thelma Pickles, a student at the Liverpool Institute College of Art. For a time Thelma and John dated. When Hunter Davies interviewed her for his authorized biography of the Beatles, she commented: "He was so different and original. But I just couldn't see what he could be famous at. Perhaps a comedian, I thought." This remark is astute because some of Lennon's most cutting and damning indictments of people were done in jest. However, many people were reluctant to talk in-depth about Lennon due to this caustic personality trait.

In Hamburg, Germany, Tony Sheridan willingly recalled his experiences with Lennon. As he reminisced about the Chief Beatle, Tony selected his words carefully and intelligently. Sheridan remembers Lennon as a person of extremes as he recalls the "golden years on the Reeperbahn." The revolutionary impact of the Beatles music, Sheridan believes, was due largely to John's influence. The biting, sarcastic nature of Lennon's character shaped the uniqueness of the Beatles' songs. Sheridan emphasized that Paul McCartney was so romantically inclined that he was unable to write the "raw energy" type of rock and roll music essential to commercial success. McCartney's songwriting was heavily influenced by traditional pop music, and he spent an inordinate amount of time viewing musical films starring Bing Crosby, Grace Kelly, Frank Sinatra and Dean Martin. So the rock and roll energy

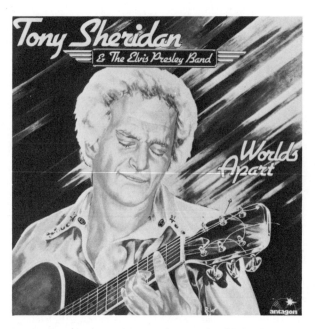

in the Beatles' music was the result of John Lennon, and he was able to persuade Paul McCartney to help write the rock and roll songs which made the Beatles famous. The blend of Lennon's offensive neo-punk pesonality with McCartney's musically skilled and romantically inclined behavior was solid gold.

In a quiet, reflective moment Tony Sheridan summed up the Lennon-McCartney songwriting magic. He pointed out that their songs were the first since Chuck Berry's to define the daily problems and aspirations of young people. They also dealt with subjects that most songwriters ignored because they were commercially too controversial. But the most important part of the Lennon-McCartney collaboration was the music's quality. It was amazing that John Lennon and Paul McCartney were able to write so many hit songs considering how busy they were with club appearances, concerts and promotional activity in the early 1960s.

Despite his songwriting successes with McCartney, "Lennon," Sheridan believes, "was a misfit and a rebel." The lack of a stable home life hurt John, and he assumed a tough guy stance as a reaction against his lack of parental love. "I liked him because he was not pretentious," Sheridan said. Although he had a hard outer shell, Tony believes that Lennon also had a sense of musical destiny. "He was ambitious, and he carefully planned the Beatles' live performances." Sheridan suggested that John projected a feeling that he could accomplish any task. "I was sure he would become a rock music superstar." In jest, John mentioned that he had made a pact with the devil to insure musical stardom. Many of John's contemporaries were frightened by this rumor. However, this story was no more than an indication that John had read the tale of American bluesmen who had sold their soul to the devil at the "Crossroads" in return for a successful musical career. Robert Johnson was one of many legendary bluesmen who fit this story, and Lennon loved to recreate this story in candle-lit sessions in a small room at the Top Ten Club. Although Tony Sheridan was present during these sessions, he never took them seriously.

The bond of friendship between Lennon, who went on to make millions, and Sheridan, who faded into relative obscurity, produced a number of interesting stories. In February, 1963, for example, Lennon urged Tony Sheridan to join the Beatles on the Helen Shapiro tour. Sheridan refused. In 1968 John Lennon quietly returned to Hamburg and attempted to visit Tony Sheridan. Unfortunately, Tony was not in town at the time, but John spent a great deal of time looking for his old buddy in the bars and clubs near the Reeperbahn. Sitting in the Blockhutte pub, just down the street from the Kaiserkeller, John regaled the audience with tales of Tony Sheridan's guitar magic. John commented that Tony's lyrical and musical qualities were unappreciated, but his work was among the best ever done in Hamburg.

During this visit to Hamburg, Lennon recalled a night in December, 1962 at the Star-Club when he appeared on stage with a toilet seat draped over his head. John was upset over the action of the management at the Star-Club and the toilet seat was a symbolic protest. Tony Sheridan counseled John to simply speak his mind, and he comforted the troubled Lennon. The high point of this trip came when Tony and John went to dinner at the Fleurs Schanke restaurant to celebrate the Beatles' success. The dinner was a farewell celebration, and they laughed and talked late into the night. John reminisced that his fondest memories were ones associated with Hamburg's British Sailor's Society. Jim Hawke, the manager of the Sailor's Society, is well-known for providing the Beatles with inexpensive meals. But equally important to John Lennon was the mission's hospitality and comfortable hominess. There were dances, social hours, and a chance to read the latest British and American magazines and newspapers. The British

Sailor's Society also had a chaplain who listened to Lennon's troubled questions about his life's direction.

In the early 1960s religion and an interest in the occult held a strange dual fascination for young John Lennon. At the mission, John often engaged in lengthy discussions on the meaning and importance of religion with Frau Prill. As Frau Prill cooked John's bacon, eggs, sausage, chips, beans and toast, he rambled on about the meaning of religious values. This was one of the earliest contradictions in John's life. He could talk at one moment about Christianity, and in the next breath celebrate the occult.

As Tony Sheridan looked back upon his years as John Lennon's friend, he recalled many bittersweet memories. The hard-driving, constantly troubled Lennon was, in Sheridan's opinion, a brilliant person. However, John never was able to experience much happiness, because of the emotional conflict from his troubled youth. In Hamburg, as Lennon matured, he displayed an irrational, virtually uncontrollable temper, but he also possessed an acerbic wit. The result was that John was a person who inspired either fanatical devotion or zealous hatred. Lennon was a man of extremes, Sheridan recalled, who climbed onto the rollercoaster of fame and fortune only to find misery and sadness.

Quite a different view of John Lennon's life is provided by his uncle, Charlie Lennon. Presently, a man in his mid-60s, Charlie has very distinct memories of young John Lennon. Sitting in the Grapes Pub late one Friday afternoon in May, 1983, Charlie recalled the Lennon's family history. As he slowly drank a Guiness Stout, Charlie reflected on a series of video-taped interviews that he had recently completed for Albert Goldman's John Lennon biography. It was difficult for Charlie to articulate his thoughts because the press so often twisted his comments. The questions about John's life obviously brought back a lifetime of mixed memories, but Uncle Charlie was eager to clarify many of the misconceptions about John's family background. The significance of Charlie Lennon's reminiscences is that they provide an excellent personal recollection of the family history and its influence upon young John Lennon. In many respects, Charlie's remarks validate Tony Sheridan's later observations.

The most significant family influence upon John Lennon was his father Alfred Freddie Lennon. Born on December 14, 1912, to Jack Lennon and Mary Maguire, Freddie, as he was known, was a magnificent singer and an accomplished amateur actor. When his father died from a liver ailment in 1921, Freddie was placed in the

Charlie Lennon

Bluecoat School. Much like his son John, Freddie's childhood was traumatic. His mother, Mary Maguire, a beautiful woman with long dark hair rolled in a small bun on the back of her head, attempted to raise the family alone. The lack of a strong father figure is one of the most revealing aspects of the Lennon family history. Mary Maguire raised her children in an atmosphere where male roles were never clearly defined.

In 1927 as Freddie Lennon walked through Sefton Park, he met Julia Stanley. The 13 year old Julia, born on March 12, 1914, in Liverpool, was one of George and Annie Stanley's five daughters. Julia's family was successful in a marginal sort of way as George worked for the Liverpool Salvage Company as a deep sea skipper. Since he was frequently away on business, Julia's mother raised the family. Like Freddie's home there was no clearly defined father figure in the Stanley household. The result was that neither Freddie nor his bride-to-be had exposure to traditional family roles.

For more than a decade Freddie and Julia were close friends. As Julia Stanley grew up, she exhibited bizarre and often unconventional behavior. She was a rebellious young girl with an extraordinary intellect. She was a poet, a philosopher, and most significantly a fine musician. But she was also a young girl living in the midst of a depressed economy as well as an unstable family. Therefore, Freddie Lennon was an escape for Julia. In 1930, when 18 year old Freddie Lennon went to sea, Julia cried for a week. They continued to see each other when he came home. Freddie often stayed at the Stanley house in Wavertree, and he taught Julia to play the piano. The music of Fats Waller, Louis Armstrong and Memphis Minnie were just a few of the influences that Freddie brought home from his voyages.

On December 3, 1938, Freddie and Julia were married at the Mount Pleasant register office, but neither the Lennon nor Stanley families were present for the wedding. After the ceremony the newlyweds went to the Trocadero Theater, and then they each went their separate ways. The next day Freddie Lennon left for a three-month assignment on a ship destined for the West Indies. Although he was constantly at sea, Freddie did come home periodically.

The sporadic relationship between Freddie Lennon and his young bride led to increased marital disputes. However, when John Winston Lennon was born on October 9, 1940, the differences in the marital pact temporarily subsided. As Charlie Lennon pointed out, Freddie and Julia were united by John's presence, and the marriage seemed to improve with the new baby.

When problems in the Lennon's marriage resurfaced it was due to World War II. It was impossible for Freddie and Julia to remain together, because Freddie was forced to go to sea. The couple drifted apart during World War II. Young John grew up with little knowledge of his parent's problems.

It was Freddie Lennon's desire fror a show business career which hindered their marriage. To the casual observer it did not seem that Julia and Freddie had any problems. They were both free spirits who disliked conventional social mores and the rigors of middle-class Liverpool values; Freddie and Julia were quiet rebels against the staid conformity of English society. But Freddie was also an unsteady provider, and he was prone to irrational, almost uncontrollable, fits of anger. Julia found it difficult to collect her support payments from the shipping line, and she soon looked elsewhere for a provider. It was a difficult period in her life for young Julia because she had little to offer but her beauty and intellect. The 1940s were an uncertain time for most people and Julia Lennon had great difficulty stabilizing her life during World War II.

After Freddie had been absent from Liverpool for almost two years, Julia assumed he was either missing or dead, and she began to date other men. As Hitler's terror reigned over Europe, Julia dreamed of family security and still spent many hours crying for Freddie. Although still a free spirit, Julia was understandably nervous about her personally rebellious nature. She longed for serenity and calm. Unknown to Freddie she had received religious instruction from a local Anglican clergyman. This brief foray into Orthodox religion did not satisfy Julia, though, and soon she was reading about the wonders of India and the diversity of Moslem religions. Clearly, Julia was an inquisitive and exceptionally bright young woman.

Julia Lennon's search for religious answers coincided with John's birth on October 9, 1940 during an unusually heavy German air raid. It is ironic that Freddie Lennon was not present at his son's birth, just as John was later not present at his son Julian's birth. It was as a result of Freddie's continual absences that Julia's sister, Mimi Stanley, began to exert a great deal of influence over young John Lennon. Mimi Stanley was not only Julia's sister, but she was the Stanley daughter who had married most successfully. Aunt Mimi was the first person to visit John in the Maternity Hospital on Oxford Street. Almost immediately she was fixated by John Lennon and spent an inordinate amount of time with the young boy. The main reason for Aunt Mimi's instant love for John was her belief that he could be her surrogate son.

In 1944 John went to live with Aunt Mimi and Uncle George in Mendips. It was a nice time for John as he had a yard to play in and a loving family environment. John's mother, however, experienced some hard times. In 1945 Julia Lennon gave birth to another son who was promptly adopted by a Norwegian couple. In the suburbs of Oslo, Norway, John Lennon's half brother is a businessman who has an uncanny resemblance to the famed Beatle guitarist.

Despite his parent's personal difficulties, John was growing into a fine boy. In 1944-1945 his grandfather, George Stanley, spent a great deal of time walking and talking with John. Young John also played a great deal at Aunt Mimi's and took long walks with Charlie Lennon. It was not until John Lennon's mother was killed on July 15, 1958 that his life was struck by tragedy. For years Julia Lennon had boarded the bus where she lived in Spring Wood and spent 25 minutes riding the bus to see John. She usually visited without announcing herself. This caused Aunt Mimi a great deal of concern, and the two sisters fought with each other over when Julia was to see John. There was a great deal of guilt in Julia because she felt that she had abandoned her son. As a result Julia tried to show John her best possible side. When John and Pete Shotton played hookie from school they went to Julia's house for lunch. She welcomed them with open arms and assured John and Pete that their truancy was of no concern to her. It was not until Julia's death that the family filled John in on his mother's erratic personal behavior. This was a mistake because in a fit of youthful rage, John Lennon vowed never to think of his mother again. This emotional reaction soon subsided and John was forced to rethink his mother's role. As a little boy, John was used to women attempting to win his favor. This trait manifested itself throughout his short but brilliant adult life. As a result John was hopelessly confused about the role of women in his life. "It was a tragedy that John did not know his mother and father as a young man," Charlie Lennon remarked.

When he returned from his erratic travels after World War II ended, Freddie Lennon had a means of explaining his absence. During World War II, he alleged, he had been arrested and imprisoned in North Africa for stealing a bottle of vodka from the Captain's quarters. In a moment of guilt, Freddie wrote Julia that he was going to prison and he was not much of a father. Perhaps Julia would prefer a new husband. This was a sign to Julia that Freddie no longer wanted her and she began to date other men. He regretted his impulsive behavior because his wife was important to Freddie Lennon. As Uncle Charlie suggested, "Freddie never forgave himself for this act."

The problems that John's parents experienced were not unique ones. The World War resulted in many families disintegrating due to the unusual pressures of the times. What is intriguing, according to Charlie Lennon, is how inaccurate some of the descriptions are of John's father's background. Freddie Lennon was not the black sheep, in Charlie's view, that Peter Brown suggests in *The Love You Make: An Insiders Story of the Beatles*. Although Brown is accurate in pointing out that Freddie did not see John until he was five years old and that he was involved in black market smuggling, nonetheless, Freddie had strong feelings for his son. In 1946 when Freddie showed up in Liverpool to visit Julia, he was wracked with guilt. After making a large amount of money selling smuggled nylon stockings. Freddie was attempting to make amends with Julia and John by showing up to take them away from their misery. Much to Freddie's astonishment he found Julia happily ensconced with a new boy friend and John comfortably residing with Aunt Mimi.

Although he was only five years old, John was happy to see his parents temporarily back together.

One of the positive aspects of Freddie Lennon's return was that he persuaded Julia and Aunt Mimi to allow him to take John north to Blackpool for a holiday. A small, sleepy town, Blackpool is an excellent city for long walks and quiet talks. Freddie and John soon became fast friends and they plotted a trip to New Zealand. "The brief vacation made quite an impression upon John," Charlie Lennon reflected. It was the first time that John was able to get to know his father. But this idyllic vacation was interrupted when Julia suddenly showed up in Blackpool and demanded to take John home. In anger Freddie bellowed that he and John were moving to New Zealand. Julia grabbed a table lamp and began pounding Freddie on the arms and chest. Eventually Julia left with young John. This scene remained a living nightmare for John, and only after he went through primal therapy with Arthur Janov did he realize how devastating these early confrontations had been to his self-image.

From 1946 to 1964 John did not see or hear from his father. Aunt Mimi continually reinforced the notion that Freddie Lennon was no good. John spent a great deal of time in the early 1960s reflecting on his parents. It was a frustrating time as John Lennon remarked to Tony Sheridan and Charlie Lennon that his "roots" were so bothersome that he had no idea what to think about his mother and father. "Rock music is me salvation," John remarked. When John gained his initial popularity as a Beatle in the early 1960s, Freddie decided that he would not bother his son. "Freddie didn't want to see a Beatle," Charlie Lennon reflected. "He wanted to see his son. Aunt Mimi caused a great deal of torment in the Lennon family, because she built an internal hatred in John," Charlie concluded. Many of John's negative attitudes and psychological problems were, according to Uncle Charlie, the direct result of Aunt Mimi's constant interference in his life.

On December 24, 1963, the Beatles performed in their annual Christmas show at the Empire Theater in Liverpool and the next three nights they were at the Finsbury Park Astoria Theater in London. Charlie Lennon went to the Empire Theater Show and the next day took the train to London. On Christmas Eve, 1963, unknown to John Lennon his dad and Uncle Charlie sat in the audience and watched the Beatles' Christmas show. "It was a proud moment for Freddie," Uncle Charlie stated, "and he was convinced that John had his unusual musical talent." Freddie

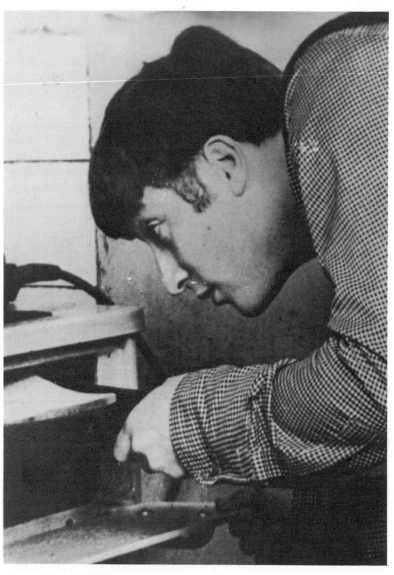

John Lennon: The Early Years

remarked that John was better off without him. However, the English press soon picked up the rumor that John Lennon's father was alive. Although he had not seen his son for years, Freddie Lennon was peripherally involved in show business. He tried to sell Tom Jones some songs and Jerry Dorsey, soon to be known as Englebert Humperdink, asked Freddie to write some tunes for him.

By 1964 Freddie Lennon had left the seamen's life and was working as a porter at the Greyhound Hotel in Hampton. Since this was close to the center of Beatlemania, it was not long before the *London Daily Express* contacted Freddie and suggested he meet with his famous son. When Freddie arrived on the set of *A Hard Day's Night*, John was aloof. It was obvious to the casual observer that John was hurt and confused by his father's sudden presence. The inner psychological turmoil which had racked Lennon's mind for years was squashed by detachment and a non-emotional front. He asked his father to leave his address, and soon John was sending Freddie $30 a week. After finding a small apartment in Kew Gardens, Freddie Lennon often wandered down to the pubs in Richmond. Soon he was friendly with young Brian Jones, and they talked for hours about the music scene. As the Rolling Stones leader became a star, he no longer visited with Freddie Lennon. But John's father was able to become a minor celebrity and he was a well-known figure on the London night club circuit.

Soon a British songwriter and entrepreneur, Tony Cartwright, persuaded Freddie to record a song. Cartwright's composition, "That's My Life," was issued in December, 1965 by Pye Records on their Picadilly label. The song faded quickly into obscurity and Freddie's show business aspirations ended. His relationship, however, with John was strained as a result of his attempt to make a hit record.

By early 1967 Freddie was working as the kitchen porter at the Tobey Jug in Surrey. During the times he had visited John at his house in Kenwood, Freddie was infatuated with one of John's employees, Pauline Jones. They eventually married and had two sons David Henry and Alfred Lennon. "John provided support for those boys until his death," Charlie reflected. Freddie Lennon died of lung cancer in 1970 while John was fighting to remain in New York. Although John attempted to pay the funeral expenses, Pauline refused to take the money. Even in death Freddie Lennon had a traumatic effect upon John. It was no different from his mother's death, John lost his father at a time he desperately needed parental help and approval.

In sum, Charlie Lennon and Tony Sheridan offer some valuable insights into John Lennon's character. The chief Beatle was complex and tormented by his enormous creative talent. As a result of his family background, the tragedy of John Lennon was that he was unable to escape the horrors of his past. He dwelled upon the unstable, lower-class problems of his youth and this created great instability in his adult life.

Breaking In All Major Markets

WHO DO YOU LOVE
THE SAPPHIRES

S-4162

CHAIN REACTION ON SWAN

The Beatles Biggest Hit Is On Swan! 19 Weeks On Englands Top 10—#3 Last Week. This Is The Record Performed On The Jack Paar Show . . .

SHE LOVES YOU
THE BEATLES

S-4152

Another Chartmaker!

AMAZONS AND COYOTES THE DREAMLOVERS

S-4167

SWAN RECORDS
8th & Fitzwater Sts.
Philadelphia, Pa.
MA 7-1500

PART III
THE MEDIA AND THE BEATLES

The Media and the Beatles

In the early 1960s the rise of Beatlemania was an English phenomena associated with a sensational form of Yellow Journalism. By November, 1963 Beatlemania had taken the United Kingdom by storm, thereby providing a subtle release from the depressing political scandal involving John Profumo's Conservative Party. Suddenly the Beatles became celebrities and the English were ready for swinging London, Carnaby Street and a brand of rock and roll music which set international records. This section of *The Beatles: Untold Tales* will examine the influence of the two major English rock music newspapers, the *New Musical Express* and *Melody Maker*, upon the growth and commercial popularity of the Beatles' music.

There always has been a name-calling tendency in British journalism. A good example of this practice occurred in the early 1960s when *Melody Maker* headlined: "Would You Let Your Daughter Go With a Rolling Stone?" This quotation helped to popularize the Rolling Stones' music, because it demonstrated that major British music newspapers were not in tune with the changes in rock and roll. In addition, the Beatles were treated rudely by *Melody Maker* in their early coverage of the Liverpool group. An essay entitled: "Will the Beatles Please Go Away? *Melody Maker*

Reacts To The New Music," argues that *MM* did not understand
the significant cultural changes occurring in English society.

Once the Beatles developed into a commercially successful
popular rock music group, there were many newspapers that
praised their innovative talents. The most perceptive English rock
newspaper, the *New Musical Express*, championed the Beatles'
music and generally applauded the rise of a distinct style of British
rock and roll. Since the 1950s the *New Musical Express* had
chronicled carefully the major developments in British rock music.
As a result the pages of the NME were filled with significant
quotations from rising rock artists, key facts about the various
groups and performers, and incisive analysis of the record
companies reactions to the new music. Because of their personal
attitude, the *New Musical Express* was able to complete in-depth
interviews with the Beatles and other rising English rock
musicians like Peter Townshend, Jeff Beck, Eric Clapton and
Jimmy Page. The result is that the *NME* stands out as the most
important source in British rock history in the 1960s. An essay
entitled: "The *New Musical Express* and the Beatles," explores the
relationship between this pioneer British newspaper and the
Liverpool group.

Since hype and scandal are the ingredients of many rock and
roll successes and failures, it is important to analyze how the
Beatles fared at the hands of the press and to demonstrate what
positive and negative press coverage did to change the direction of
the Beatles' music.

MELODY MAKER

Will the Beatles Please Go Away?
Melody Maker Reacts to the New Music

In the early 1960s the British musical press witnessed a revolutionary change in rock music. As the small clubs increased, and the local dance halls flourished in the United Kingdom a new and distinct brand of English rock music was developed by small groups and individual performers. The rise of this new talent happened so quickly that English music critics felt like foreigners in their own land. Not only was the music different, but the artists were unique to British culture. No longer was the music predictable. The initial British rock stars, Tommy Steele, Cliff Richard, Billy Fury, Terry Dene, and Dickie Pride had hits on the British charts from 1956 to 1960 with Elvis Presley or Buddy Holly type songs. These artists were little more than American clones. One of the original rock talents in England in 1956 was a middle-aged band leader, Tony Crombie, whose band, The Rockets, was very similar to Bill Haley and the Comets. There were other groups like Crombie's Rockets, Art Baxter and the Sinners and Rory Blackwell's Blackjacks who played a watered down brand of American rock music in ballrooms and dance halls throughout the United Kingdom. In response to the demand for rock music in February, 1957 BBC-TV began broadcasting a teenage music show, Six-Five Special on Saturdays. This British version of Dick Clark's American Bandstand was the first means of promoting local rock music talent. The initial explosion of rock performers and the early television and radio shows helped to lay the foundation for the second stage of England's rock revolution in 1962-1963.

In the early 1960s larger numbers of new bands from small clubs and little towns were invading London. A good example of this phenomena was Belfast, Ireland singer Van Morrison and his group Them. When they arrived in London to record and perform they were so broke that Them slept in Hyde Park the first night. When Van Morrison appeared on the TV show "Ready, Steady, Go," one music critic was amazed at how much he sounded like the Black American blues singers. Big Joe Williams, Muddy Waters and John Lee Hooker were Morrison's musical inspirations, and he had an uncanny ability to recreate their music. While American rock musicians were ignoring the blues, the British were preparing for a major assault upon the American marketplace by bringing back original versions of American blues, rhythm and blues and "roots" rock and roll music. A good example of another group of British performers who had blues roots was Eric Burdon and the Animals. This exciting new group from the Newcastle-on-Tyne area took London by storm, and their music reflected the raw intensity of Bo Diddley, Jimmy Reed and Sonny Boy Williamson. These bands had a personal fury which left some music critics perplexed about the new direction of English rock and roll. But there was nothing startling about English rock music, as it simply combined American soul, blues, and rhythm and blues influences with traditional rock music. Many of the major musical newspapers in London, notably *Disc* and the *New Musical Express,* welcomed the revolutionary changes in British music during the 1960s. A number of obscure magazines in the mid-1960's, notably *Rave* and *Fabulous,* also applauded the music, but these magazines built their circulation around the teenage fashion revolution and its connection to the music. In the early 1960s, as the Beatles and other British groups struggled for recognition, there were only two significant British music weeklies, the *New Musical Express* and *Melody Maker.* In time the *Disc Weekly,* which later evolved into *Disc* and finally *Music Echo* provided one of the best views of British rock and roll. As British rock music experienced profound changes in content, so did the rock music weeklies. Some adjusted and adapted to the new music, others were overly critical of it. This essay will examine the reaction of *Melody Maker,* England's best-known music newspaper, to the Beatles' music during 1962-1963.

Melody Maker did not initially recognize the importance of rock music as a developing art form, because the newspaper's coverage was so heavily attuned to traditional jazz. When Alexis Korner began popularizing the blues, *Melody Maker* ignored Korner's excellent pub performances, and his direct influence upon a new generation of experimental musicians. Much like Mitch Miller, the chief A and R man for Columbia Records in America, *Melody Maker* did not believe that there was a commercial future to the British rock revolution. In addition to a generally negative attitude toward the new music, *Melody Maker* reserved a vitriolic criticism for the Beatles. It was almost as if *Melody Maker* blamed the changes in the music business upon the Beatles and the emerging Merseyside sound.

The reasons for *Melody Maker*'s intensive criticism of the Beatles' music remains a mystery, but there is no doubt that the new British rock music was not looked upon favorably by *MM* staffers. As a result the newspaper's coverage often assumed a personal as well as a professional tone in the criticism of club performances, records and musical directions of the major English groups. The reporting of Beatle activity generally seemed designed to embarrass the Liverpool group. A good example of *Melody Maker* attempting to make the Beatles' management look silly occurred when Brian Epstein issued an internal memo to John Lennon requesting that John not wear his glasses in public If John was photographed publicly wearing his glasses, Brian reasoned, it would lessen the Beatles' sex appeal for young girls. A great deal of Brian's reporting strategy centered around coverage which emphasized the "teen idol" aspect of the Beatles' music. When *Melody Maker* discovered John Lennon's glasses were considered too intellectual and Brian Epstein assigned Neil Aspinall to remind John not to be seen with his glasses on, the *MM* staffers exploited the story. Soon *Melody Maker* devised a strategy to take as many pictures as possible of John wearing his glasses, and subsequent *Melody Maker* issues featured pictures and stories centering around Lennon's eye attire. In sum, *Melody Maker* believed that the eye glasses memo was a restriction upon free speech. It was this attitude which made *Melody Maker* a thorn in the Beatles side throughout much of 1962 and 1963.

Melody Maker delighted in making fun of the Beatles' well-organized and generally sensible management policies. This type of journalistic behavior is easy to understand because *Melody Maker* sensationalized its product in typical English journalistic fashion to

reach a wider market. There was, however, a strong distaste for
rock music amongst many *Melody Maker* staffers, and this made
the newspaper's criticism uneven, one-sided and often inaccurate.
The rival rock newspapers, *Disc* and the *New Musical Express* were
very fair to the Beatles' music, whereas *Melody Maker* was a trendy
publication intent upon deriding rock music.

The British press tends to pander toward the sensational
stories about rock music and entertainment personalities. When
pop singer Helen Shapiro was ejected from a dance in Carlisle, for
instance, the *London Daily Express* treated this minor escapade as
front-page news. It was an innocuous event which occurred when
one of Shapiro's friends wore a leather jacket which was
unacceptable to the Young Conservative Hotel's management. This
story helped Shapiro to sell large numbers of records, and it is a good
example of the English media's ability to invent racy stories. This
type of pseudo-event was one of *Melody Maker*'s favorite means of
creating stories to titillate the English public. *Melody Maker*
became the premier practitioner of this form of journalism as it
constantly created Beatle news.

In order to understand how *Melody Maker* used pseudo-events,
it is necessary to examine some of their earliest interpretive news
stories. In an attempt to discredit the Beatles' music, *Melody Maker*
wrote a glowing article on the Manchester invasion. This English
city, very close in proximity to Liverpool, was a natural rival to the
Merseyside sound. With the exception of the Hollies and Freddie
and the Dreamers, however, the Manchester groups did not provide
the excitement of the Merseyside sound. Another means used by
Melody Maker to denigrate the Beatles was reporting that the
Beatles turned down an offer to appear on ATV's "Sunday Night at
the London Paladium" as well as rejecting a movie. What *Melody
Maker* failed to report was that the Beatles signed more lucrative
television and movie contracts. Finally, *Melody Maker* quoted John
Lennon as saying that the Rolling Stones were simply a cloned
version of the Beatles. It was difficult for the Beatles to escape
Melody Maker reporters because Brian Epstein required that the
Beatles spend an inordinate amount of time with the press. As John
Lennon lamented to Ray Coleman and Chris Roberts: "On our day
off, we get lumbered with...guys like you."

There are many news stories which reflect *Melody Maker*
hostility to the Beatles, and these news items help to explain *MM*'s
distaste for the Liverpool sound. When the Beatles released "Love
Me Do," it rose to number 11 on the *Melody Maker* charts. This is

not surprising, because EMI did not publicize the Beatles' first release adequately. On October 4, 1962 "Love Me Do" was shipped to the record stores, but most of EMI's executives were not optimistic about the Beatles future. Radio Luxembourg, a commercial radio station broadcasting from the European continent, beamed an EMI sponsored program after 8 p.m. to England. During the first month after "Love Me Do" was released, EMI played the song only six times. Chris Montez' "Let's Dance" and Tommy Roe's "Sheila" received the most airplay of any contemporary songs, and American artists continued to dominate the English charts. It was not until the Beatles accompanied Helen Shapiro, Tommy Roe and Chris Montez on an extended English tour in February and March, 1963 that *Melody Maker* became interested in the Beatles music. Tommy Roe recalled the frenzy and excitement of that Beatle tour: "After one night it was necessary for the Beatles to close the show as they were the crowd favorite," Roe explained. "The Beatles sounded better in person than they did on records in the early days, and they were able to control the crowds with their tight stage show." Roe, who rode the tour bus sitting alongside John Lennon, noted that none of the other performers had the appeal or charisma of the Beatles on this early tour. What impressed Roe was how eager John Lennon was to learn the proper chords to Roe's hit record "Sheila." "I spent hours working with John on the chord progression, and he was the nicest, easiest person to teach," Roe recalled. John Lennon felt very close to Roe on this tour, and John informed Bob Wooler that Roe's conversation was "insulation from the press." During this tour *Melody Maker* reporters were demanding and overly critical of the Beatles' music, and they often complained about not receiving exclusive stories. John Lennon laughingly commented that *Melody Maker* wouldn't recognize an exclusive story, because the magazine failed to understand rock music. The Beatles preferred to talk to *New Musical Express* reporters, because the Beatles sensed that the *NME* understood their music. Brian Epstein quietly put *Melody Maker* reporters in their place by occasionally denying them access to the Beatles. This was a mistake, because it led to a festering hatred among some *Melody Maker* staffers.

There is no doubt that the Beatles' first commercial breakthrough was when the February 16, 1963 issue of *Melody Maker* rated "Please Please Me" as its number 2 song. Most other British music newspapers listed "Please Please Me" as number 1, and as early as January 31, *Mersey Beat* had rated it number 1.

Although *Mersey Beat* was a Liverpool-based newspaper, nonetheless, the general feeling among British rock critics was that the Beatles were creating an entirely new generation of record buyers. HMV, the Oxford Street Record store, reported that the Beatles had revolutionized the 45 record market, and they were having trouble maintaining an adequate stock of Merseyside records. *Melody Maker* ignored these changes. The London-based newspaper simply failed to interpret the revolutionary changes brought about by the Beatles' music.

The main reason that the Beatles were treated so poorly by *Melody Maker* was because its staff was composed of jazz aficianados who were unhappy with the rise of rock music. As late as 1965 when British rock critic Nick Jones went to work for *MM,* they asked him to get a haircut. In 1962-1963 *Melody Maker* staffers were determined to stamp out this "rock and roll rot," and return Cliff Richard's music to the top of the charts. The Shadows, Acker Bilk and Lonnie Donegan were treated so well by *MM* that their records often had artificial sales in the early 1960s. The best example of creating a hit record was the support that *Melody Maker* gave to Jet Harris and Tony Meehan. Due to Harris' popularity with the Shadows, his recording "Diamonds" was number 1 in 1963. Although Harris was a talented musician prone to self-destruction, *Melody Maker* accorded him better coverage than the Beatles. The reason was that Harris and Meehan's music had a mainstream, pop quality to it.

There is no doubt that *Melody Maker*—which had so thoroughly dominated jazz music coverage, suddenly felt threatened by the new rock and roll invasion. No longer was *Melody Maker* able to direct the musical tastes of the British public. Pete Townshend of the Who, a struggling art student in the early 1960s, was typical of the fledgling British musician who ignored the description of the music scene by *MM* staffers. In fact, in one *Melody Maker* interview in the mid-1960s, Townshend pointed out that the Beatles inspired groups like the Who to create their own type of music. In comparing the Who and the Beatles, Townshend pointed out that Lennon like Townshend was an art student. Although the Beatles played a different type of rock music than the Who, Townshend emphasized that the Beatles were still much like the Who playing "pop art with standard sound equipment." Townshend's remarks reflected the revolt against the narrow musical interpretation of *Melody Maker*'s staff. It was as though *Melody Maker* hoped that British rock and roll music would go away and traditional jazz, skiffle and American blues would continue to dominate the music scene. By examining *Melody Maker*'s coverage of the Beatles carefully in 1963, it is possible to analyze the emergence of this new form of British rock music.

It was difficult for the rock revolution to succeed in England during the 1960s due to government regulations. The government-regulated BBC radio and television outlets carefully selected songs for the pop charts and monitored the amount of music airplay. The British teenager was incensed by the lack of popular music on the airwaves, and, as a result, on March 27, 1964, Radio Caroline began broadcasting as a pirate radio station. By this time the Beatles were already commercially successful, but groups like the Who, the Kinks and the Rolling Stones benefitted from Radio Caroline's airplay. In 1962-1963, however, the BBC Light Programme was the only means of listening to rock music. The term, "light programming," was intended to reflect a music selection which appealed to all age groups. Due to the limited amount of rock music on the BBC controlled airwaves, it was only natural for pirate stations to emerge.

Ronan O'Rahily, the owner of London's Scene Club, helped to establish the pirate radio station operation by pointing out that a ship beyond the three-mile limit in international waters could safely transmit to London and most of southern England. After Radio Caroline went on the air in May, 1964, it was joined by Radio Atlanta. In 1962-1963 there were already signs of this impending revolution as BBC was flooded with letters complaining about their programming. *Melody Maker* failed to notice this discontent, while virtually every other London-based rock music newspaper reflected on the growth of record sales and the demand for more rock music on the airwaves. Prior to the radio revolution the sole means of influencing record sales was the rock music newspaper.

The rock newspapers published separate record ratings. Many artists found themselves on a newspaper's play list for cooperating with its reporters. In 1960 Ricky Valance's "Tell Laura I Love Her" was number 1 on the *Melody Maker* charts simply because of one review. An even better example of *MM*'s musical culpability was the praise accorded to B. Bumble and the Stingers number 1 hit "Nut Rocker." In 1962 B. Bumble was described by *Melody Maker* as the new direction in rock music. Bob Wooler commented that "B. Bumble and the Stingers were the worst group to play at the Cavern." John Lennon remarked that the rotound B. Bumble sat in his room reading history books while the rest of the band appeared confused by England. *Melody Maker*'s penchant for these acts created hostility in the Beatles camp, and this was one of the reasons that they were generally uncooperative with many of its staffers.

The question of payola in the English record business has not been analyzed in detail by historians. Julie Burchill and Tony Parsons, reporters for the *New Musical Express,* co-authored a quirky, but excellent, book on the decline of rock and roll entitled: *The Boy Looked at Johnny: The Obituary of Rock and Roll* which suggested that drugola, gangsters and sycophantic press agents were destroying the creative energies of rock music. What is refreshing about the Burchill-Parsons book is that it equates the problems of punk musicians with those of the Beatles in the early 1960s. Almost a quarter of a century later, the forces which hampered the Beatles rise to popularity continue to plague the rock music business.

By 1963 shrewd record company executives were entertaining the key writers for the *New Musical Express, Melody Maker* and a number of other British rock newspapers. The major record labels also began catering expensive parties to publicize new record releases. The artists were made available to the press, and there was a tacit understanding that a good review would lead to further considerations. Since nationally recognized Top 40 radio did not exist in England, the music newspapers were inordinately important in promoting new record releases. Decca Records was one of the first companies to realize the importance of advertising in the rock music newspapers, and soon this form of payola helped the career of groups like the Who. Although the Who's music was strong enough for commercial success, Decca Records spent a great deal of money on related advertising. When Radio Caroline went on the air in 1964, Decca spent thousands of pounds on advertising and as a result the station was instrumental in the rise of the Who. Decca often sponsored Radio Caroline programs devoted entirely to the Who's music. In reality, this was a technique pioneered earlier in the 1960s by Brian Epstein, and it was designed to give maximum commercial exposure to a group's music. When "Love Me Do" was released in October, 1962, for example, Brian spent large sums of his own money promoting the Beatles' first record. It was certainly not the first skillful entertainment publicity campaign, but Brian Epstein was able to make it look like a ground swell of public sentiment in support of the Beatles' music. It was Brian's ability to generate an apparently spontaneous reaction to the Beatles' music which helped to make "Love Me Do" a modest 1962 English hit.

All of the major record charts, whether from newspapers like the *New Musical Express* or from *Melody Maker* did reflect a portion of the public's musical taste. Most of the charts, with the possible exception of *Melody Maker*'s, were a modestly accurate gauge of record purchasing activity. There is no evidence that *Melody Maker* engaged in any form of payola, however *Melody Maker*'s record rankings indicated that its critics were not listening carefully to the new music. This well-known music newspaper found it difficult to recognize the quality of some of the more innovative music in England's small clubs.

A good example of *Melody Maker*'s problem in analyzing the changing music scene occurred from 1958 to 1960 when Tony Sheridan was the featured act at the 2-Is coffee bar in London's Soho district. He was such a popular artist that the 2-Is was packed nightly, but there was scarcely a word of its impact in *Melody Maker*.

The 2-Is coffee bar, located at the Wardour Street end of Old Compton Street, was the closest thing to a rock music scene in the late 1950s and early 1960s. The Heaven and Hell was another coffee bar near the 2-Is where the basement served as a performing venue for local artists. The basement was referred to as Hell, but it was one of the most important venues in England. Brian Locking and Hank Marvin, who later went on to fame with the Shadows, were two excellent musicians who started in these clubs. In time, Locking and Marvin backed Tony Sheridan in the 2-Is Coffee Bar and eventually became Cliff Richard's back-up band. Soon young musicians like Peter Green, Eric Clapton, John Mayall and Peter Townshend were wandering into the 2-Is to watch the local acts. The 2-Is provided an inspirational environment for its musicians who later achieved fame in the mid-1960s.

By 1962 the 2-Is was no longer the main force in British rock music, but it was the club which began England's first rock revolution. It was also an important source of musical talent for American rock stars who toured England and the European continent. The 2-Is often provided the musicians for touring American artists like Gene Vincent, Eddie Cochran, Little Richard and Conway Twitty. When Gene Vincent arrived in London in December, 1959, he went to the 2-Is and hired Tony Sheridan to provide musical support; *Melody Maker* failed to report that Vincent raved over Sheridan's talent. They also ignored Vincent's insightful comments about the rise of England's own rock talent. Conway Twitty also selected Sheridan to back him on tour, and his comments on Tony's career were totally ignored by *Melody Maker*. This is one of the main reasons that Tony Sheridan moved to Hamburg, because he believed it was a better place to achieve musical stardom. In addition to Vincent and Twitty, Ray Charles and Jerry Lee Lewis commented that Sheridan was an original talent. Much like the Beatles were ignored by *Melody Maker* in the early 1960s, Sheridan was not given the press coverage necessary to launch a successful English recording career.

Although Sheridan appeared on popular programs like Jack Good's British TV show, "Oh Boy," he was not signed to a major English record label. The tendency of British rock historians to blame Sheridan's erratic personal life style for his show business misfortunes is not the main reason for Sheridan's commercial failure. A more plausible answer is that publications like *Melody Maker* failed to publicize Sheridan's strong, live performances. Since Tony could not find an English label to record his music, his unique brand of rock and roll was not available to English record buyers. One of the reasons that the major record companies did not sign Sheridan was because BBC radio and TV programming played so few rock and roll songs. While "Oh Boy" did present rock artists, the corporation bosses in London believed that Cliff Richard's "Move It" was typical of rock music, and, as a result, it was difficult for anyone with a different sound to achieve recognition. Sheridan's music was considered too racous and blues oriented for commercial success. When Sheridan finally recorded in German, his songs "My Bonnie" and "Skinnie Minnie" sold more than a half of a million records each. Had Brian Epstein been around to help Tony Sheridan, he might have become one of England's early rock and roll music stars.

When rock and roll music became a widely accepted English phenomena in 1962-1963, Tony Sheridan was in exile in Hamburg and *Melody Maker* continued to champion traditional jazz. Acker Bilk was still praised by *MM* staffers and they were strongly anti-intellectual in analyzing the reasons for rock music's success. In sum, this attitude was largely due to the notion that the new music was not intellectually or commercially acceptable for the English market.

Despite *Melody Maker*'s distaste for rock music in general and the Beatles' songs in particular, the Liverpool group and other new English singers were beginning to slowly dominate the English charts. On January 19, 1963, for example, "Please Please Me" entered the *Melody Maker* Top 50 at the number 47 position, and *MM*'s editors finally recognized that Beatle music was not a one hit phenomena. Although the Beatles' first hit, "Love Me Do," slipped from number 21 to 26, nonetheless, *Melody Maker* reported the mild popularity of the provincial Liverpool group. It was impossible for *MM* staffers to ignore the growing love affair between the British public and the Beatles.

In January and February, 1963, *Melody Maker* did not report the obvious signs of the Beatles' growing popularity. In January, after returning from their last engagement in Hamburg, the Beatles toured Scotland and began a series of concerts in England's countryside. On January 7, 1963, the first indications of the Beatles enormous popularity occurred at the Majestic Ballroom in Birkenhead. Not only did the concert sell out, but 500 ticketless fans milled around outside the ballroom. The following week "Please Please Me" was released and the song generated strong sales outside of London. Most English rock journalists dismissed the Beatles' success, because they believed that Brian Epstein's promotional work was solely responsible for the Beatles' record sales. The *Melody Maker* Top 50 reflected this attitude as Jet Harris and Tony Meehan's middle of the road song "Diamonds" was number 1.

Despite *Melody Maker*'s propensity to ignore the Beatles, the newspaper did recognize Brian Epstein's managerial skills. In its early coverage of the Beatles, *Melody Maker* implied that Epstein was the only literate member of the group's entourage. This angered John Lennon and Paul McCartney, and they talked privately about boycotting the newspaper's reporters. Suddenly John and Paul decided to take a hard line attitude toward *MM* reporters. An example of this new attitude occurred on February 23, 1963, when McCartney was interviewed in the *Melody Maker* office. McCartney was tired because the previous night the Beatles had recorded performances for BBC's "Talent Spot" and "Saturday Club." Those tapings had not gone well, and the Beatles were forced to continually redo their part of the show. Obviously irritated, McCartney said as little as possible during the interview. When asked if being a Beatle was hard work, McCartney replied: "This isn't a job. It's a dedication." The *Melody Maker* reporter failed to follow up on McCartney's remarks about his frustrations with the Beatles. *Melody Maker* was too intent upon low-level criticism, and they failed to pick up the early dissatisfaction among the Beatles.

The Beatles: An Early Publicity Shot

There was no apparent reason for dissension among the Beatles. Brian Epstein was paying them 200 pounds a week each, and they were constantly touring and performing on radio and television. As the Beatles' music became successful, the strain of touring and constant recording, increased stress and caused problems. John Lennon remarked to Bob Wooler that the demands upon the Beatles were excessive ones and that he was having trouble writing songs. John eventually began to isolate himself from his fans and the other Beatles to write his parts of the Lennon-McCartney songs. On January 31, 1963, Andrew Logg Oldham, who later went on to manage the Rolling Stones, was hired to handle the Beatles' publicity. This was the first indication that the group's business was becoming too involved for Brian Epstein.

As a result of growing national interest in the Beatles, *Melody Maker* increased its coverage of the group's activity. When "Please Please Me" reached number 1 on the *Melody Maker* Top 50 on March 2, 1963, it was an acknowledgment of the Beatles' success. The growth in the group's popularity convinced *Melody Maker* to include a feature story on the Beatles. On March 23, 1963 Chris Roberts' article "The Beat Boys" analyzed the Merseyside sound and compared it to American rhythm and blues music. Roberts labelled Liverpool the Nashville of Britain. This reference was designed to point out that English rock musicians were heavily influenced by such artists as Carl Perkins, Roy Orbison, Elvis Presley, Jerry Lee Lewis and the emerging Stax-Volt sound. A small section of Roberts' article dealt with the reasons why the Liverpool sound was a revolt against Cliff Richard's type of music. What Roberts failed to note was the intensity of the revolution erupting in the English music scene. Yet Roberts did believe that the Beatles were headed toward stardom, because they had mastered an American sound which was very commercial in England: "They were one of many groups (the Beatles) who had achieved a near-enough coloured sound..." He also had latent praise for Lennon and McCartney's songwriting skills. Most other English rock newspapers, notably *Disc* and the *New Musical Express,* were already effusive in their reviews of the Beatles' original songs. Roberts' article should have warned *Melody Maker*'s editors about the Beatles' new popularity, but much of the editorial content continued to demonstrate a hostile attitude toward the Liverpool groups music. Privately, Brian Epstein and John Lennon agonized over the hostility of Britain's premier musical newspaper. One night Brian and John went to a private club near Picadilly Circus to drown their sorrows. After quietly downing half a dozen drinks the two men stumbled into the street and gave a startled newsman 10 pounds for his remaining issues of *Melody Maker.* John Lennon then walked into one of the dark side streets adjacent to Soho and lit the bundle of newspapers into a fiery blaze. The Lennon-Epstein incident illustrates the tension surrounding the making of Beatlemania. Brian Epstein was determined to avoid publicly attacking *Melody Maker*'s coverage of the Beatles. But Brian also urged the Beatles to defend themselves verbally against the newspaper.

The Beatles' new aggressiveness toward the press was demonstrated on April 27, 1963, when George Harrison remarked to a *Melody Maker* reporter: "Don't mention work. We're off on holiday and that's all we can think of at the moment." As Harrison sat on a plane to America to see his sister, it was apparent that he resented *Melody Maker*'s prying attitudes.

Since *Melody Maker*'s relationship with the Beatles was so cool, its reporters began to concentrate upon other new groups. On May 25, 1963, when the Hollies entered the *Melody Maker* charts with a song entitled, "Just Like Me," *Melody Maker* described the

Manchester group as one with a solid musical style. Graham Nash of the Hollies remarked that "there's every chance of Manchester catching up with the Merseyside success story." Nash suggested that Freddie and the Dreamers were another Manchester group destined for as much success as the Beatles. But even *MM* staffers realized that musical change was dramatic in the U.K.

On June 8, 1963, *Melody Maker* grudgingly acknowledged that Cliff Richard and Adam Faith were no longer the most popular English acts. However, *Melody Maker* did not report how effusively Cliff Richard had praised the Beatles' music, and concluded that the Merseyside sound was the future of English rock.

During the summer of 1963 *Melody Maker* slowly changed its attitude concerning the Beatles music. When the Beatles third Parlophone release "From Me to You" stayed on the *Billboard* English charts for 17 weeks and eventually rose to number 1, it was awarded a silver record for half-a-million sales. *Melody Maker* took note of this success, and perceptibly softened their criticism of the Beatles. Yet, *Melody Maker* could not leave the Beatles personal lives alone—like many English newspapers, it was critical of John Lennon's alleged neglect of his new-born son Julian. Although John's marriage was not officially revealed by the British press until mid-July, 1963, nonetheless, there were numerous snide remarks and rumors in the press about the possibility of a married Beatle. This made John look somewhat insensitive since he had just ended a tour the previous month with Tommy Roe and Chris Montez, and the British public believed that Lennon should be home with his wife.

On April 16, 1963, just two days before Julian's birth, John appeared with the Beatles on BBC-TV's "The 6.5 Show," and Brian Epstein kept the Beatles busy by scheduling a series of promotions in and around London. The Beatles had planned a two-week vacation beginning on April 29, 1963, and Brian eagerly was publicizing the recently released record "From Me to You." On April 21, the Beatles performed at the Empire Pool in Wembley at a concert to celebrate the *New Musical Express* poll winners. The publicity generated from this appearance was important to selling records. Brian also had John appear at press conferences with Duffy Powers, who had recently recorded "I Saw Her Standing There," and Billy J. Kramer, who was promoting his recently released record, "Do You Want to Know a Secret." These Lennon and McCartney songs were doing well by other artists, and Brian Epstein believed that the Beatles' songwriting was potentially as lucrative as records and live performances. Brian and John were very visible in Beatles' promotions, and as a result when they left for a twelve-day vacation in the Canary Islands there was gossip about a homosexual affair. It was common knowledge that Brian Epstein was gay, but the Beatles and Brian denied it. Simon Napier-Bell, a rock music entrepreneur during the 1960s, remarked that: "Brian was playing games all the time, with himself as much as anyone else." Napier-Bell's astute observation suggests the difficulty that the Beatles organization had in maintaining a hip, yet respectable, public image.

Brian Epstein was concerned that he might become a target for *Melody Maker*'s vitriolic journalism. As rumors spread through London about Brian's vacation with John Lennon, there was an insidious level of malicious gossip directed toward the chief Beatle. This hurt Brian, and he confessed his feelings one night in a long talk with his friend singer Alma Coogan. "Why can't the press leave us alone," Brian remarked to Alma. As Brian and Alma drank brandy late into the night, they commiserated about the problems of appeasing the English press. Coogan, a well-known recording star, was worried that her personal life might affect her career. Brian confessed that he was at wits end over *Melody Maker*'s journalism. But Brian and John Lennon were not the only ones to feel these journalistic barbs. Since drugs were not yet a major concern, and the "hip, swinging Carnaby Street scene" was a few years in the future, *Melody Maker* concentrated upon the individual character of rock personalities.

Ringo Starr became a target of *Melody Maker* critics as a result of their penchant for making exciting news. When he joined the Beatles, Ringo was the quietest and least obtrusive member of the group. It took two years to perfect the ad-libs which made Ringo a media favorite. This transformation was the product of careful training and constant experience during British press conferences. *Melody Maker* continually badgered and hounded Ringo for quotes, but they failed to print many of his more intelligent remarks. It was a frustrating experience for Ringo, because he was the most cooperative Beatle with *Melody Maker* reporters. After a particularly demanding concert, Ringo was asked about his drumming. "I'm not as good as some of these top boys," Ringo remarked, "because I should really practice more than I do." Ringo was complaining about the Beatles exhausting schedule which left neither time for practice nor for a personal life. *Melody Maker* gloatingly featured Ringo's remarks while ignoring Ringo's

Ringo Starr

substantial historical comments upon the English music scene. Personally, *MM* staffers ignored Ringo and often commented that he was the least important Beatle. The result was that he developed an antipathy toward the newspaper's reporters.

The main reason that Ringo became reticent to talk openly with *Melody Maker* reporters was due to a John Lennon story. On August 3, 1963, *Melody Maker* reported that Lennon was personally critical of the Rolling Stones. This story was the result of an article which attempted to establish a controversy between the two British rock groups. Since Ringo was present during the interview, he found it difficult to trust *Melody Maker*'s staff in future interviews. Equally indignant, John Lennon in a fit of rage informed two *Melody Maker* reporters that they were stretching the truth. John Lennon privately complained to close friends that *Melody Maker*'s staffers were the most arrogant and ill-informed people he had encountered.

Another reason for John's unhappiness with *Melody Maker* was a story which stated that Lennon believed that the Beatles would be finished as a money-making group by 1967. Not only did John refute this statement, but he resented the continual attempts to elicit controversial quotations. *Melody Maker* referred to John as the

Beatle who was going to make all the money before the group disbanded. This remark suggested that John's songwriting was strictly a money-making device. *Melody Maker* not only refused to recognize Lennon's considerable songwriting skills, but they also ridiculed John for mercenary financial attitudes.

Unwittingly, *Melody Maker* shaped many of John Lennon's views. Growing up in Liverpool John had witnessed oppressive social and economic forces, and these conditions strengthened his working-class views. In *Melody Maker*'s staff, John once remarked to Bob Wooler, there was an attempt to "play at culture" and to describe the average worker's reaction to English music. This approach failed miserably because *Melody Maker* had little understanding of England's working class. Its reporters were "processed middle-class college graduates" who displayed little sensitivity to blue-collar problems. In later years, John continued his reflections on media deception when he stated: "The workers are dreaming someone else's dream." This idea was developed in Lennon's song "Working Class Hero." In this song there is an indication that the media obscures reality from the working class. In fact, the media presents a view of success which is impossible for the average worker to achieve, but he or she is kept so busy striving for this goal that revolutionary attitudes never form. John chides the worker for developing a pseudo-sophistication which blind them to the world's problems. Due to his unhappiness with *Melody Maker*'s reporting, John frequently complained to Paul McCartney about the "vindictive nature" of the British music newspapers, and John predicted that the press could adversely influence the Beatles' future success.

As a result of *Melody Maker*'s reporting, McCartney was not as cooperative as he had been in the past. A good example of his new attitude occurred when Paul stated that he and John did not begin writing songs until 1961. It was common knowledge that Lennon and McCartney had written together for a number of years, but Paul was intent upon letting *Melody Maker* know that he was unhappy with their coverage of the Beatles. In particular, McCartney was furious over *Melody Maker*'s report that Paul came out on stage at the Cavern Club with newspapers shredded under his pants and that John often wore plastic bags on his shoes. *Melody Maker* reporters also liked to point out that the Beatles often came on stage with no shirts and only jackets and ties. These stories were examples of the good-time attitudes of the Beatles, but Paul

McCartney was incensed over these obvious attempts to ridicule the group.

But Paul McCartney was not the only Beatle to complain about *Melody Maker* coverage. When George Harrison remarked that the Beatles were very successful and making excellent money prior to Brian Epstein's management, the story was printed as fact. Harrison's attempt at irony was twisted into a news item which attempted to bring about a personal confrontation between Epstein and Harrison. The August 3, 1963, issue of *Melody Maker* refused to report that George smiled and rolled his eyes when he made the comment. "Before Brian Epstein saw us working, we were earning quite a lot of money really," George jested. In the same issue, Ringo interpreted the Beatles economic status differently: "Financially, things are much different for me now. Now we eat with the nobs." Brian Epstein was furious with this contradictory type of reporting, and he called *Melody Maker* to voice his unhappiness.

Yet Brian had little to complain about since the Beatles were on the verge of an enormously successful year. On July 22, 1963, the Chicago-based Vee Jay record firm released the Beatles first American album, *Introducing The Beatles.* In August, the first issue of *The Beatles Monthly,* a 28-page book of news, photos and little-known facts was mailed to the growing legion of fans. On August 10, 1963, *Melody Maker* reported that the Beatles LP "Please Please Me" was number 1 and two 45 record releases, "Twist and Shout" and "From Me to You" were number 4 and 24 respectively on the *Melody Maker* Top 50. The following month "She Loves You" reached number 1 and the *MM* Top 50 and *Please Please Me* remained the U.K.'s top album.

As a result of the Beatles firmly established popularity, *Melody Maker* compared the Liverpool group to English rock star Cliff Richard. The September 7, 1963 issue of *Melody Maker* featured an innocuous article: "Cliff versus the Beatles." It was a juvenile comparison of the two musical careers and styles which had little in common. The zealous fan complaints about *Melody Maker*'s journalism may have prompted the magazine to select the Beatles as the U.K.s top vocal group for 1963. *MM* also announced that "From Me to You" was England's most popular record. This type of reporting was typical of English journalists who criticized for no other reason than to generate titillating tales. *Melody Maker* believed that controversy would sell its product.

An interesting aspect of *Melody Maker*'s coverage of the English rock music in 1963 was the continual reference to the

The Beatles: A Foreign Movie Ad

Beatles' money. In October, for example, *Melody Maker* reported that the Beatles were earning 250 to 350 pounds a week. This was a subtle, yet pervasive, attempt to suggest that the Beatles were in the rock music business for monetary reasons only.

In November, 1963, Beatlemania reached its peak in England. The term itself was coined just after the Beatles' appearance on November 4th in the Royal Variety Show at the Prince of Wales theater. After this critically acclaimed performance before the Queen Mother, Princess Margaret, and Lord Snowden, the *London Daily Mirror* used the term "Beatlemania" in a headline, and soon all of England was abuzz. The *Daily Mirror's* circulation increased by 30% due to Beatle coverage, and the *London Daily Express* ran five front-page stories on the Beatles. The *London Daily Mail* entered the journalistic battle for supremacy on the Beatle front not by using the group's name, but by printing a cartoon logo depicting the group to announce its coverage. Even the staid *London Times* devoted a Sunday issue to an examination of the Beatles' impact upon English culture.

Not only were the Beatles regularly selling out concerts, but they often sold out a theater within an hour without prior advertising. A good example of this phenomena occurred on November 1, 1963 when the Beatles appeared at the Odeon in Cheltenham. The concert was not publicly announced, but it sold out within an hour. Yet the Beatles continued to travel to and from their concert appearances in a bus that driver Ron King described as "average." King often stopped at small greasy-spoon restaurants in the English countryside, and John Lennon good naturedly remarked that Cliff Richard didn't have to eat in such "fryups." George Harrison was busy taking home movies of the fourth British tour and Paul McCartney concentrated upon writing new songs. The Beatles were still infatuated with their first record. As a result they continually played "Love Me Do" on the bus and would then follow it with the Contours inspired version of "Do You Love Me."

In 1963 there was still a party atmosphere around the Beatles. Neil Aspinall and Mal Evans alternated in lugging the Beatles' equipment around England in a VW van, and John Lennon was often seen helping with the sound gear. When the Beatles' entourage stopped at a restaurant or gas station, John proudly stated that he was the Beatles' equipment manager. It was a bit of fun that would soon be impossible for the Beatles, because success was changing the Liverpool group's environment.

When the English newspapers reported that "She Loves You" had sold 750,000 copies and that Beatles record sales were two million, there was no longer any personal freedom for the group. Suddenly young girls were knocking at their homes, and the concert tours necessitated tight security. The Beatles topped the *Melody Maker* charts in September, 1963, and there was a noticable change in the newspaper's attitude. It appears that the *London Daily Mirror,* which was part of the publishing conglomerate which owned *Melody Maker*, pressured the rock newspaper into taking a more positive view of the Beatles. As the Fleet Street newspaper discovered the Beatles, their lives became a part of daily newspaper coverage. In many respects the Beatles became psychological relief from the turmoil of a serious political scandal. It was the good fortune of the Beatles when a Conservative Party Cabinet Minister, John Profumo, was entertained by a 22-year-old call girl Christine Keeler. The ensuing scandal dominated the London newspapers while the Conservative Party attempted to explain away the sordid affair as insignificant. So the British desperately needed some good news. The Beatles were proclaimed as a positive side of the nation, and the English were infatuated with the youth revolution. Although Christine Keeler and her friend Mandy Rice-Davies provided the British public with titillating news, this coverage soon grew old. As a result London newspapers concentrated upon youth, sex, and social conflict in the United Kingdom. The publicity barrage surrounding the Beatles created new interest in their music, and this led to "She Loves You" reentering the music charts and rising to number 1 on the *Melody Maker* Top 50. It was the first time in British rock history that a song rose for the second time to number one on the charts.

Despite their negative coverage of the Beatles, the *Melody Maker* poll to select the most popular musical group for 1963 resulted in the Beatles topping the list. It was not accidental that *Melody Maker*'s award coincided with the *Daily Mirror*'s in-depth story on the "Four Frenzied Little Lord Fauntleroys" who were earning $12,500 a week. Rather than concentrating upon the Beatles music or their impact upon English culture, the *Daily Mirror* emphasized the gyrations of pre-pubescent 14 year old Lolitas who dogged the Beatles' footsteps.

What much of the English press failed to recognize was that a demographic revolution had occurred in the United Kingdom in the early 1960s. When the Conservative Party government of Harold MacMillan abolished compulsory military service, London was suddenly inundated with thousands of young men who no longer had to plan their lives around military conscription. The English economy also provided comfortable salaried positions for educated as well as working-class youths. A sputtering technology flourished by 1963 and suddenly stereos, radios, and televisions flooded the department stories on Oxford Street. HMV, the largest London record store, reported that 30% of young people's paychecks were spent on entertainment-related goods.

Another important controversy spawned by the Beatles' success was the debate over the roles of the mods and rockers in English society. As swinging London emerged in the 1960s, the mods were distinguished by a carefully groomed look. Mods often attended art college and spent every penny of their paycheck on clothing. The pin-collar shirt, high buttoned jackets and pointed Spanish boots typified the Mods' dress. The rockers were essentially blue-collar youths who traced their lineage to the teddy boys of the 1950s. The rockers were visually frightening as they sported grotesque tatoos and leather jackets. There was a neo-Gene Vincent look to the rockers, and they loved to show up at dances attended by the Mods to pick fist fights. The Beatles were unique, because they dressed like Mods while acting like rockers. The

Liverpool group was a hybrid that both mods and rockers identified with in the 1960s. Although the Beatles had a style which was arty, once they began playing their music a raw rock and roll energy ensued. By appealing to all elements in English society the Beatles were able to merchandise their music in a large marketplace.

It was the expansion of the Beatles record market and the continual demand for interviews, product information and press releases which made it difficult for Brian Epstein to remain in Liverpool. For some time Brian had considered locating his burgeoning musical empire in London. When he asked Bob Wooler if he would consider accompanying the Beatles organization, Bob declined. Despite the fact that many key people were unwilling to relocate in London, Brian announced that it was time to merchandise his product in England's financial center.

Just prior to embarking on a November, 1963 English tour, Brian Epstein moved the Beatles organization to London. There was a symbolism to the Beatles relocation in London. As Bob Wooler recalled: "It meant that the boys were a million-pound property." Suddenly at London clubs like the Wips and the Ad Lib, a rock music aristocracy began to congregate to drink, talk and listen to the new music. Ray Coleman remarked that the Beatles never seemed to have any money. This was one indication that things were not going well financially for the Beatles. Coleman did not mention that Brian Epstein was spending the Beatles' earnings to promote their records. There were already inquiries about a possible tour for the Beatles from American promoters. As a result of this interest, Brian spent an inordinate amount of money publicizing the Beatles records.

The notion that Brian Epstein was not a competent financial manager began to circulate around London in late 1963 as a result of cash flow problems. The problem with the Beatles' management was that Brian had signed a series of contracts for concert bookings which were not very lucrative. These contracts were signed before Beatlemania emerged, and the concert fees were no more than 300 pounds a night. Since he was a gentleman, in addition to a businessman, Brian honored the old contracts. In an attempt to reorganize the Beatles finances, Brian hired the accounting firm of Bryce, Hanmer and Isherwood. For the moment the Beatles financial problems were pushed into the background. In time the Beatles would have to face the possibility of bankruptcy, but in 1963 the Beatles were happy that Brian incorporated their assets and deposited their money in a Bahama Island bank. On the surface this

The Beatles: Mid-1960s

appeared to be a smart business move because it diverted large sums of the Beatles' money away from British tax authorities. *Melody Maker* failed to report these cataclysmic changes in Beatle management. What is even more astonishing is that the Beatles began squabbling publicly among themselves over money.

As the Beatles' financial woes became public, two events took place which placed these problems in the background. The first was the blooming of Beatlemania in November, 1963; the press was too busy covering the Beatles' music to notice the discontent over alleged monetary difficulties. The second development was the rise of American interest in the Beatles. As negotiations proceeded to bring the Beatles to New York, the four Liverpool lads temporarily settled their differences and concentrated upon their upcoming appearance on the Ed Sullivan TV Show and their first American tour.

The intensity suddenly surrounding the early part of the Beatles career was reflected in a statement by their press agent Tony Barrows: "I have never known anything like this before—it would be a difficult job arranging for the Beatles to get in and out of the places they're playing." Like any pop cultural phenomena,

Beatlemania depended upon a special feeling. British television, not noted for its fondness for rock music, helped to provide an uninterrupted barrage of Beatles' music. Since their first appearance on the "Sunday Night at the Palladium" on Britain's independent ATV network, there was a special relationship between the Beatles and television audiences. In addition to appearing on "Juke Box Jury" and "Thank Your Lucky Stars," the Beatles also had a limited series on BBC entitled "Pop Goes the Beatles." By Christmas, 1963 the Beatles were ready to invade America.

As the final details were worked out for the American tour, there was a noticeable change in *Melody Maker*'s attitude. They were no longer as critical of the Beatles. One of the main reasons for the new attitude of the British press was due to Brian Epstein orchestrating Beatle press conferences so that the wit and comic genius of the group dominated the question and answer sessions. "We were funny because the whole atmosphere of those press conferences gave us just the right mock-serious setting," John Lennon remarked. Paul McCartney recalls that the non-serious nature of the questions led to a proliferation of humorous answers. Unwittingly, these remarks helped to establish the Beatles as the first rock music group with serious intellectual qualities.

The classic Beatle one-liners have been preserved on a number of albums, and they attest to one of the main reasons for Beatlemania. When Ringo was asked why he wore so many rings on his fingers, he replied, "Because I couldn't get them through me nose." One of John Lennon's favorite remarks when asked who does the best cover versions of Beatle songs, he responded: "The Beatles." These light moments were a means of fighting the pressures of fame and fortune. Professor Richard Poirier, chairperson of the English department at Rutgers University, summed up the intellectual quality of the Beatles in an article, "Learning From the Beatles," which appeared in the Fall, 1967 issue of the *Partisan Review*. The Beatles, Poirier wrote, had "a self-delighting inventiveness that has gradually exceeded the sheer physical capacities of four such brilliant musicians." In his stilted academic prose, Poirier reflected both the intellectual depth and the popular appeal of the Beatles.

The intellectually provocative remarks by the Beatles were the result of their press agent Tony Barrow. When Barrow joined the NEMS organization on May 1, 1963, he was a respected journalist for the *Liverpool Echo* and considered an extraordinarily gifted publicist. In a column he wrote for the *Liverpool Echo,* Barrow used the pen name "DISKER." This allowed him to praise the Beatles as a critic while still working for Brian Epstein. By hiring Barrow, Brian shrewdly placed the Beatles' publicity in the hands of a professional. Epstein also stroked Barrows' ego by asking his advice on a recording contract, and making Barrows believe that he was instrumental in the Beatles' success.

Another aspect of Tony Barrows' career that remains unexplained is his relationship with Paul McCartney. Barrows and McCartney developed close personal ties, and much of Paul's wit during Beatle press conferences was the result of Barrows' training. The lesson that Barrows imparted to McCartney was to charm the critics with the intellectual quality of the Beatles music. In essence, Barrows trained McCartney to act as a rock music superstar, and in later years this impressive ability manifested itself in McCartney's solo career with Wings.

The impact of *Melody Maker* upon the Beatles' career was an important aspect of their inauguration into the music business. The trendy, pseudo-intellectual nature of *MM* staffers made the Beatles wary of pretentious newspeople. They learned to handle themselves very well with the press, and this was one of the reasons that the Beatles had such a dramatic impact upon cultural attitudes in England and America. *Melody Maker* initially hoped that the Beatles would go away and their resistance to the British rock revolution helped to reinforce its growth. *Melody Maker* reflects how one rock newspaper reacted to Beatlemania. It is ironic that in the 1980s, *Melody Maker* has now changed its approach so that its staffers praise almost any new act. The extremes of the early 1960s simply give way to a type of *Melody Maker* rock journalism in the late 1960s and early 1970s.

In 1968 *Melody Maker* introduced "progressive" rock music journalism. This type of reporting concentrated upon long album and concert reviews. During the next few years *Melody Maker's* circulation doubled and it surpassed the *New Musical Express* as the most widely read rock newspaper in the United Kingdom. In the February 6, 1971 issue of *Melody Maker* the editor commented: "The scene we report...is now accepted as a great deal more serious and creative than previously...." Despite these altruistic statements, *Melody Maker* reverted to a style of rock journalism in the 1970s which emphasized one-upmanship or hip coverage. Suddenly *Melody Maker* informed U.K. audiences whom the next important musicians were and what songs would be hits. The record buying public was not impressed. In contrast, the *New Musical Express* continues to offer a sociological interpretation of British music, whereas *Melody Maker* views the music as a reflection of consumer tastes. Due to *Melody Maker*'s reactionary attitude, they are unable to provide a balanced view of musical development. Perhaps John Lennon's glasses live on in the 1980s.

THE NEW MUSICAL EXPRESS

The New Musical Express and the Beatles

In 1962 the Beatles emerged as an unknown, but highly popular English club band. No one realized that the gruelling night-long performances at the Kaiserkeller, Top Ten, and Star-Club in Hamburg—as well as the lengthy, innovative sets at the Cavern in Liverpool—were molding the Beatles into a highly original musical group. In addition, the songwriting skills of John Lennon and Paul McCartney came to the fore just as the rock music industry was beginning to recognize the singer-songwriter. As a result, Lennon-McCartney songs entered a highly commercial rock and roll marketplace. Like Elvis Presley, the Beatles offered a new generation of rock music fans a sound to define their times.

The British press initially ignored the Beatles' growing reputation and rock music in general. There was little interest in a musical group which ran counter to English tradition. The historians, sociologists and free-lance writers who analyzed popular culture in the early 1960s paid virtually no attention to rock music. The only reliable source of rock music in the early 1960s was the specialized music newspapers. In order to understand the influence of the British rock newspapers, it is necessary to trace their history and influence.

In 1926 *Melody Maker* published its initial issue and became the first British music newspaper. The focus of *Melody Maker's* journalism for thirty years was on jazz and dance band music. Since *Melody Maker* was not a youth-oriented music newspaper, it was highly critical of the blues, non-traditional jazz, rhythm and blues and rock music. When Elvis Presley's "Hound Dog" hit the British charts, *Melody Maker* suggested that Elvis "hits a new low...." The smooth stylings of Ella Fitzgerald and Frank Sinatra were what pleased *Melody Maker* critics.

The growing interest in music among the general British population led to the publication of the *New Musical Express*. By 1952 *NME* was reviewing records aimed at a younger crowd, and the *New Musical Express* became the first music newspaper to establish an accurate list of British record ratings. As a result *Melody Maker* followed *NME*'s lead and announced that the creation of the *MM* Top 50, a highly accurate reflection of record sales. Soon the two magazines were squabbling over which rating system was most accurate, and this dissension spawned one of the most important innovations in the rock music business—the hyping of record sales. Neither the *Melody Maker* nor the *New Musical Express* ratings were necessarily accurate barometers of record sales. However, the music magazines soon exerted an enormous influence upon consumer buying habits. As a result, Britain's major record labels suddenly bought extensive advertising in *Melody Maker* and the *New Musical Express*. In an attempt to foster favorable coverage the major record companies took the papers' staffers to dinner and generally provided inside information about record releases. The development of new promotional techniques indicated that rock and roll music was developing new merchandising tactics. The use of hype, the first signs of payola, and the selection of chart songs due to personal whims was an important factor in the first period of British rock music from 1958 to 1963. The smart English promoters like Larry Parnes could easily take advantage of the press, and he was often able to provide excellent newspaper coverage for acts which were minimally talented.

The early British music newspaper was very much like a fan magazine. The stories were often juvenile and failed to provide investigative journalistic analysis. However, the *New Musical Express* was able to establish itself as a major force in British journalism because it did provide intelligent coverage of the music scene by the late 1950s. Rather than engaging in vitriolic attacks on the new music like *Melody Maker*, the *New Musical Express* attempted to understand the new current musical trends. The changes in British culture intrigued *NME* reporters, and they spent an inordinate amount of time reflecting on the reasons for phenomena like Cliff Richard and Tommy Steele. The interest in rock music was manifested in the growing popularity of English music newspapers.

When the Beatles' "Love Me Do" appeared on the *NME* charts in 1962, the newspaper's circulation was almost 300,000 copies a week. Because rock music was thought of as a working-class phenomena, the *New Musical Express* spent a great deal of time describing the Beatles as "blue collar musicians." This association created an image helpful to the Beatles' success. But the Beatles' music also prompted the blue and white collar worker in the United Kingdom to take another look at the burgeoning rock music revolution. In 1963 *London Times* critic William Mann reviewed the Beatles' career, and this was the first time that rock music appeared in the *Times* art section.

When the Beatles emerged as a national phenomenon in 1963, the *New Musical Express* was the only music newspaper to understand and appreciate rock and roll. It was difficult for the staunchly conservative English press to take four young men with long hair, unusual clothes and loud music seriously. The *New Musical Express* accorded the Beatles serious consideration because the newspaper firmly believed that their music represented a significant change in British culture. But *NME* also recognized that Tony Sheridan's innovative white blues, Alexis Korner's blues music and the struggling bands and singers in clubs like the 2-Is were important forces in the British music scene. When the Beatles released "Love Me Do" in 1962, there was no doubt in the minds of *NME* reporters that a change in musical direction was imminent.

As a result of this belief the *New Musical Express* covered the development of the Beatles' early years very thoroughly. Their coverage of the Liverpool group was often highly critical, but they were also very fair in analyzing the Beatles' contribution to British culture. In order to understand the rise of Beatlemania in England, it is necessary to focus upon the *New Musical Express'* reporting of the Beatles' early years. Not only did *NME* provide in-depth coverage of the music scene, but they were also able to garner a great deal of inside historical information. As a result the *NME* is one of the best and most reliable sources concerning the Beatles' musical origins.

In January, 1962, however, there were few encouraging signs for the Beatles. The *New Musical Express* reported that Elvis

Presley was the most popular artist on its charts. The top-ranking English acts on the *NME* list were Cliff Richard, Helen Shapiro and The Shadows. This type of musical talent represented a mainstream, pop approach to rock music. Much like American rock music in the early 1960s, British rock and roll was trite, predictable, and lacked the spontaneous energy of the 1950s. Cliff Richard and the Shadows were the British reincarnation of Bobby Vee, Frankie Avalon, and Fabian. While Richard and his band were exceptionally talented musicians and still remain an integral part of the British music scene, nevertheless, the Cliff Richard sound was too mainstream for most rock enthusiasts. The English rock and roll crowd was searching for something new.

A good example of the impending rock revolution was *Mersey Beat*'s 1962 readers poll which selected the Beatles as the newspaper's favorite Liverpool group. The day after the poll's results, the Beatles played at the Cavern with the Collegians. At the same time Bob Wooler announced that the Beatles' popularity was spreading beyond Northern England. On January 17, 1962, the Beatles were on a Cavern show with the Remo Four and Ian and the Zodiacs while Ray McFall, the Cavern's owner, quietly ushered in a group of London promoters to watch the night's entertainment. The new "beat clubs" intrigued the visiting musical entrepreneurs, and they suddenly realized that the Cavern Club was a potentially lucrative musical venue.

Another important influence upon the fledgling British rock sound was the rise of pub music. Pub bands were not numerous in the early 1960s. But there were enough to lay the foundation for the late 1960s and early 1970s when Nick Lowe, Dave Edmunds, Elvis Costello, Graham Parker, and Joe Jackson created another English musical renaissance. The pubs were also a training ground for many of the groups who dominated the British and American charts in the mid-1960s. The Beatles were an example of a band which played many inconspicuous pubs like the Iron Door in Liverpool. It was in these clubs that they crafted their highly commercial musical sound.

In addition to the pubs, the British were heavily influenced by expatriate American rockers like Gene Vincent, Eddie Cochran and Bruce Channel. While these artists varied in their talent and in their approach to rock music, they provided an example of songwriting and musical skills previously unknown to many British bands. Gene Vincent was the favorite of nearly every young UK rock and roller, and soon artists like Rod Stewart were performing acts that were carbon copies of these American rock idols. A good example of this influence occurred when John Lennon tuned in the January and February, 1960 appearances that Eddie Cochran made on the British television program "BOY MEETS GIRL." British recording artist Marty Wilde introduced Eddie who sang Ray Charles', "Hellelujah, I Love Her So," and his own hits "C'mom Everybody" and "Somethin' Else." John Lennon was mesmerized by Cochran's performance. He had never seen this type of live guitar work and Cochran's swaggering stage manner was an impressive show for the English audience. Not only did Lennon come away intrigued by Cochran's showmanship, but Peter Townshend of the Who and Mick Jagger of the Rolling Stones also watched Cochran perform "Twenty Flight Rock." It was ironic that the Beatles, the Who and the Rolling Stones all at one time or another experimented with "Twenty Flight Rock" as a concert song. The diversity of Cochran's music influenced Lennon, Townshend and Jagger, and they were all convinced that the ballad performed by Cochran "Have I Told You Lately That I Love You" was indicative of the breadth necessary for a rock musician. It was the roots of American rock and roll in Cochran's music which had such a dramatic impact upon these young English musicians. Not only did they watch Cochran but Gene Vincent was another excellent example of pioneer American rock music. In addition, a number of obscure British acts like Joe Brown and His Bruvvers played an American brand of rock and roll music.

The trend toward American rock was demonstrated in 1962 when the *New Musical Express* listed Joe Brown and His Bruvvers as the 10th most popular English rock group. Billy Fury was another important influence upon the resurgent English rock and roll market. From 1959 until 1963 Fury's Buddy Holly type vocals were an original sound which contributed greatly to English rock music. Fury's raw performing energy was influenced directly by Cochran's and Vincent's styles. When Eddie Cochran performed J.P. Richardson's "White Lightning" on a British TV show, he was joined by Gene Vincent, and soon young bands all over the U.K. were performing this rockabilly musical classic. Had it not been for Billy Fury's rockabilly sound, the Cochran and Vincent influences might not have been translated into live performances by hundreds of obscure British garage bands. Dave Edmunds and Nick Lowe would soon become major figures in reviving this type of music in the English pubs.

The Beatles: An Interview

The visual impact of Eddie Cochran and Gene Vincent was also important to the fledgling English rock music audience. John Lennon never forgot the black leather clothing and the menacing figure that Gene Vincent projected on stage. Eddie Cochran's aggressive guitar solos also convinced John that it was necessary to exaggerate the music to create a crowd reaction. When Lennon finally met Gene Vincent, a few years later, he was amazed how quiet and introverted Vincent was off stage. Clearly, John Lennon envisioned rock and roll music as a form of expression which fit his own personality. The black leather vest and pants worn by Vincent intrigued Lennon, and he soon took to dressing in this manner. John was not just a Teddy Boy, but an Englishman disguised as a "roots" American rock and roller. Cochran and Vincent's duet on British TV demonstrated the visual impact of rock music during a live performance. There was enough of the artist in John to realize that rock music not only combined an artistic sense but a distinct musical direction. When the Beatles' became an important British rock act, many of their best concert songs were old American rock and roll tunes. Chuck Berry's "Roll Over Beethoven," the Marvellettes' "Please Mr. Postman," and the Shirelles' "Boys" were the Beatles favorite American rock songs during their early concert performances. In concert the Beatles discovered that the Motown sound, the Chess Record artistry of Chuck Berry and the music of the girl groups appealed to British audiences. In addition the Beatles popularized the music of obscure American artists like Arthur Alexander. When Alexander released "Anna (Go to Him)" on Dot Records in September, 1962 it failed to hit the American charts. It became one of the Beatles' strongest concert songs and made Alexander a cult figure among Beatle fans. But the roots of American rock music was only one influence upon the Beatles.

The *New Musical Express* featured a number of stories which demonstrated that the Liverpool Institute was an important factor in the maturation of the Beatles' talent. Both John Lennon and Paul McCartney were products of this school. John was an art student and Paul studied education and literature. It was the creative atmosphere within the Liverpool Institute which influenced Lennon-McCartney compositions. However, the Beatles initially did not view their music as a cultural phenomena. When a *New Musical Express* reporter asked Paul McCartney if it was difficult to write a song, Paul replied: "I suppose writing is the wrong word, really. John and I just hammer out a number on our instruments." What Paul McCartney meant was that the Beatles did not consider songwriting an art. It was simply part of the business, and McCartney casually remarked that they wrote their best songs prior to a concert. Then John and Paul would work out the number on stage before a live audience. This was possible in 1962-1963 before the Beatles became international superstars. At this time the *New Musical Express* was England's only rock newspaper to recognize the Beatles' talent for musical experimentation. Clearly, Lennon and McCartney viewed songwriting as a job, whereas *Melody Maker* chided them for this attitude. In contrast, however, the *New Musical Express* recognized that the Beatles were writing not only their own hit songs but those of other artists. A good example of the pressures placed upon the Beatles to write songs for other people occurred when McCartney stated that "Misery" was written for Helen Shapiro, who was going to Nashville for a recording session. The completion of this song was purely business, McCartney stated, because it would help the Beatles' music break into the U.S. market.

For some time the rumor persisted that American record companies were interested in the Beatles. The *New Musical Express* was the first British rock newspaper to recognize the Beatles' potential commercial appeal in America. In January, 1963, Brian Epstein signed a contract with the Chicago based Vee-Jay Record company to release Beatle material. There were also other contracts signed with European distributors after the Beatles received extensive airplay on Western European radio stations. On February 4, 1963, "Love Me Do" was released in Canada. American rock giant Little Richard was effusive in his praise of the Beatles. "I've never heard that sound from English musicians before," Little Richard remarked. "Honest, if I hadn't seen them with my own eyes I'd have thought they were a colored group from back home."

The first signs of Beatlemania were recognized by the *New Musical Express* in the midst of a February, 1963, English tour. Not only did *NME* report that the Beatles were a strong tour draw, but also that there was an even greater demand for their records. In the middle of this tour the Beatles were brought into London for a twelve-hour recording session, and the *NME* predicted future stardom for the Liverpool group. The result of these sessions was the Beatles' first English LP *Please Please Me*. In addition to the songs on this LP, there were a number of excellent Beatles' tunes not initially included in the album. Among them were "Bad to Me," "I'm in Love," "Hold Me Tight," 'Keep your Hands Off My Baby," and "I'll Keep You Satisfied." On March 27, 1963, the Beatles' first album entered the English charts and by May 8 it was the number 1 LP. *Please Please Me* not only remained in the *New Musical Express* Top Ten for 63 weeks, but it was the LP which remained for the longest time at number 1 of any record on the *NME* album charts.

In fact, just five days after completing their first LP, the Beatles were informed that "Please Please Me" was number 1 on the *NME* 45-record listings. The *Record Retailer, Record Mirror,* and the *BBC* charts reported "Please Please Me" at the number 2 position. The Beatles believed that their record would soon hit the American charts. But the celebration was premature as Jay Livingstone of Capitol Records in America wrote George Martin that "Please Please Me" would not be released in the United States because it lacked commercial appeal. Despite the rebuffs from the American market, the Beatles continued to tour steadily in England in early 1963. They developed huge followings in the United Kingdom, and the sold-out movie houses made local promoters realize there was a potentially lucrative market for rock music concerts.

As the Beatles perfected their craft in small theaters and dingy halls, a number of strange business decisions were made. In late

February, 1963, Northern Songs Limited was founded with the four Beatles, Brian Epstein and Dick James as partners. The fact that James had a larger share of the corporation than Brian, John, or Paul indicates that Epstein and the Beatles were inexperienced in this area. "From Me To You" was the first song published by Northern Songs Limited. It was written during the night of February 28, 1963 as John and Paul rode on their tour bus from York to Shrewsbury, and was based on a letter column "From You to Us," which appeared in the *New Musical Express*. As John Lennon rode on the bus with the *NME* reporters, he was happy that "Please Please Me" was England's number one single. John pointed out that the song was almost the flip side of "Love Me Do." But George Martin thought that the initial recording was too fuzzy. As a result the Beatles decided to release "Please Please Me" at a later date after rerecording it. "We changed our minds only because we were so tired the night we did "Love Me Do," John remarked. When the Beatles rerecorded "Please Please Me," they believed that it was a number one hit. John Lennon was so happy that while eating dinner in a West End restaurant he put on his glasses and signed autographs as Shadows' guitarist Hank Marvin. (From time to time one of John's favorite recreations was to impersonate the Shadows' guitarist.) As the Beatles were celebrating after recording "Please Please Me," a young girl burst into the London restaurant and asked if John was a member of the Tornados. It was a pleasant and frivolous time, and the Beatles were still able to go out publicly without being hounded.

In February and March, 1963 the complex touring and recording schedule made it more difficult for the Beatles to have any free time. In February there were only twelve concert dates but the following month the Beatles performed twenty-three days of concerts. There was also an increased demand for Beatle records. As a result on March 4, 1963 the Beatles recorded their third single, "From Me To You," and a song entitled "Thank You Girl" for the b side. After recording these songs the Beatles took a train to Manchester where, on March 6, they recorded an interview and three songs at the Playhouse Theater for the radio program "Here We Go." Bob Wooler helped to organize a small army of Liverpool fans who rode the bus to Manchester to cheer their hometown idols. In April, Brian Epstein and John Lennon were scheduled to leave for a vacation in the Canary Islands. The day before their departure the *New Musical Express* named the Beatles the most promising newcomers in England. They performed in an April 1, 1963 show at the Empire Pool, Wembley at a special show sponsored by the *NME*. Despite these honors the *New Musical Express* was still capable of criticizing the Beatles. "Admittedly they still need better production, and a good choreographer, tailor and barber," the *NME* editorialized, "but they are the most exciting newcomers in Britain today."

Although the Beatles were successful in early 1963 there were other Liverpool groups who experienced similar stardom. Gerry and the Pacemakers' song "How Do You Do It" not only sold as well as the early Beatle records, but it also appeared in the *NME* top ten. There was a great deal of talk in London about the Merseyside sound, and Brian Epstein was already expanding his burgeoning musical stable by signing new acts. During the Canary Island vacation with Brian, John Lennon wrote "Bad To Me" for Billy J. Kramer as a means of thanking Brian for believing in the Beatles.

In April, 1963, vacations and some relaxation brought the Beatles not only a welcome respite from their touring and recording grind, but they also made a number of new friends. Bruce Welch of the Shadows had a birthday party for Cliff Richard and the Beatles were invited. Sitting in Welch's living room the Shadows and Beatles performed the Chiffon's "He's So Fine" and Ernie Maraseca's "Shout." When the party ended at 4:30 a.m., a blurry eyed John Lennon realized that he had misjudged the Shadow's pristine public image. They were much like the Beatles, working-class musicians who had reached the apex of stardom in the U.K.

As the Beatles and Cliff Richard talked about their music, Cliff noted the early Beatles songs all contained "Me" or "You" in their title, Such songs as "Love Me Do." "Please Please Me," "From Me to You," and "Do you Want to Know a Secret," followed this pattern. Paul McCartney laughed when he was asked about the significance of the "Me" or "You." "We didn't plan it that way. It just happened. These days if we think up a tune very quickly we know we've got a hit." It was simplicity which Paul McCartney stressed in his songwriting.

The success of the Beatles' music prompted a bootleg of the song "Some Other Guy" to surface in May, 1963. This bootleg 45 was issued in a 400 copy pressing in Liverpool. The bootlegger commented that "it was a crime that Parlophone wouldn't release the best Beatle songs." In Paris, France, a bootleg EP with Tony Sheridan was released, but this record quickly vanished from the market.

An indication of the Beatles' impact upon the music business occurred on May 18, 1963 when they performed at the Adelphi Theater in Slough with Roy Orbison and Gerry and the Pacemakers. After this performance Orbison was effusive in his praise of the Beatles, and he indicated that they would have a great deal of chart success in America. "These boys have enough originality to storm our charts... with the same effect as they've already done here," Orbison commented. He emphasized that the Beatles had something new which would make them very successful in the United States. It was Roy Orbison's remarks which convinced Brian Epstein to alter his marketing of the Beatles by emphasizing their British origins. A shrewd judge of musical trends, Orbison believed that the American record buying public was ready for an English invasion.

On May 25, at the City Hall in Sheffield, Roy Orbison was preparing to go on stage when John Lennon threw a bag of jelly beans on Roy's lap. "It's me ninth bag today, Roy," John remarked. Orbison was amazed at the candy, gifts and personal favors British girls were showering on the Beatles, and he pointed out that they would be bigger one day than Elvis Presley. "It's a change to see new stars who are not just watered-down versions of Elvis," Orbison stated. An interesting sidelight to the Orbison tour is that Roy abandoned the private, chauffeured limousine arranged by the promoter and rode the tour bus with the Beatles. Each night he sat and laughed with the boys and told stories about Sam Phillips and the Sun Record label, the antics of recording artists like Johnny Cash, Elvis Presley and Carl Perkins, and the importance of rockabilly music in Orbison's sound. It is not surprising that the Beatles recorded such legendary rockabilly songs as "Honey Don't" and "Everybody's Trying to Be My Baby." One afternoon in Manchester the Beatles and Roy Orbison went to see the movie "55 Days In Peking." It was a typical war movie and Orbison delighted in explaining the subtle nuances of American movies to the young Liverpool lads.

The increasing Beatle popularity outside of England was demonstrated on May 27, 1963, when Vee Jay records in Chicago released the Beatles "From Me To You" and "Thank You Girl." Although it was the second American release on Vee Jay, "From Me To You" was the Beatles' first *Billboard* chart record, peaking at the 116th position.

George Martin reflected on the Beatles' rising popularity, and he informed the *New Musical Express* that the Beatles were developing a unique sound. Martin also praised the Beatles for their willingness to experiment with new musical ideas. "From Me To You," Martin pointed out, was originally intended to have a guitar introduction. But Martin believed that they should sing the opening with a harmonica accompaniment, and this gave the song unusually strong appeal to a wide variety of listeners. Another indication of the Beatles' success was the increase in cover versions of their songs. Duffy Power recorded "I Saw Her Standing There" for the English market, and Johnny Halliday recorded it in France. "Misery" was released in England by Kenny Lynch and in France by Dick Rivers.

On June 14, 1963, the Beatles performed one of their best concerts with Gerry and the Pacemakers at the New Brighton Tower Ballroom. After the concert the jubilant Beatles piled into Paul McCartney's car and drove to the Blue Angel, one of Alan Williams' clubs, to celebrate. At this party, John Lennon stood up and proclaimed the Beatles would be bigger than Elvis in the American market. Everyone laughed and continued to party into the night. Lord Woodbine wandered in and was seen walking on the ledge of the club's roof at 4 in the morning. It was a marvelous time as the Beatles recalled their old Liverpool days. That night George Harrison went home to stay with his parents. He awoke the next morning to hear a furious pounding on the door. As George opened the door, a young girl asked if Paul McCartney lived there. George replied "No," and the girl left.

There was no doubt that the Beatles' lengthy concert tours had brought them a new audience. In July, 1963, the *New Musical Express* half-year poll rated Cliff Richard as the top British rock artist, and the Beatles were in second place. On June 26, 1963 the Beatles' first EP was released and it included a cover version of the Isley Brothers hit "Twist and Shout," as well as "Do You Want To Know a Secret," "There's a Place," and "A Taste of Honey."

In July, 1963 the American rock artist Del Shannon saw his cover version of "From Me To You" reach number 87 on the *Billboard Hot 100*. Although the Beatles' song was released prior to Shannon's, American disc jockeys were not yet playing the original version. But "From Me To You" was number 15 in Australia and number 10 in Norway. What was strange about the British music scene in July, 1963, was that three versions of "Twist and Shout" reached the charts. Brian Poole and the Tremelos had a number 7 hit, the Beatles were in number 13 and the Isley Brothers were in the number 22 position, all with "Twist and Shout." The Beatles'

The Author in Front of the Kaiserkeller, 1983

EP *Twist and Shout* became the first English EP in history to enter the British Top 10. It reached number 8 on July 24, 1963, and only Elvis with his "Follow That Dream" EP had come close in 1962 when Presley's disc reached the number 11 postion.

The popularity of the Liverpool sound brought the Beatles into the ABC-TV studios on June 29, 1963, to record an all Liverpool show for the "Thank Your Lucky Stars" program. When this television show aired on October 9, 1963, it became the highest-rated musical program of the year. By July and August, 1963, the Beatles were finding it difficult to escape the large, admiring crowds. On July 29, 1963, London recording sessions were cancelled due to crowd problems. By September 1, 1963, the Beatles were forced to cancel a concert at Marmouth ABC because the large, uncontrollable crowd was a threat to the Beatles' security. Beatlemania was in full bloom, and no one was sure how to handle it.

On August 9, 1963, the *New Musical Express* provided its first in-depth profile of a Beatle. Paul McCartney was the first member of the group featured in an article written by Alan Smith. As McCartney talked about the Beatles, he pointed out that he and

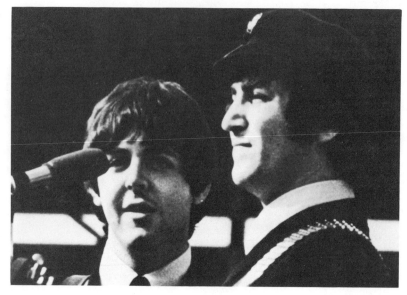

Paul and John, 1964

John had written more than 100 songs before they recorded "Love Me Do." It was this catalog of early songs, McCartney explained, which allowed the Beatles to consistently turn out hit records. A week later Alan Smith featured George Harrison, followed by Ringo Starr and John Lennon. These interviews provided Beatle fans with an inside view of the Liverpool and English music scene, as well as some important Beatle opinions. Brian Epstein had not yet clamped down on Beatle press comments, and the interviews were amazingly candid. George Harrison pointed out that when the Beatles auditioned for the Carroll Levis' Discoveries show in Manchester they were proceeded by Ronald Wycherly who sang "Margot." Wycherly later changed his name to Billy Fury and became one of England's early rock stars. Graham Nash, of the Hollies, was also present during this audition, and Nash told Harrison that he had an idea for a group which employed three or four part harmony. A few years later Harrison saw the Hollies perform, and he remembered Nash's original musical concept. But George Harrison was also very candid about his own career.

On his songwriting efforts George commented that after he heard the Shadows' "Apache," he teamed with John Lennon to write:

"Cry For a Shadow." "The result wasn't a bit like 'Apache,' but we liked it and we used it in the act for a while. Now it's on our Polydor EP," George concluded. Another interesting aspect of Harrison's interview was his effusive praise for Bob Wooler. Not only did he acknowledge Wooler's in-depth musical skills, but he thanked Wooler for his astute advice.

Of these early interviews, John Lennon's was the most revealing. It was a combination of Bill Haley, Chuck Berry, Lonnie Donegan, and Elvis Presley music which formed John's songwriting directions. "It was Elvis who got me hooked on beat music," John remembered. "When I heard 'Heartbreak Hotel' I thought this is it, and I started trying to grow sideboards and all that gear."

During his years in Liverpool John often did Johnny Ray impersonations while singing Carl Perkins "Blue Suede Shoes." Lennon also confessed that art college was no longer significant due to rock and roll music, and he missed his first exam while in Scotland backing Johnny Gentle. During his early years with the Beatles, John spent an inordinate amount of time writing a play entitled *Pilchard*. It was a drama which followed Jesus as he returned to live in the London slums in the 1960s. *Pilchard* was an example of John Lennon's writing talent, but no one realized that it was the beginning of a serious literary career.

The Beatles were no longer able to effectively conduct their business in Liverpool, and in early October, 1963 they moved to London. On October 10, 1963 the Beatles new London office announced that Lennon was married, and the NEMs Enterprises office indicated that there would be a new direction in the Beatles career. The following month Beatlemania officially became a part of English history. Had it not been for the *New Musical Express* the impact of the Beatles' early music upon English culture would not have been as dramatic.

Appendix I
Early Beatle Performances
1956-1963

May 24, 1956: Quarrymen's First Performance from the back of a truck at an open air party in Roseberry Street, Liverpool.

June 15, 1956: The Quarrymen perform at a garden party across from St. Peter's Paris Church in Woolton. At the party, Ivan Vaughn introduces John Lennon to Paul McCartney. Colin Hanton on drums, Pete Shotton on Washboard, Eric Griffith on guitar, Ivan Vaughn on guitar, and Gary Vaughn on guitar make up the the Quarrymen.

January, 1957: George Harrison is introduced to the Quarrymen at the Morgue Club, Old Roan, Liverpool. Harrison plays two songs "Guitar Boogie Shuffle" and "Raunchy" with the Quarrymen.

August 29, 1958: The Quarrymen play at the opening of the Casbah Club in the basement of Mona Best's home at 8 Hayman's Green, West Derby, Liverpool 12. Ken Brown is on drums during this performance and the Quarrymen perform Little Richard's "Long Tall Sally and "Three Cool Cats," a Leiber-Stollersong.

October, 1958: Appearance at the Rainbow Club.

November, 1958: Performance as the Nurk Twins, Bending, Berkshire.

June, 1959: Johnny and the Moondogs audition for the Carroll Levis' Discovery Show in Manchester.

July, 1959: Performance at the Casbah Club.

May 5, 1960: The Quarrymen audition for the position of backup band for singer Billy Fury at the Wyvern Social Club on Seel Street, Liverpool.

Mid-May 1959: Johnny Gentle and the Silver Beatles tour Banff, Stirling, Nairn Inverness and other parts of Scotland. Tommy Moore, a fork-lift driver from Garston is hired as the drummer replacing Johnny "Hutch" Hutchinson on drums.

May, 1960: Neston Institute, Merseyside, two nights.

May 25, 1960: Rory Storm and the Hurricanes introduce rock and roll at the Cavern Club, Liverpool.

June 6, 1960: The Silver Beatles and Gerry and the Pacemakers perform at the Grosvenor Ballroom, Wallasey.

June, 1960: Appearances at the New Cabaret Artists Club, Liverpool.

July, 1960: Jacaranda, Liverpool.

August 16, 1960: Pete Best becomes the Beatles new drummer and Stu Sutcliffe convices Paul McCartney and John Lennon to use the name Beatles.

August 18, 1960: The Beatles open at Bruno Koschmider's Indra Club and the Beatles move to the Kaiserkeller in October, 1960.

October 17, 1960: Kaiserkeller Club performances until mid-December, the Beatles probably closed at the Kaiserkeller on December 17, 1960.

December 19, 1960: Performance at the Top Ten Club, Hamburg.

December 24, 1960: The Beatles perform at the Grosvenor Ballroom, Wallasey.

December 27, 1960: The Beatles perform a "Welcome Back from Germany" concert in Litherland Town Hall, Hatton Hill Road, Litherland, near Crosby. It was Bob Wooler's idea to bill the Beatles as "direct from Germany."

January 6-20, 1961: The Beatles perform at the Star Club in Hamburg.

January 25, 1961: The Beatles perform at Hambleton Hall, Liverpool.

February 24, 1961: The Beatles perform at the Grosvenor Ballroom, Wallasey.

March 16, 1961: Iron Door Club, Temple St., Liverpool.

March 21, 1961: The Beatles perform for the first time at the Cavern Club.

April-May 1961: A two-month engagement at the Top Ten Club, Hamburg.

June 1961: The Beatles return to Liverpool but Stu Sutcliffe remains in Germany to enroll at the Hamburg Academy of Art.

July 1961: The Beatles perform with Gerry and the Pacemakers as one group, the Beatmakers, at Litherland Town Hall.

July 6, 1961: The first issue of *Mersey Beat* appears with an article by John Lennon on the history of the Beatles.

July 7, 1961: Iron Door Club, Temple St., Liverpool.

July 14, 1961: A performance at the Cavern Club. This is a welcome home concert with Johnny Sandon and the Searchers.

July 21, 1961: Lunchtime performance at the Cavern Club.

July 25, 1961: Evening performance at the Cavern Club with the Bluegenes, Gerry and the Pacemakers, the Remo Four and the Four Jays.

July 26, 1961: An evening performance at the Cavern Club with the same lineup as the previous night.

August 5, 1961: An evening session at the Cavern Club with the Panama Jazzmen, Kenny Ball's Jazzmen, Mike Cotton's Jazzmen and the Remo Four.

August 31, 1961: The first Beatles fan club is formed in Liverpool by Bernard Boyle, Jennifer Dawes and Maureen O'Shea.

September 1, 1961: Lunchtime session at the Cavern Club with Karl Terry and the Cruisers and an evening session with Dizzy Burton's Jazzband.

September 5, 1961: An evening session at the Cavern Club with the Bluegenes, the Remo Four and Gerry and the Pacemakers.

September 6, 1961: A lunchtime session at the Cavern Club with Gerry and the Pacemakers.

September 6, 1961: An evening session at the Cavern Club with Ian and the Zodiacs, Johnny Sandon and the Searchers.

September 7, 1961: An evening session solo at the Cavern Club.

September 13, 1961: An evening session at the Cavern Club with the Remo Four.

September 15, 1961: A lunchtime session at the Cavern Club.

September 19, 1961: A lunchtime session at the Cavern Club.

September 20, 1961: An evening session at the Cavern Club with Ian and the Zodiacs, and Karl Terry and the Cruisers.

September 21, 1961: A lunchtime session at the Cavern Club.

September, 1961: Four separate performances at Litherland Hall.

October, 1961: John Lennon, Paul McCartney and Jurgen Vollmer vacation in Paris and the Beatle haircut is allegedly born.

October 18, 1961: An evening session at the Cavern Club with the Four Jays and Ian and the Zodiacs.

October 28, 1961: Raymond Jones attempts to purchase "My

Bonnie" from Brian Epstein at NEMS.

November 9, 1961: Brian Epstein goes to a lunchtime performance by the Beatles at the Cavern Club.

November 10, 1961: "Operation Big Beat" takes place at the Tower Ballroom in New Brighton. The Beatles, Gerry and the Pacemakers, Rory Storm and the Hurricanes, the Remo Four, and Kingsize Taylor and the Dominoes perform. The Beatles also play an 8:30 concert at the Village Hall in Knotty Ash. They sandwich this between the 6:30 and 10:30 concerts.

November 16, 1961: A concert at Litherland Hall.

November 18, 1961: A concert at the Cavern Club with the White Eagles Jazz Band.

November 22, 1961: An evening session at the Cavern with Kingsize Taylor and the Dominoes and the Undertakers.   ,

November 23, 1961: A concert at Litherland Hall.

November 29, 1961: An evening session at the Cavern with Johnny Sandon and the Searchers and Ian and the Zodiacs.

December 1, 1961: A concert at the Tower Ballroom, New Brighton with Rory Storm and the Hurricanes, Dale Roberts and the Jaywalkers, Kingsize Taylor and the Dominoes, Derry and the Seniors and Steve Day and the Drifters. The concert lasted from 7:30 pm to 1:00 am.

December 2, 1961: An evening session at the Cavern Club with the Zenith 6.

December 6, 1961: An evening session at the Cavern Club with the Remo Four and the Strangers.

December 8, 1961: The Davy Jones Show at the Tower Ballroom, New Brighton. A Sam Leach production featuring Rory Storm and the Hurricanes, Gerry and the Pacemakers, the Remo Four and the TTs. The show started at 7:30 and ended at 2:00 am. Admission was 8.6. Alan Ross was the compere.

December 12, 1961: The Casbah Club, West Derby

December 13, 1961: An evening session at the Cavern Club with the Ravens and the Four Jays. A contract signed at the Casbah after the concert with Brian Epstein.

December 15, 1961: A performance at the Tower Ballroom, New Brighton. Rory Storm and the Hurricanes, Derry and the Seniors and Dale Roberts and the Jaywalkers are on the bill. The show starts at 7:30 and ends at 1:00 am.

December 23, 1961: A performance at the Cavern Club in which Mike Smith of Decca Records is in the audience at Brian Epstein's invitation. This helps to arrange an audition with Decca Records.

December 24, 1961: Stu Sutcliffe and Astrid Kirchheer arrive in Liverpool.

December 27, 1961: An evening session at the Cavern Club with Gerry and the Pacemakers and Kingsize Taylor and the Dominoes.

December 29, 1961: An evening session at the Cavern Club with the Yorkshire Jazzband.

December 31, 1961: The Beatles travel to London for their Decca audition and spend the night at the Royal Hotel in Woburn Place, London, WC1. Bed and breakfast for one night is one pound 371/2 pence each.

January 1, 1962: The Beatles spend a part of New Year's day auditioning in the Decca Studios in West Hampstead, London.

January 4, 1962: *Mersey Beat's* readers polls selects the Beatles as their favorite Liverpool group.

January 6, 1962: An evening session at the Cavern Club with the Collegians.

January 10, 1962: An evening performance at the Cavern Club with Gerry and the Pacemakers.

January 12, 1962: An evening session at the Cavern with the Mike Cotton Jazzmen.

January 17, 1962: An evening session at the Cavern with the Remo Four and Ian and the Zodiacs.

January 24, 1962: The Beatles sign a new management contract with Brian Epstein's NEMS Enterprises.

February 3, 1962: An evening session at the Cavern with Gerry and the Pacemakers and the Saints Jazzband.

February 9, 1962: An evening performance at the Cavern with Gerry and the Pacemakers.

February 14, 1962: An evening at the Cavern Club with Johnny Sandon and the Searchers and the Strangers.

February 15, 1962: A Tower Ballroom New Brighton Concert with Terry Lightfoot and His New Orleans Jazzmen.

February 16, 1962: The Cavern solo.

February 21, 1962: Performance at the Cavern with the Remo Four, and Steve Day and the Drifters.

February 24, 1962: An all night session at the Cavern with the Red River Jazzmen, Tom Smith's Jazzmen and Saints Jazzband.

February 28, 1962: An evening session at the Cavern with Gerry and the Pacemakers and Johnny Sandon and the Searchers.

March 2, 1962: An evening session at the Cavern Club.

March 3, 1962: An evening session at the Cavern with Jim McHarg's Jazzband.

March, 1962: A number of performances at clubs in Southport, Chester and Gloucester.

March 23, 1962: An evening session at the Cavern with Gerry and the Pacemakers.

March 24, 1962: Afternoon Performance at the Jazz Club in Heswell, in the Wirral.

March 24, 1962: An evening performance at the Women's Institute in Branston with the Pasadena Jazzmen. The show lasts from 7:30 until 11:15 pm.

March 28, 1962: An evening performance at the Cavern with Gerry and the Pacemakers and the Remo Four.

March 29, 1962: Performance a the Odd Spot with the Mersey Beats.

March 30, 1962: An evening session at the Cavern with the Dallas Jazzband.

April 2, 1962: A performance at the Pavilion Club with the Royal Show Band.

April 4, 1962: An evening session at the Cavern with the Dominoes and the Four Jays.

April 5, 1962: A fan club night at the Cavern with the Four Jays. This is prior to departing for Hamburg for a seven week engagement at the Star Club.

April 13 through June 4, 1962: An engagement at the Star Club, Hamburg.

April, 1962: Brian Epstein meets music publisher Syd Coleman and plays the Decca audition tape for him. Coleman is responsive to the tape and introduces Brian to George Martin who promises a Parlophone audition.

May 9, 1962: Brian Epstein sends a telegram to *Mersey Beat* announcing that the Beatles have signed with Palophone. This turns out not to be true.

June 4, 1962: The Beatles return from Hamburg and celebrate their audition for EMI—Parlophone with Brian Epstein at the National Milk Bar, Liverpool.

June 6, 1962: The Beatles audition for Parlophone in EMI's number 3 studio in London and play "Love Me Do," "P.S. I Love You," "Ask Me Why," "Hello Little Girl," "Besame Mucho," and "Your Feet's Too Big" as well as other numbers.

June 9, 1962: A welcome back night at the Cavern with the Red River Jazzmen, Ken Dallas and the Silhouettes and the Four Jays. The concert is from 7 to 12.

June 11, 1962: The Beatles travel to Manchester to perform on a BBC Light Programme. A busload of fans travel for the program entitled: "The Beatles in Concert." The program is broadcast over BBC radio.

June 12, 1962: Performance at the Cavern with Mark Peters and the Cyclones.

June 13, 1962: Performance at the Cavern with the Dennisons.

June 15, 1962: An evening session at the Cavern with the Spidermen.

June 16, 1962: An evening session at the Cavern with Tony Smith's Jazzmen.

June 19, 1962: A performance at the Cavern with the Bluegenes and Ken Dallas and the Silhouettes.

June 20, 1962: A performance at the Cavern with the Sorrals and the Strangers.

June 21, 1962: A concert at the Tower Ballroom, New Brighton with Bruce Channel. Channel's harmonica player Delbert McClinton teaches John Lennon the riffs used in "Love Me Do." Bob Wooler is the compere and the acts include Howie Casey and the Seniors, the Big Three and the Four Jays. The show starts at 7:30 and ends at 1:00 am.

June 22, 1962: Performance at the Cavern Club with the Cyclones.

June 27, 1962: An evening session at the Cavern with the Big Three.

June 28, 1962: Performance at the Majestic Ballroom, in Birkenhead which begins a season of Thursday night concert engagements for the Beatles. (10 mins by train from Liverpool)

June 29, 1962: The Tower Ballroom in New Brighton for a BBC radio show entitled: "Pop Go the Beatles."

July 1, 1962: Performance at the Cavern Club with Gene Vincent. The Sounds Incorporated and the Bluegenes are also on the bill.

July 4, 1962: A performance at the Cavern with the Four Jays and the Spidermen.

July 6, 1962: Riverboat Shuffle with Mr. Acker Bilk and His Paramount Jazz band.

July 8, 1962: The Cavern solo.

July 11, 1962: The Cavern with the Statesmen and the Morockans.

July 15, 1962: The Cavern with the Four Jays, and the Saints.

July 18, 1962: The Cavern with Ken Dallas and the Silhouettes and the Spidermen.

July 21, 1962: Performance at the Tower Ballroom, New Brighton with a return engagement by Bruce Channel and Howie Casey, the Big Three and the Four Jays.

July 22, 1962: The Cavern at night with the Red River Jazzmen.

July 25, 1962: The Cavern with the Dennisons, the Dakotas and Ian and the Zodiacs.

July 26, 1962: Performance at Cambridge Hall, Cambridge with Joe Brown and His Bruvvers.

July 27, 1962: A performance at the Tower Ballroom, New Brighton, with Joe Brown and His Bruvvers.

July 28, 1962: Majestic Ballroom, Birkenhead. The Mersey Beat Ball with the Swinging Bluegenes and Billy Kramer and the Coasters. (a 7:30 to 11:30 concert) Dee Fenton and the Silhouettes and the Red River Jazzmen also appeared.

July, 1962: Monday night concerts at the Plaza Ballroom, St. Helen.

July, 1962: Undated concerts at Rhyl, Crewe, Warrington, Manchester, Southport, Stroud and Doncaster.

August 1, 1962: An evening session at the Cavern with Gerry and the Pacemakers.

August 2, 1962: A concert at the River Park Ballroom, Chester. Pete Best was not present due to illness.

August 5, 1962: An evening session at the Cavern with the Saints Jazzband.

August 8, 1962: An evening session at the Cavern with Shane Fenton and the Fentones and the Big Three. (Shane Fenton was Bernard Jewry and he later changed his performing name to Alvin Stardust.)

August 9, 1962: Grafton Ballroom, Liverpool, Holiday Spectacular with Gerry and the Pacemakers and the Big Three.

August 15, 1962: The Cavern Club, Liverpool.

August 16, 1962: At the Beatles' request, Pete Best is informed that he will be replaced as the group drummer by Ringo Starr of Rory Storm and the Hurricanes.

August 16, 1962: Riverpark Ballroom, Chester (Pete Best is replaced for the night by Johnny "Hutch" Hutchinson of the Big Three (formerly Cass and the Cassanovas).

August 17, 1962: The Cavern and Pete Best plays his last time with the Beatles.

August 18, 1962: The Cavern Club with Ringo Starr on the drums for the first time.

August 23, 1962: John and Cynthia are married at the Mount Pleasant Registry Office in Liverpool. A lunchtime reception is held at Reece's Cafe and the Lennon's move into his Falkner Street flat. *Mersey Beat* runs a story on Pete Best's firing. That night the Beatles play at the Riverpark Ballroom in Chester.

August 27, 1962: Pete Best fans demonstrate and the Beatles play the Cavern.

August 28, 1962: An evening performance at the Cavern with the

Bluegenes, Gerry Levine and the Avengers and the new Beatle lineup with Ringo on the drums.

August 30, 1962: The Riverpark Ballroom, Chester.

September 3, 1962: Queens Hall in Widnes with Billy Kramer and the Coasters and Rory Storm and the Hurricanes.

September 4, 1962: The Beatles travel to London and register at the Chelsea Hotel. In EMI's Studio 2 in St. John their first single, "Love Me Do" is recorded. Session drummer Andy White sits in for Ringo. Dezo Hoffmann takes a series of publicity shots.

September 6, 1962: Performance at the Riverside Ballroom, Chester.

September 8, 1962: Performance at the Majestic Ballroom, Birkenhead.

September 9, 1962: Performance at the Cavern with Billy Kramer and the Coasters and Clinton Ford with Cyril Preston.

September 10, 1962: Queen's Hall in Widnes with Rory Storm and the Hurricanes and Geoff Stacey and the Wanderers.

September 12, 1962: Performance at the Cavern with Freddie and the Dreamers, Group One and the Spidermen.

September 16, 1962: Performance at the Cavern with the Red River Jazz Band, and Gerry and the Pacemakers.

September 17, 1962: Performance at Queen's Hall, Widnes with Billy J. Kramer and the Coasters, and the Vikings.

September 19, 1962: Performance at the Cavern with Peter MacLaine with the Dakotas and the Big Three.

September 22, 1962: Performance at the Majestic Ballroom, Birkenhead.

September 23, 1962: An evening performance at the Cavern with the Saints Jazz Band and the Dominoes.

September 26, 1962: Lunchtime session at the Cavern.

September 26, 1962: Evening session at the Cavern with the Spidermen and the Dominoes.

September 28, 1962: Lunchtime session at the Cavern.

September 30, 1962: Evening session with the Red River Jazzmen and Clay Ellis and the Raiders.

October 1, 1962: The Beatles sign a contract for 5 years with Brian Epstein.

October 3, 1962: The Beatles perform an evening concert at the Cavern with the Echoes, and Billy Kramer and the Dakotas.

October 5, 1962: The Beatles first single is released in England, "Love Me Do," backed with "P.S. I Love You."

October 6, 1962: The Beatles sign copies of their record at Dawson's Music Shop in Widnes.

October 7, 1962: An evening session at the Cavern with the Red River Jazzmen, the Bluegenes and the Zodiacs.

October 8, 1962: A lunchtime performance at the Cavern.

October 10, 1962: Lunchtime and evening performances at the Cavern with the Four Jays and Ken Dallas and the Silhouettes.

October 11, 1962: "Love Me Do" becomes the first Beatle song to make the British charts entering the *Record Retailer* Top 50 at number 49.

October 12, 1962: Tower Ballroom, New Brighton, The Little Richard Show with the Big Three, Pete MacLaine and the Dakotas, Billy Kramer and the Coasters, Rory Storm and the Hurricanes, Lee Curtis and the All Stars, the Mersey Beats, the Undertakers, Gus Travis and the Midnighters, Peppermint Twisters and the Four Jays. The show started at 7:30 and ended at 1:00 am.

October 13, 1962: An evening session with the Zenith Six and Group One at the Cavern. This show is taped by Grenada TV and the song "Some Other Guy" is aired on the "People and Places" program on November 7, 1962 program.

October 15, 1962: The Majestic Ballroom, Birkenhead.

October 17, 1962: Lunchtime and evening performances at the Cavern.

October 19, 1962: Lunchtime concert at the Cavern.

October 19, 1962: B.Bumble and the Stingers play the Cavern and the Beatles watch the show.

October 20, 1962: Royal Lido, Prestatyn.

October 21, 1962: The Cavern with the Swinging Bluegenes, the Red River Jazzmen and the Four Most.

October 22, 1962: Queen's Hall Widnes with Lee Curtis and the Allstars and the Merseybeats. The show started at 7:30 and ended at 1:00 am.

October 24, 1962: "Love Me Do" charts at no. 27 during the week on the *New Musical Express* Top 30.

October 25, 1962: Manchester taping for Grenada TV, the Beatles sing "Love Me Do." The program is broadcast on October 26, 1962 as part of the BBC Light Programme. The show is entitled "People and Places: Teenager's Turn."

October 26, 1962: Lunchtime performance at the Cavern.

October 28, 1962: Empire Theater, Liverpool with Little Richard, Craig Douglas, Jet Harris and the Jetblacks, Kenny Lynch, the Sounds Inc., and the Breakaways.

November 1 to 14, 1962: The Star-Club, Hamburg.

November 17, 1962: Recordings for Grenada TV "People and Places" show.

November 18, 1962: Evening session at the Cavern with the Merseybeats.

November 19, 1962: A lunchtime performance at the Cavern Club followed by an evening show at the Majestic Ballroom, Birkenhead.

November 21, 1962: Lunchtime session at the Cavern Club.

November 22, 1962: Performance at the Majestic Ballroom, Birkenhead with the Zodiacs and Johnny Templer and the Hi-Cats.

November 23, 1962: Lunchtime show at the Cavern followed that evening by a performance at the Twelfth Annual Arts Ball at the Tower Ballroom in New Brighton. The Llew Hird Jazz Band, Billy J. Kramer and the Coasters, and the Pipes and Drums of the 1st Battalion Liverpool Scottish Regiment perform.

November 25, 1962: Evening performance at the Cavern Club with the Zenith Six, the Fourmost and the Denisons.

November 26, 1962: "Please Please Me," "Ask Me Why," and "How Do You Do It" recorded at EMI's Number 2 studio in London. The Beatles flub the Mitch Murray song, "How Do You Do It," because they do not like it.

November 27, 1962: The Beatles record an appearance for BBC's Light Programme, "The Talent Spot," at the BBC Paris Studio in Regent Street. It is the first time that the Beatles have recorded at the BBC London studios. Three songs are featured, "Love Me Do," "P.S. I Love You," and "Twist and Shout."

November 28, 1962: An evening performance at the Cavern with the Remo Four and Dee Young and the Pontiacs.

November 29, 1962: Performance at the Majestic Ballroom, Birkenhead.

November 30, 1962: Lunch time performance at the Cavern with Peter MacLaine and the Dakotas.

December 2, 1962: Peterborough with Frank Ifield.

December 4, 1962: The Beatles appear on the Talent Spot which is a BBC program.

December 5, 1962: The Beatles' welcome home concert with the Statesmen, Gerry and the Pacemakers, the Remo Four and Johnny Sandon and the Searchers.

December 7, 1962: The Cavern at a lunchtime concert.

December 9, 1962: An evening performance at the Cavern with the Zenith Six, the Swinging Bluegenes and the Four Most.

December 10, 1962: The Beatles perform at the Embassy Theater, Peterborough with Frank Ifield, Kingsize Taylor and Julie Grant.

December 11, 1962: The La Scala Ballroom with Johnny Sandon and the Searchers, the Remo Four and the Merseybeats.

December 12, 1962: The Beatles at the Cavern with George Martin in the audience. That same night George Martin also saw Gerry and the Pacemakers at the Majestic Ballroom in Birkenhead. Robin Hall and Jimmy MacGregor, the Fourmost and the Mersey Beats were on the bill with the Beatles.

December 15, 1962: Majestic Ballroom, Birkenhead.

December 16, 1962: The Cavern with the Red River Jazzmen, Gerry and the Pacemakers and the Fourmost.

December 17, 1962: The Beatles make their television debut on Granada TV's "People and Places" program broadcast from Manchester. They play "Some Other Guy" and receive approximately $87 for the taping.

December 18-December 31, 1982: The Beatles play the Star-Club in Hamburg and an album is taped which is released as a double LP in 1977. On Christmas Day Kingsize Taylor tapes more than 20 of the Beatles songs.

December 20, 1962: "Love Me Do" reaches no 17 in *Record Retailer*. A total of 100,000 copies of the single are allegedly sold.

December 29, 1962: "Love Me Do" reaches no 17 on the *Record Mirror* chart.

December 31, 1962: The Beatles return from Hamburg.

January 1-5, 1963: Beatle tour of Scotland.

January 7, 1963: Performance at the Majestic Ballroom, Birkenhead. Not only is the hall sold out but more than 600 people mill outside.

January 10, 1963: Performance at the Grafton Ballroom, Liverpool.

January 11, 1963: Taping session for ABC-TVs "Thank Your Lucky Stars." The Beatles sing "Please Please Me," and "Ask Me Why." The show is broadcast on January 18. The Beatles record songs for Radio Luxembourg's "The Friday Special" before an invited audience of 120 people at EMI's studio. "Carol," "Lend Me Your Comb," and "Please Please Me" are the songs taped at this time.

January 12, 1963: "Please Please Me" is issued as the Beatles second single.

January 16, 1963: Recordings for BBC Radio.

January 17, 1963: Lunchtime at the Cavern Club.

January 17, 1963: The Majestic Ballroom, Birkenhead.

January 18, 1963: The Beatles appear on Radio Luxembourg's "The Friday Spectacular." This show is a January 11 taping.

January 20, 1963: The Cavern Club, an evening session with the Bluegenes and the Dominoes.

January 22, 1963: With George Martin acting as supervisor the

Liverpool sound expands as Gerry and the Pacemakers record "How Do You Do It" as their initial single. The same day the Beatles appear on BBC's "Pop-In" program. Recordings are completed for a BBC Talent Spot on the Saturday Club.

January 25, 1963: Brian Epstein signs a contract with Vee Jay Records in Chicago to release Beatle material in the United States.

January 30, 1963: The Cavern Club an evening session with the Remo Four and Peter MacLaine with the Dakotas.

January 31, 1963: A lunch performance at the Cavern Club.

January 31, 1963: A show at the Majestic Ballroom Birkenhead. Because of the demand for tickets the Beatles play two separate shows.

February 2, 1963: The Beatles perform on ABC-TV's "Thank Your Lucky Stars" in an appearance arranged by Dick James. This is the Beatles debut on national British television.

February 2, 1963: The beginning of the Helen Shapiro tour throughout Britain. The tour will last through March 3 and includes Helen Shapiro, Danny Williams, Kenny Lynch, the Kestrels, the Honey, Dave Alland and the Red Price Orchestra. The first concert on the evening of February 2 was at the Gaumont, Bradford, and parts of the performance were recorded by ABC-TV for broadcast on "Thank Your Lucky Stars."

February 4, 1963: Capitol Records releases "Love Me Do" in Canada.

February 5, 1963: A concert at the Gaumont Theater, Doncaster.

February 6, 1963: A performance at the Granada Theater, Bradford.

February 7, 1963: A concert at the Odeon Theater, Wakefield.

February 8, 1963: A performance at the ABC Theater, Carlisle. A post-concert party held at the Midlands Hotel is not attended by the Beatles because hotel management will not let them in dressed in their leather jackets. Ringo Starr is the first Beatle ejected for being scruffy and the rest leave the hotel.

February 9, 1963: Performance at the Odeon Theater, Sunderland.

February 10, 1963: A concert at the Embassy Theater, Peterborough.

February 11, 1963: The Beatles travel to London and spend 12 hours in the recording studio turning out their first album: *Please Please Me*. An interesting sidelight is that a number of songs were recorded but not used on the album. Among them were "Bad to Me," "I'm In Love," "Hold Me Tight," "Keep Your Hands Off My Baby," and "I'll Keep You Satisfied."

February 14, 1963: A Valentine day concert at the Locarno Ballroom, Liverpool.

February 16, 1963: "Please Please me" reaches No 1 on the *New Musical Express* Top 30 and is No. 2 on the *Record Retailer, Record Mirror* and BBC charts.

February 18, 1963: Jay Livingstone of Capitol Records in Hollywood informs George Martin that "Please Please Me" is not commercially appealing to American audiences and the record will not be released in the United States.

February 16-22, 1963: The Beatles leave the Helen Shapiro tour to fulfill other contract commitments.

February 23, 1963: The Beatles rejoin the Helen Shapiro tour with a Concert at the Granada Theater in Mansfield. Helen Shapiro is moved to second billing on the tour and the Beatles close the show.

February 24, 1963: A performance at the Coventry Theater, Coventry. Northern Songs Limited is incorporated and "From Me To You" is the first song published by Northern Songs Ltd.

February 26, 1963: : A performance at the Gaumont Theater, Taunton.

February 27, 1963: A concert at the Rialto Theater, York.

February 28, 1963: A concert at the Granada Theater, Shrewbury. John and Paul write "From Me To You" on the bus from York to Shrewbury, and the song is based on a *New Musical Express* column entitled "From You To Us."

March 1, 1963: A performance at the Odeon Theater, Southport.

March 2, 1963: A concert at the City Hall, Sheffield.

March 3, 1963: A concert at Gaumont Hall, Henley.

March 4, 1963: The Beatles travel to London and record their third single, "From Me To You," backed with "Thank You Girl."

March 6, 1963: The Beatles record an interview and three songs, "Misery," "Do You Want to Know a Secret," and "Please Please Me" at the Playhouse Theater, Manchester for the radio show "Here We Go." The show is broadcast on March 12.

March 9, 1963: A concert at the Granada Theater in East Ham begins a new English concert tour with American singers Tommy Roe and Chris Montez. There are also a number of English acts including the Viscounts, Debbie Lee, Tony Marsh and the Terry Young Six.

March 10, 1963: A performance at the Hippodrome Theater, Birmingham.

March 12, 1963: A concert at the Granada Theater, Bedford. The Beatles appear for the fifth time on the radio programme "Here We Go." This will be the last time they appear on this particular program.

March 13, 1963: A concert at the Rialto Theater, York.

March 14, 1963: A performance at the Gaumont Theater, Wolverhampton.

March 15, 1963: A concert at the Colston Hall, Bristol.

March 16, 1963: A performance at the City Hall, Sheffield.

March 17, 1963: A concert at the Embassy Theater, Peterborough.

March 18, 1963: A concert at the ABC Theater, Gloucester.

March 19, 1963: A performance at the ABC Theater, Cambridge.

March 20, 1963: A performance at the Ritz, Romford.

March 21, 1963: A concert at the ABC Theater, Croydon. The Beatles record an interview and three songs to be broadcast on March 28. The songs are "Misery," "Do You Want to Know a Secret," and "Please Please Me."

March 22, 1963: *"Please Please Me"* is released as the Beatles' first LP. That night the Beatles perform at the Gaumont Theater, Doncaster.

March 23, 1963: City Hall, Newcastle.

March 24, 1963: A concert at the Empire Ballroom, Liverpool.

March 26, 1963: A performance at the Granada Theater, Mansfield.

March 27, 1963: A concert at the ABC Theater, Northhampton.

March 28, 1963: A performance at the ABC Theater, Exeter. The Beatles also appear via tape on the radio show "On the Scene."

March 29, 1963: A concert at the Odeon Theater, Lewisham.

March 30, 1963: A performance at the Guild Hall, Mortsmouth.

March 31, 1963: A concert at De Montford Hall, Leicester.

April 1, 1963: The Beatles win the promising newcomers poll for the *New Musical Express* magazine, and they perform in a poll winners' concert at the Empire Pool, Wembley. The concert is held on April 21, 1963.

April 2-11, 1963: John Lennon and Brian Epstein vacation in Spain and John writes "Bad to Me" for Billy J. Kramer.

April 8, 1963: The birth of Julian Lennon: Official Name: John Charles Julian Lennon.

April 11, 1963: Tony Barrow, a Liverpool journalist, goes to work for the Beatles as their press agent.

April 12, 1963: "From Me To You" is the third Beatle single release. The Beatles LP *Please Please Me* hits the English hit parade in the top spot and remains there for 30 weeks. That night the Beatles perform at the Cavern with the Dennisons, Faron's Flamingos and the Roadrunners.

April 16, 1963: The Beatles appear on BBC-TV's the 6.5 show and perform three songs.

April 17, 1963: "From Me To You" reaches no. 6 on the *New Musical Express* Top 30.

April 20, 1963: "From Me To You" enters the *Melody Maker* charts at no. 19.

April 21, 1963: The Beatles perform at the *New Musical Express* poll winners concert at the Empire Pool, Wembley.

April 26, 1963: Billy J. Kramer releases his first single, a Lennon-McCartney tune, "Do You Want to Know a Secret," and it is backed with another Lennon-McCartney song "I'll be on My Way." Duffy Powers version of "I Saw Her Standing There" is released in the U.K.

April 29-May 9, 1963: The Beatles leave England for a 12-day vacation in Tenerife in the Canary Islands.

May 9, 1963: The Beatles perform at the concert "Swinging Sound 62" at the Royal Albert Hall, London. It is a concert broadcast live between 9:10 and 10:15 pm with the Beatles appearing from 10:03 to 10:08. Jane Asher and Paul McCartney meet during this show.

May 11, 1963: A concert at the Imperial Ballroom, Nelson.

May 14, 1963: A concert at the Rank Theater, Sunderland.

May 15, 1963: A concert at the Royalty Theater, Chester. Gerry and the Pacemakers are the opening act.

May 17, 1963: The Beatles pose in Dezo Hoffmann's studio wearing their grey suits. A performance on the BBC-TV program "Pops and Lennie" is broadcast.

May 18, 1963: A concert at the Granada Theater, Slough, is the opening of the Beatles third concert tour through the United Kingdom. The Beatles share top billing with Roy Orbison and Gerry and the Pacemakers. There are other English acts including David Macbeth, Louise Cordet, Erkey Grant, Ian Crawford, the Terry Young Six and Tony Marsh.

May 19, 1963: A concert at the Gaumont Theater, Henley.

May 20, 1963: A concert at the Gaumont, Southhampton.

May 21, 1963: At the Playhouse Theater in Manchester the Beatles record six songs for BBC radio's Saturday Club to be broadcast on May 25, 1963.

May 22, 1963: A performance at the Gaumont Theater, Ipswich.

May 23, 1963: A concert at the Odeon Theater, Nottingham.

May 24, 1963: A performance at the Granada Theater, Walthamstow.

May 25, 1963: A concert at City Hall, Sheffield. A part of the show was recorded for future broadcast on BBC radio's Saturday Club.

May 26, 1963: A concert at the Empire Theater, Liverpool.

May 27, 1963: A performance at the Capitol Theater in Cardiff, Wales. In the US, Vee Jay records releases the 45 single "From Me To You" and "Thank You Girl."

May 28, 1963: A performance at the Gaumont Theater, Worcester.

May 29, 1963: A concert at the Rialto Theater, York.

May 30, 1963: A performance at the Odeon Theater, Manchester.

May 31, 1963: A concert at the Odeon Theater, Southend.

June 1, 1963: A concert at the Granada Theater, Tooting.

June 2, 1963: A concert at the Hippodrome Theater, Brighton.

June 3, 1963: A performance at the Granada Theater, Woolwich.

June 4, 1963: A performance at the Town Hall, Birmingham. The Beatles begin a 15 week series on programs on BBC radio entitled "Pop Go The Beatles." A three record bootleg LP documents this series of performances.

June 5, 1963: A concert at the Odeon Theater, Leeds.

June 7, 1963: A performance at the Odeon Theater, Glasgow.

June 8, 1963: A concert at the City Hall, Newcastle.

June 9, 1963: A performance at the King George Hall in Blackburn ends the Beatles third tour of the United Kingdom.

June 12, 1963: The Beatles perform at the charity concert in aid of the National Society for the Prevention of Cruelty to Children at the Grafton Ballroom, West Derby Road, Liverpool.

June 14, 1963: A concert at the Tower Ballroom, New Brighton with Gerry and the Pacemakers.

June 16, 1963: A concert at the Odeon Theater, Romford with Gerry and the Pacemakers and Billy J. Kramer and the Dakotas.

June 18, 1963: Paul McCartney's birthday party. The Beatles perform at the Winter Gardens in Margate that night.

June 20, 1963: *Mersey Beat* prints an article by Howie Casey on the Beatles' performances in Hamburg, Germany.

June 22, 1963: The Beatles fly by helicopter to Abergavenny to perform at the Town Hall. The helicopter trip is necessary because John Lennon appears on BBC-TV's "Juke Box Jury."

June 23, 1983: The Beatles appear on the BBC Radio Light Programme "Easy Beat."

June 26, 1983: The Beatles EP, 4 songs, entitled *Twist and Shout* is released.

June 28, 1963: A performance at the Queen's Hall, Leeds.

June 29, 1963: The Beatles record a show for ABC-TV's "Thank Your Lucky Stars" as part of the program devoted in its entirety to Liverpool musicians. The show is broadcast on October 9 and repeated on November 13. John's earlier recorded appearance on "Juke Box Jury" is broadcast.

June 30, 1963: A concert at the Regal Theater, Yarmouth.

July 1, 1963: The Beatles go into the studio and record "She Loves You" and "I'll Get You." Dezo Hoffmann photographs the Beatles in a number of settings.

July 3, 1963: The Beatles travel to Manchester to tape a performance on the BBC Light Programme, "The Beat Show." They perform three songs and the show is broadcast July 4.

July 6, 1963: A concert at the Plaza Ballroom, Oldhill. Denny Laine and the Diplomats are included on the bill.

July 7, 1963: A performance at the ABC Theater, Blackpool.

July 8-July 13, 1963: A week of concerts, two shows per evening, at the Winter Gardens Theater in Margate with Billy J. Kramer and the Dakotas.

July 15, 1963: "All My Loving" is recorded for the new LP.

July 16, 1963: BBC Radio's "Pop Go The Beatles" first show in the second series is broadcast. The series consists of ten 30 minute shows weekly.

July 21, 1963: A concert at the Queen's Theater, Blackpool. 4000 fans without tickets show up and this is an early sign of Beatlemania.

July 22, 1963: Vee Jay Records releases the first Beatle LP in America. It is entitled: *Introducing the Beatles.*

July 22-27, 1963: A week of concerts at the Odeon Theater in Weston Super-Mare. Other acts on the bill are Gerry and the Pacemakers and Tommy Quickly.

July 28, 1963: A performance at the ABC Theater, Great Yarmouth.

July 29, 1963: A concert at the Southend Odeon is cancelled and the Beatles go into the studio to record "She Loves You" and "I'll Get You" for a new 45 release. Other songs are recorded for album cuts.

July 30, 1963: The Beatles continue to record.

July 31, 1963: A performance at the Imperial Ballroom, Nelson.

August 1, 1963: The first issue of the Beatles Monthly Book. The Beatles play in Southport.

August 2, 1963: Concert at the Grafton Ballroom, Liverpool with the Undertakers, the Dennisons, Sonny Webb and the Cascades and Chick Graham and the Coasters.

August 3, 1963: The Beatles perform for the 292 time at the Cavern Club in Liverpool. It is also their last performance at the Cavern. The other acts include the Escorts, the Merseybeats, the Roadrunners, Johnny Ringo and the Colts and the Sapphires.

August 4, 1963: The Beatles perform at the Queen's Theater, Blackpool.

August 6, 1963: The Beatles appear at a Twist and Shout Dance in Abbotsfield Park, Urmston, Manchester. Three other acts are on the bill: Brian Poole and the Tremeloes, the Dennisons and Johnny Martin and the Tremors.

August 6-9, 1963: The Beatles perform nightly at the Springfield Ballroom, St. Helier, Jersey.

August 10, 1963: "From Me To You" reaches its highest position on the American *Billboard* charts peaking at no. 116.

August 11, 1963: A performance at the ABC Theater, Blackpool.

August 12-17, 1963: A week of concerts at the Odeon Theater in Llandudno, Wales with Billy J. Kramer and the Dakotas and Tommy Quickly.

August 18, 1963: A performance at the Princess Theater, Torquay.

August 19, 1963: A performance on Granada TV's "Scene at 6:30." The Beatles sing "Twist and Shout," "This Boy," and "I Want to Hold Your Hand."

August 19-24, 1963: A week of appearances at the Gaumont Theater in Bournemouth with Billy J. Kramer and the Dakotas.

August 20, 1963: "Glad All Over" and "I Just Don't Understand," two songs the Beatles did not record are sung in the studio for the show "Pop Goes the Beatles."

August 23, 1963: "She Loves You/I'll Get You" the Beatles fourth single is released. EMI has orders for 500,000 copies of this record.

August 24, 1963: The Beatles appear on ABC-TV's "Thank Your Lucky Stars-Summer Spin."

August 25, 1963: A concert at the Queen's Theater, Blackpool.

August 26-31, 1963: A week of concerts at the Odeon Theater, Southport with Gerry and the Pacemakers and Tommy Quickly.

August 30, 1963: The Fourmost, a Liverpool band managed by Brian Epstein, releases a Lennon-McCartney song, "Hello Little Girl."

September 1, 1963: A performance at the Regal Theater, Yarmouth is cancelled. The Beatles tape a show for ABC-TV's "Big Night Out" in an empty theater.

September 3, 1963: A performance at the Queen's Theater, Blackpool.

September 4, 1963: "She Loves You" hits number 1 on the *New Musical Express* charts. The Beatles perform at the Gaumont Theater in Worcester. This begins a brief tour with Mike Berry and Freddie Starr and the Midnighters.

September 5, 1963: A concert at Gaumont Theater, Taunton.

September 6, 1963: A concert at the Odeon Theater, Luton. Cilla Black is signed to a recording contract by Brian Epstein.

September 7, 1963: ABC broadcasts "Big Night Out" and the Beatles perform live at the Fairfields Theater in Croydon.

September 8, 1963: A concert at the ABC Theater, Blackpool.

September 10, 1963: BBC Radio's "Pop Goes The Beatles" includes Chuck Berry's "Too Much Monkey Business" and Chan Ramero's "The Hippy Hippy Shake."

September 12, 1963: "She Loves You" is number 1 on the *Record Retailer* charts.

September 13, 1963: A concert at the Public Hall, Preston.

September 14, 1963: A performance at Memorial Hall, Nantwich. "She Loves You" reaches number 1 in *Record Mirror* magazine.

September 15, 1963: A concert at the Royal Albert Hall, London.

September 17, 1963: The Beatles perform at the Queen's Theater, Blackpool. An edition of "Pop Goes The Beatles" features Little Richard's "Lucille."

September 19, 1963: The Beatles take a three-week vacation. Paul and Ringo go to Athens, Greece, John and Cynthia go to the George V Hotel in Paris and George travels to Benton, Illinois to visit his sister, Louise.

October, 1963: The Beatles follow Brian Epstein to London.

October 5, 1963: A concert at the Concert Hall in Glasgow begins a brief tour of Scotland.

October 6, 1963: Regal Theater, Kirkcaldy, Scotland.

October 7, 1963: A performance at Caird Hall, Dundee, Scotland.

October 9, 1963: BBC-TV broadcasts "The Mersey Sound" a documentary about the Liverpool musical scene.

October 10, 1963: The British press finally announces that John Lennon is married and the father of a young son.

October 11, 1963: The Beatles receive their first gold record for "She Loves You." That evening they play at the Trentham Gardens, Stroke-on-Trent.

October 12, 1963: A concert in Leicester.

October 13, 1963: A live performance at the London Palladium. The show is part of ATV's "Sunday Night at the London Palladium." The Beatles perform "I Want to Hold Your Hand," "This Boy," "All My Loving," "Money," and "Twist and Shout."

October 14, 1963: The term Beatlemania is used for the first time in the press.

October 15, 1963: A concert at the Floral Pavilion, Southport.

October 18, 1963: A concert at Shrewsbury Music Hall, Shrewsbury.

October 19, 1963: A concert at Buxton, Derbyshire. A recording session for "I Want to Hold Your Hand" and "This Boy" is held. The Beatles also record a special single to be sent as a Christmas present to the fan club members.

October 20, 1963: An ABC-TV crew films in Birmingham for a "Thank Your Lucky Stars" broadcast. The show is broadcast on October 26, 1963.

October 24, 1963: A concert at the Karlaplan Theater, Stockholm, Sweden. This begins a week-long tour of Sweden. The show is taped for Swedish radio.

October 25, 1963: Two shows in Kavlstdt, Sweden. The Beatles win five awards from the British Association of Songwriters, Composers and Authors. The awards are known as the Ivor Novello awards. (No relation to Father Sarducci)

October 26, 1963: Two shows at the Kungliga Tennishallen. Other acts include the Violents, Suzie, Joey Dee and Jerry Williams and Roadwork. Brian Epstein is on BBC-TV's "Juke Box Jury."

October 27, 1963: Two concerts in Goteburg, Sweden.

October 28, 1963: A concert in Boras, Sweden.

October 29, 1963: A concert in Eskilstuna, Sweden.

October 30, 1963: The Beatles tape a segment for Swedish TV's "Drop In" program which will be broadcast on November 3.

November 1, 1963: The Beatles perform at the Odeon Theater in Cheltenham to begin a new tour with the Brook Brothers, Peter Jay and the Jaywalkers, the Kestrels and the Vernon Girls. The EP Beatles No. 1 is released as well as two singles by other artists which feature Lennon-McCartney songs. The songs are Billy J. Kramer and the Dakotas' "I'll Keep You Satisfied," and the Rolling Stones' "I Wanna Be Your Man."

November 2, 1963: A concert at the City Hall, Sheffield.

November 3, 1963: A concert at the Odeon Theater, Leeds.

November 4, 1963: The Royal Family is in the audience as the Beatles perform at the Royal Variety Show at the Prince of Wales Theater in London.

November 5, 1963: The Beatles perform at the Adelphi Theater, Slough.

November 6, 1963: A concert at the Odeon, Leeds.

November 7, 1963: A concert at the Ritz Dublin, Ireland.

November 8, 1963: A performance at the Adelphi Theater, Belfast.

November 9, 1963: A concert in England at the Granada Theater in East Ham.

November 10, 1963: A performance at the Hippodrome Theater, Birmingham. The Beatle Fan Club of Holland is founded by Har

Van Fulpen, who is officially recognized by Brian Epstein and the Beatles as their representative.

November 12, 1963: A concert at the Guild Hall Theater in Portsmouth is cancelled because Paul McCartney has the flu. It is rescheduled for December 3, 1963.

November 13, 1963: The Beatles perform at the ABC Theater in Plymouth. BBC reruns the documentary "The Mersey Beat" due to viewer requests.

November 14, 1963: A performance at the ABC Theater, Exeter.

November 15, 1963: A concert at Colston Hall, Bristol.

November 16, 1963: A performance at the Winter Gardens, Bournemouth. An American film crew shoots this concert for future use in publicity and promotion. On January 3, 1964, the American-based Jack Paar show on NBC-TV broadcast a segment of this tape.

November 17, 1963: A concert at the Coventry Theater in Conventry is photographed by America's *Life* magazine.

November 18, 1963: A performance at the Gaumont Theater, Wolverhampton.

November 20, 1963: "She Loves You" is number 1 on the *NME* charts. The Beatles play at the Ardwick Apollo, Manchester and the Pathe British News records an 8 minute film. This film displays the early signs of Beatlemania as they perform "She Loves You" and "Twist and Shout."

November 21, 1963: A concert at the ABC Theater , Carlisle.

November 22, 1963: A concert at the Globe Theater in Stockton. A new LP, *With the Beatles* is released and includes vocals by all members of the group. It also has a George Harrison song, and the LP has a 250,000 advance order.

November 23, 1963: A concert at the City Hall, Newcastle.

November 24, 1963: A performance at the ABC Theater, Hull.

November 25, 1963: Capitol Records in Canada releases an LP *Beatlemania With The Beatles*. There are orders for 100,000 copies and growing indication of a Beatle movement in Canada.

November 26, 1963: A concert at the ABC Theater, Cambridge.

November 27, 1963: A concert at the Rialto Cinema, York.

November 28, 1963: A performance at the ABC Theater, London. "She Loves You" returns to the No. 1 position on the *Record Retailer* charts, and this is the first time a former no. 1 record returns to the no. 1 position.

November 29, 1963: A concert at the ABC Theater in Huddersfield.

November 30, 1963: A concert at the Empire Theater in Sunderland.

December 1, 1963: A concert at De Montfort Hall, Leicester.

December 2, 1963: A performance at the Grosvenor House, London, for a charity for children.

December 3, 1963: The rescheduled concert at Guild Hall, in Portsmouth.

December 6, 1963: Members of the Beatles fan club receive their novelty record for Christmas.

December 7, 1963: Two performances at the Liverpool Odeon Theater and that afternoon the Beatles fan club hears a special performance at the Liverpool Empire.

December 8, 1963: A concert at the Odeon Theater, Lewisham.

December 9, 1963: A performance at the Odeon Theater, Southend.

December 10, 1963: A performance at the Gaumont Theater, Doncaster. The Beatles' van runs out of gas and they hitchhike to the concert.

December 11, 1963: A concert at the Futurist Theater, Scarborough.

December 12, 1963: A concert at the Odeon Theater, Nottingham.

December 13, 1963: A performance at the Gaumont Theater, Southhampton.

December 14, 1963: A performance at the Wimbledon Palais for the Southern England Fan Club Convention and 3000 fan members turn out.

December 21, 1963: The first preview of the Beatles' Christmas Show is held at the Gaumont Theater, in Bradford. The show includes Rolf Harris, Billy J. Kramer and the Dakotas, the Fourmost, Cilla Black, Tommy Quickly and the Barron Knights.

December 22, 1963: A second preview show is held at the Empire Hall in Liverpool.

December 23, 1963: Radio Luxembourg broadcasts the first program of a weekly series entitled: "It's The Beatles."

December 24, 1963: The Beatles Christmas Show begins at the Finsbury Park Astoria Theater in London. A helicopter stands by to take the Beatles back to Liverpool to spend Christmas with their families.

December 25, 1963: A Special Christmas edition of "Thank Your Lucky Stars" is broadcast with the Beatles, Cilla Black, Billy J. Kramer and the Dakotas, Gerry and the Pacemakers as well as other acts.

December 26, 1963: The Beatles have a two hour radio special on BBC Light Programme.

December 26-31, 1963: The year closes with the Christmas show continuing. In fact, it runs through the night of January 11, 1964.

Appendix II
Bob Wooler's Reminiscences

Re: Cavern Club, Liverpool, etc.

I was Merseysides's first disc jockey. I first got involved with the Mersey Beat scene through a skiffle group which formed largely in the railway office where I worked in 1957. The skiffle group was called the Kingstrums Skiffle group and lasted until the end of 1957, a matter of only six months or so. I was soon to find that the 'life' of a skiffle-type group was short-lived, and that the Kingstrums was typical of so many other Liverpool groups of the time. One such group was called the Quarrymen, who later, with a different line-up, were to become the Beatles.

I first met the Quarrymen at a labour club talent contest in the autumn of 1957. I went to a heat with my group, the Kingstrums. I am sorry to say that my group got nowhere. I do not remember much about the Quarrymen. They did not strike me as being at all outstanding. At the time—over a quarter of a century ago—they were just another group, doing much the same as every other group.

I, of course, was rooting for the Kingstrums—my group from Garston, where I was born. They unfortunately did not get anywhere, and like I have said, they split up at the end of 1957. I also met a group of youngsters called the Mars Bars who later, with some changes, became Gerry and the Pacemakers.

In 1958 I joined the Winter Gardens Ballroom in Garston where there was a teenage dance on a Friday night. This was in the main a disc hop, although a group called the Rockin' Rhythm Coasters used to play at the Winter Gardens now and again. I used to put on the records and do the announcements. These days the dance would be called a discotheque.

The Winter Gardens, which was opposition to Charlie Mac's Hall, Garston, lasted until the end of 1958, when trouble caused the promoters to pull out. Early in 1959, I went as resident Dee Jay/Compere to Holyoake Hall, near Penny Lane. This was a Wally Hill promotion, which I did for him on a Saturday and a Sunday. I also did Thursday evenings at Wavertree Town Hall (now a pub/wine bar scene at the back of which George Harrison lived during the war and the immediate postwar years, in Arnold Grove.) I also did Blair Hall, Walton Road on Wednesday evenings, and for a time Mondays at the David Lewis Ballroom. These were all promotions run by Wally Hill, whom I last heard (about ten years ago) was running a cab in Chester.

I was still a railway clerk at Garston Docks, although it seemed inevitable that I should go full time. When Allan Williams persuaded me to run his Top Ten Club in Soho Street, I seized the chance to go full time. This was at the end of November 1960. The first group to play at the Top Ten in Liverpool was Howie Casey and the Seniors, with Negro singer Derry Willkie, who were also the first group to play Hamburg in the late summer of 1960. When the Top Ten Club burned down after six nights, I was to obtain work with North End promoter Brian Kelly (Litherland Town Hall, Lathom Hall, Aintree Institute, Leigh Co-op Ballroom) during the evenings, whilst I promoted midweek at Hambleton Hall, Huyton, and did the Cavern Club lunchtime sessions. Later in 1961, I was to meet Brian Epstein, who ran Nems Record Store in Whitechapel City Center, and also do promotions for him. All in all, the Beatles played at the cavern club 292 times, their last appearance there being on Saturday, August 3, 1963.

Bob Wooler
Dated: June 15, 1983

Bibliographic Essay

Interviews

The essays in *The Beatles: Untold Tales* are based largely on interviews with people close to the group. In Hamburg, Tony Sheridan, Horst Fascher and Tom Shaka provided in-depth interviews about their lives, the Beatles', and the general Hamburg music scene. The influence of the British Sailors Society was recounted in interviews with Joseph Provenzano, Frau Prill, Frau Jensen and David C. Sams. Corey at the Blockhutte also answered a number of questions and Christian Kluver was my guide through the underside of Hamburg.

In Liverpool Bob Wooler, Joe Flannery and Clive Epstein graciously provided a great deal of information about the Beatles. Jim and Liz Hughes filled in much of the historical material and their Cavern Mecca Beatles Museum was an excellent historical source. Charlie Lennon provided four separate interviews and graciously shared his knowledge of the Liverpool music scene and John Lennon's life. Allan Williams and Willie (Lord) Woodbine provided minor caveats of knowledge.

There are a great many knowledgable people on the Liverpool scene. Among those who helped in this book are Sam Leach, David

Caryl, Dave Smith, Eddie Porter, Patricia Daniels, Alan Graham, George Matty O'Brian, Brian Kelly and Pat Kelly.

The American rock artists who toured England and played with the Beatles were also helpful in this study, Tommy Roe, Bo Diddley, Guitar Mac, Mary Wells, Little Willie Littlefield and Memphis Slim all provided examples of important influences that the Beatles had upon their careers, music in general and the rise of rock and roll as a cultural force. Melody Jean Vincent was particularly insightful upon her dad, Gene Vincent, and she confirmed much of my research with her vast knowledge of English rock music.

Specialized Studies of the Beatles

The interest in the Beatles' music has led to a wide variety of specialized studies on their career. In analyzing their songwriting Malcolm Doney's, *Lennon and McCartney* (London, 1981) was an indispensible source. Nicholas Schaffner, *The Boys From Liverpool: John, Paul, George, Ringo* (New York, 1980) is a study which offers valuable insights into the Beatles' personality and intellectual makeup. John Blake, *All You Needed Was Love: The Beatles After the Beatles* (New York, 1980), confirms many of the conclusions in this book. Billy Shepherd, *The True Story of the Beatles* (New York, 1964) was written by *Record Mirror* editor Peter Jones under the pseudonymn, Billy Shepherd, and it is an engaging book. Derek Taylor's, *As Time Goes By* (London, 1974) and Simon Napier Bell's, *You Don't Have To Say You Love Me* (London, 1982) are witty, intelligent, well-written gossip books on important aspects of the British rock revolution in the 1960s.

The Beatles attempt at corporate dealings can be examined in Peter McCabe and Robert D. Schonfeld, *Apple To the Core* (New York, 1972) and Richard DiLello, *The Longest Cocktail Party; An Insider's View of The Beatles* (New York, 1972).

Hunter Davies' authorized biography, *The Beatles* (New York, 1968) remains an important source. Although receiving little publicity there are three books which reflect very well on the Beatles, see, Julian Fast, *The Beatles: The Real Story* (New York, 1968); Anthony Scaduto, *The Beatles: Yesterday, Today and Tomorrow* (New York, 1968) and John Swenson, *The Beatles: Yesterday and Today* (New York, 1977).

One of the rarest and most revealing sources on the Beatles is a book entitled *Love Me Do* by an American, Michael Braun. This mass market paperback is a history of the Beatles' concerts in England in 1963. Using selected concert sites, Braun details the origins of Beatlemania. This is one of the best books ever published on the Beatles and it deserves a reprint.

Edward E. Davis edited a book, *The Beatles Book* (New York, 1968) which is a collection of 14 insightful essays on the Beatles. This book was very important in analyzing the Beatles' intellectual impact as was Don J. Hibbard and Carol Kaleialoha, *The Role of Rock* (Englewood Cliffs, N.J., 1983). B. Lee Cooper, *Images of American Society in Popular Music: A Guide to Reflective Teaching* (Chicago, 1982) provides an excellent means of testing the intellectual validity of rock music. Steve Chapple and Reebee Garofalo, *Rock N Roll Is Here To Pay* (Chicago, 1977) is a much maligned but very important book in analyzing the business side of the Beatles career.

Dave Marsh's *Before I Get Old: The Story of the Who* (New York, 1983) is an important book which says more about the Beatles than many of their biographers. Equally significant in assessing the influences of the Beatles with other superstar rock groups is Philip Norman, *Symphony For the Devil: The Rolling Stones Story* (New York, 1984) and Britt Hagarty, *The Day The World Turned Blue: A Biography of Gene Vincent* (Vancouver, 1983) reminds us how important "roots" American rock and roll artists were to the Beatles' development.

The two most useful books on the Beatles for this study were Peter Brown, *The Love You Make: An Insider's Story Of The Beatles* (New York, 1983); and Philip Norman, *Shout* (London, 1981). The Brown and Norman books are often disagreed with in this study, but they are model rock music studies. They exhibit clarity, intelligent analysis and a sense of history not found in most rock music books.

The Beatles recording career is an important part of this book and the following were useful: Mark Wallgren, *The Beatles on Record* (New York, 1982); Harry Castleman and Walter J. Podrazik, *All Together Now: The Only Complete Beatles Discography, 1961-1975* (Ann Arbor, 1975); J.P. Russell, *The Beatles On Record* (New York, 1982); Neville Stannard, *The Beatles, The Long and Winding Road: A History of the Beatles on Record* (New York, 1982) and Tim Rice, et al, *The Guinness Book of British Hit Singles* (Fourth Edition, London, 1983). In assembling Beatle concerts the following are important, Jan Van de Bunt, et al., *The Beatles: Concert-ed Efforts* (Holland, 1979); H.V. Fulpen, *The Beatles: An Illustrated Diary*

(London, 1983): and Tom Schultheiss, *The Beatles: A Day In The Life, The Day-By-Day Diary, 1960-1970* (New York, 1981).

An excellent set of sketches on British and American rock pioneers is Stuart Coleman, *They Kept On Rockin: The Giants of Rock N Roll* (London, 1982). George Martin, *All You Need is Ears* (New York, 1979) is an important inside examination of the Beatles' career. Simon Frith's *Sound Effects: Youth, Leisure, and the Politics of Rock N Roll* (New York, 1981) offers a valuable analysis of rock music as a cultural, political and economic phenomena.

Allan Williams, *The Man Who Gave The Beatles Away* (New York, 1975) is an implausible tale of one individuals' relationship with the Beatles. This book is highly emotional and does not accurately depict the Beatles' early years.

Reference Tools: The Basics

Bill Harry, *The Beatles: Who's Who* (New York, 1982) is an excellent collection of little facts on the Beatles by someone quite close to the group. Charlie Gillett, *The Sound of the City: The Rise of Rock 'n' Roll* (2nd edition, New York, 1984) is a history of rock music and this study employed it as a reference tool. Gillett's work, along with Greil Marcus' *Mystery Train: Images of America in Rock 'n' Roll Music* (New York, 1975), are the two best interpretive accounts of rock music. They served as reference tools for this book. The *Illustrated Encyclopedia of Rock*, by the editors of the *New Musical Express* (London, 1977) was useful. Barry Miles, *The Beatles In Their Own Words* (New York,1978) and *John Lennon In His Own Words* (New York, 1981) were also important sources. Phil Hardy and Dave Laing, *The Encyclopedia of Rock: From Liverpool to San Francisco* (London, 1976), volume 2, is the single best encyclopedia dealing with British rock and roll music.

General Interpretive Works on the History of Rock Music

Roy Carr and Tony Tyler *The Beatles: An Illustrated Record* (2nd ed., New York, 1978) is an excellent source for small bits of information. Robert Christgau, *Any Old Way You Choose It: Rock and Other Pop Music, 1967-1973* (Baltimore, 1973) is an interpretive work somewhat beyond the scope of this book, but there are a number of important ideas in Christgau's work. Equally provocative is Robert Christgau's "John Lennon, 1940-1980," *Village Voice*, December 10, 1980, p. 1. Perhaps the most astute English writer on the Beatles is Maureen Cleave, see Cleave's, "Old

Beatles, A Study in Paradox," *New York Times Magazine*, July 3, 1966.

For the emergence of John Lennon as a writer see Leonard Gross, "John Lennon: Beatle on His Own," *Look,* December 13, 1966, pp. 58-60. Bill Harry, *Mersey Beat: The Beginnings of the Beatles* (London, 1977) is a collection of early *Mersey Beat* newspapers and contains some excellent comments on the rise of Beatlemania.

A great deal of information about John Lennon and the Beatles' early life is examined in Jonathan Cott and Christine Doudna, *The Ballad of John and Yoko* (New York, 1982); Andrew Kopkind, "John Lennon After The Fall," *Ramparts* April 1971; Robert Palmer, "John Lennon: Must An Artist Self-Destruct?" *New York Times*, November 9, 1980; and Tom Spence, "Beat City, The Home of the Mersey Sound," *London Daily Worker*, November 2, 1963.

To understand the early 1960s in relationship to other artists who were developing during the Beatles' era see, Howard A. DeWitt, *Chuck Berry: Rock N Roll Music* (2nd edition, Pierian Press, Ann Arbor, 1985), Howard A. DeWitt, *Van Morrison: The Mystic's Music* (Fremont, 1983); and Anthony Scaduto, *Bob Dylan* (revised edition, New York, 1979). Chuck Berry adjusted to the changes the Beatles brought to rock music, Van Morrison represented the singer-songwriter in England and Bob Dylan matured as an artist with influences from Chuck Berry , Van Morrison and the Beatles. These three books reflect the changes in the music industry due to the emergence of these artists.

In order to understand the history of London's Soho district and the 2-Is coffee bar see Patrick Doncaster and Tony Jasper, *Cliff* (London, 1981) and George Tremlett, *The Cliff Richard Story* (London, 1975). Although not as useful as the books already mentioned, also see the publications of the International Cliff Richard Movement for important information on how Cliff Richard influenced the early English rock music industry.

An important book in understanding the rock music newspaper business is Robert Sam Anson, *Gone Crazy and Back Again: The Rise and Fall of the Rolling Stone Generation* (New York, 1981). Anson presents a general history of *Rolling Stone* magazine and in the process examines the fascination that John Lennon and the Beatles provided for Americans. Robert Christgau's, "The Political Power of Rock and Roll," *Newsday*, July 9, 1972 is an important reflection on how John Lennon helped to change the American political atmosphere. R. Serge Denisoff, *Solid Gold: The*

Popular Record Industry (Chicago, 1972) is an excellent examination by a sociologist of the impact of gold records upon the business and creative side of the recording industry.

Morris Dickstein, *Gates of Eden: American Culture in the Sixties* (New York, 1977) is an important examination of the forces shaping American culture and it pays tribute to the Beatles influence. Marc Eliot, *Death of a Rebel* (New York, 1979) chronicles the life of Phil Ochs and the parallels between Ochs and Lennon are interesting ones.

Greil Marcus' essay, "The Beatles," in *Rolling Stone Illustrated History of Rock and Roll* (New York, 1980, 2nd edition) is one of the best short pieces on the Liverpool group.

Little Richard was one of the strongest influences upon the Beatles and Charles White's *The Life and Times of Little Richard: The Quasar of Rock* (New York, 1984) is an excellent biography of his impact upon the Beatles. There are also a number of books which indicate the strong historical roots of the Beatles' in American rock music. See, for example, Terence O'Grady, *The Beatles: A Musical Evolution* (Boston, 1983) for the historical significance of the Beatles' musical evolution. Although there is very little material on the early years, this excellent book which began as a doctoral dissertation, is an important discussion of the revolutionary nature of the Beatles sound. Wilfred Mellers, *The Twilight of the Gods: The Music of the Beatles* (New York, 1973) is a classic study of the music apart from the culture. George Melly, *Revolt Into Style: The Pop Arts* (New York, 1971) is a highly important book in placing the Beatles' music in the mainstream of American popular culture. The collector books, albums and general memorabilia connected with the Beatles, as well as an incisive examination of their career is presented in Nicholas Schaffner, *The Beatles Forever* (New York, 1978). Alfred G. Aronowitz, "Yeah! Yeah! Yeah! Music's Gold Bugs: The Beatles," *Saturday Evening Post*, March 21, 1964 remains a classic interpretation of the Beatles' impact upon American culture.

Herbert I. London, *Closing The Circle: A Cultural History of The Rock Revolution* (Chicago, 1984) is a highly personalized account of rock music in American culture. Robert Christgau's article, "Now That We Can't Be Beatle Fans Anymore," *Village Voice*, September 30, 1971 is an excellent analysis of what the Beatles meant in the 1960s. Christopher Lasch, *The Culture of Narcissism* (New York, 1979) is a poignant account of some American forces influencing John Lennon's music.

Specialized Articles on the Beatles

The best examples of articles on the Beatles used in this book are David J. Smith, "From the 'Top Ten' to Number 17," *Beatles Now*, Autumn/Winter, 1982, pp. 8-9. Smith's article examines the rise of the Beatles music in 1961-1962 and the importance of "Love Me Do" in their early career. For an excellent interview with Bob Wooler see, Daniel Beller, "Bob Wooler," *Beatles Now*, Winter/Spring, 1983, pp. 10-12. Tony Barrow's, "The Beatles and the Press," *The Beatles Book*, June, 1981, pp. iii-vi, is an excellent article on how Brian Epstein handled the press.

Steve Scott's, "The Beatles E.P.'s, " *Record Collector*, May, 1983, pp. 36-39 is an indispensible guide to these releases. An in-depth look at Brian Epstein is provided in Tony Barrow's three part article, "Brian Epstein," *The Beatles Book*, January, March, April, 1983. A help in understanding Beatlemania is the excellent Johnny Dean and Peter Jones article, "Beatle People," *The Beatles Book*, October-November, 1980. Also see, Peter Jones, "The Beatles' Incredible 1963 Stage Shows," *The Beatles Book*, September, 1980.

The Hamburg years are covered in Bill Harry's article, "Bert Kaempfert: The Man Who Gave Brian Epstein The Beatles," *The Beatles Book*, September, 1980, pp. ix-x. Ian Hines, "The Beatles Hamburg Days," *The Beatles Book*, April-May-June, 1977, is an article by a member of Tony Sheridan's backup band, The Jets, which explains many of the mysteries of the Reeperbahn.

The beginnings of the Beatles' recording success is documented in Johnny Dean's, "How 'Love Me Do' Became a Hit," *The Beatles Book*, August, 1978, pp. iii-iv. A strange guide to the Beatles' hometown is Bill Harry's article, "The Beatles' Liverpool: A Guide to All the Places Associated With John, Paul, George and Ringo," *The Beatles Book*, pp. iii-v. On the subject of the Beatles and the media see, for example, Peter Jones, "An Early Interview With the Beatles," *The Beatles Book*, June, 1980, pp. iii-vi.

On the musical popularity of the Beatles see, Tony Barrow, "Everyone Wants to Record a Lennon-McCartney Song," *The Beatles Book*, April, 1983, pp. 4-11. An interesting fan reaction to Beatle music is Diana Vero, "Outspoken But Charming: A Personal Look at the Beatles," *The Beatles Book*, December, 1964, pp. 13-15. Ms. Vero interviewed the Beatles in December, 1963 at a taping of the program "Thank Your Lucky Stars" in Birmingham, and her story adds a great deal to their early image. Kathy Lewis', "The

Beatles in 1961," *The Beatles Book*, August, 1978, p. 9 is useful in assessing their early career.

The best interview with Pete Best is Jeff Tamarkin, "Pete Best," *Goldmine*, September, 1982, pp. 6-8. For a guide to collecting early Beatles BBC broadcasts see, Richard M. Hochadel, "Yellow Matter Custard: Collecting Beatle Broadcasts," *Goldmine*, September, 1982, pp. 10-15. Also see Pierian Press' excellent book on Beatles bootlegs, Charles Reinhart's *You Can't Do That* (Ann Arbor, 1981) and Mark Lewisohn's, "A Complete Catalogue of the Beatles' U.K. Radio Broadcasts," *The Beatles Book*, March-April, 1980 is an excellent source document.

Charles P. Lamey, "The Peter Jay and Jaywalkers Story," *Record Profile Magazine*, September/October, 1984, pp. 52-55 is an interesting interview with a musician close to the Beatles in the early 1960s. Steve Phillips, "Epstein," *Beatles Now*, October-November-December, 1982, is an interesting examination of the Beatles' manager.

Special Studies of John Lennon

The number of books on John Lennon are enormous and many of these studies are simply opportunistic attempts to cash in on his untimely death. However, a number of these quickie books offer substantial insights into Lennon's character. Ed Naha, ed., *John Lennon and the Beatles Forever* (New York, 1980); George Carpozi, Jr., *John Lennon: Death of A Dream* (New York, 1980); Timothy Green Beckley, ed., *Lennon: Up Close and Personal* (New York, 1980); Ray Coleman *John Lennon: A Melody Maker Tribute* (London, 1980); and Ernest E. Schworck, *John Lennon, 1940-1980* (Los Angeles, 1981) are the best of the quickie John Lennon books. Coleman's book is the best historical source and Carpozi presented an excellent instant analysis of Lennon's death. All of these books, however, are very weak on the origins of Lennon's talents.

Among the biographers of John Lennon the useful ones were Anthony Fawcett, *John Lennon: One Day At a Time* (rev. ed., New York, 1981); Ray Connolly, *John Lennon, 1940-1980: A Biography (London, 1981);* Pete Shotton and Nicholas Schaffner, *John Lennon in My Life* (New York, 1983); Tadeu Gonzaga Martins, *John Lennon* (Brazil, 1982); Har Van Fulpen, *John Lennon, 1940-1980* (Paris, 1980); George Tremlett, *The John Lennon Story* (London, 1976); David Stuart Ryan, *John Lennon's Secret* (London, 1982), and Vic Garbarini and Brian Cullman, *Strawberry Fields Forever: John*

Lennon Remembered (New York, 1980). All of these books provided useful information, in one way or another, about John Lennon's life, and they demonstrated how complex Lennon's artistic talent was during the 1960s.

James Sauceda's *The Literary Lennon: A Comedy of Letters, The First Study of All the Major and Minor Writings of John Lennon* (Ann Arbor, 1983) is the best study of Lennon's intellectual growth. Pierian Press which published Professor Sauceda's work also has reissued Brian Epstein, *A Cellarful of Noise* (Ann Arbor, 1984) in a handsome hardcover edition. Both of these books are essential in understanding the development of John's thought process.

The worst book on John Lennon is May Pang's, *Loving John: The Untold Story* (New York, 1983). Although Henry Edwards provides an excellent writing style for Pang's story, there is little in *Loving John* to justify its publication. It adds very little to the musical career of Lennon and the soap opera narrative is embarrassing. John Greene's *Dakota Days* (New York, 1983) is the story of John's tarot card reader. It is as dull and uninspiring as the Pang book.

The best interview with John Lennon remains, Jann Wenner, *Lennon Remembers: The Rolling Stone Interview* (San Francisco, 1971). A surprisingly good interview is Peter McCabe and Robert D. Schonfeld, *John Lennon: For The Record* (New York, 1984) which contains material from a *Penthouse* interview. Andy Peebles, *The Lennon Tapes*, (London, 1981) is an excellent verbatim interview with John and Yoko on December 6, 1980, and it remains one of the most interesting sources on John's life.

There were a few other books about John Lennon which were significant in providing little caveats of knowledge, among these are: Cynthia Twist Lennon, *A Twist of Lennon* (London, 1978); John Lennon, *In His Own Write*, (London, 1963) and *A Spaniard In The Works* (London, 1965) are essential in analyzing John's thought process. Carol Bedford's, *Waiting For the Beatles: An Apple Scruffs Story* (London, 1984) is an interesting look at the zealous fan.

Jon Weiner, *Come Together: John Lennon In His Time* (New York, 1984) is the best book on Lennon's life, and it is particularly strong on the early years. Bill Harry, *The Book of Lennon* (New York, 1984) is another excellent listing of people, places, performances, records, films, publications and personal facts surrounding John's life. Jeanie Attie and Josh Brown's essay, "John Lennon," in the *Radical History Review*, no. 24, (Fall, 1980), pp. 188-190 contributed greatly to many of the ideas expressed in this book.

For a radical look at rock and roll music through the eyes of a political activist see John Sinclair, *Music And Politics* (New York, 1971). An interesting article on John Lennon's music is Steve Marinucci, "John Lennon: Music At The Heart of the Man," *San Jose Mercury News*, December 12, 1980, p. 10.

About the Author

Howard A. DeWitt is a Professor of History and Popular Culture at Ohlone College in Fremont, California. For almost two decades he has taught courses in history and popular culture. He is a widely published scholar with nine books on varying subjects. In the field of rock music his publications include *Chuck Berry: Rock N Roll Music* (1981) and *Jailhouse Rock: The Bootleg Records of Elvis Presley*, written with Lee Cotten (1983). Pierian Press will publish a second edition of the Chuck Berry book in 1985.

After completing his Ph. D. in American Studies at the University of Arizona in 1971, DeWitt taught at Cochise College, Chabot College, and the University of California at Davis. His musical experience was gained in the late 1950s when he was a promoter in Seattle, Washington and presented such acts as The Wailers, Little Bill and The Bluenotes, The Frantics, and Ron Holden and The Playboys.

He is presently completing a manuscript on Elvis Presley's early life entitled *Sun Elvis*. In 1983 he toured Europe lecturing on the career of Chuck Berry.

Other Books by Howard A. DeWitt
Popular Culture
Chuck Berry: Rock N Roll Music (Pierian Press, 1985)
Jailhouse Rock: The Bootleg Records of Elvis Presley, with Lee Cotton
(Pierian Press, 1983)
Van Morrison: The Mystic's Music (Horizon Books, 1983)

History and Government
California Civilization (Kendall Hunt, 1979)
Readings in California Civilization: Interpretative Issues (Kendall
Hunt, 1981)
In the Course of Human Events: American Government, with Alan
Kirshner (Kendall Hunt, 1983)

Ethnic Studies
*Images of Ethnic and Racial Violence in California Politics, 1917-
1930: A Survey (R and E Associates, 1975)*
Anti-Filipino Movements in California
(R and E Research Associate, 1976)
*Violence in the Fields: California Filipino Farm Labor
Unionization During the Great Depression*
(Century 21 Publishing Company, 1980)

Contributors

ELIZABETH HUGHES is a well known San Francisco rock artist. The original drawing of John Lennon is an example of Ms. Hughes' work. Her work is sold regularly at fairs. For a list of drawings write Elizabeth Hughes, 40775 Ambar Place, Fremont, CA 94539.

DENNIS LOREN designed the cover. He is the editor of America's foremost collector rock magazine RPM. For a sample copy of RPM send $1 to RPM, 24361 Greenfield, Suite 201, Southfield, MI 48075.

LEE COTTEN is the owner of Golden Oldies, 809 K Street Mall, Sacramento, CA 95814. He provided many of the records and magazines for this study.

Index